FROMMER'S

COMPREHENSIVE TRAVEL GUIDE

Amsterdam

8th Edition

by Lisa Legarde

MACMILLAN • USA

ABOUT THE AUTHOR

Lisa Legarde was born in New Orleans and graduated from Wellesley College with a B.A. in English. She has traveled extensively in Europe and North America and is the author of Frommer's Walking Tours guides to San Francisco and Paris, as well as comprehensive guides to New Orleans; New Mexico; and Santa Fe, Taos, and Albuquerque. She is also co-author of *Frommer's New England.*

MACMILLAN TRAVEL

A Prentice Hall Macmillan Company
15 Columbus Circle
New York, NY 10023

ISBN 0-02-860459-8
ISSN 0899-3181

Design by Michele Laseau
Maps by Geografix Inc. and Ortelius Design

SPECIAL SALES

Bulk purchases (10+ copies) of Frommer's Travel Guides are available to corporations at special discounts. The Special Sales Department can produce custom editions to be used as premiums and/or for sales promotion to suit individual needs. Existing editions can be produced with custom cover imprints such as corporate logos. For more information write to: Special Sales, Simon & Schuster, 1230 Avenue of the Americas, New York, NY 10020.

Manufactured in the United States of America.

List of Maps

What the Symbols Mean

⭐ **Frommer's Favorites**   Hotels, restaurants, attractions, and entertainments you should not miss

$ **Super-Special Values**   Really exceptional values

In Hotel & Other Listings

The following symbols refer to the standard amenities available in all rooms:

A/C air conditioning
MINIBAR refrigerator stocked with beverages and snacks
TEL telephone
TV television

The following abbreviations are used for credit or charge cards:

AE American Express
CB Carte Blanche
DC Diners Club
DISC Discover
ER enRoute
EU EuroCard
JCB Japanese Credit Bureau
MC MasterCard
V Visa

Trip Planning with this Guide

USE THE FOLLOWING FEATURES

What Things Cost   To help you plan your daily budget

Calendar of Events   To plan for or avoid

Suggested Itineraries   For seeing the city

What's Special About Checklist   A summary of the city's highlights

Easy-to-Read Maps   Walking tours, sights, hotel and restaurant locations

Fast Facts   All the essentials at a glance: currency, embassies, emergencies, taxes, tipping, and more

OTHER SPECIAL FROMMER FEATURES

Cool for Kids   Hotels, restaurants, and attractions

Did You Know . . . ?   Offbeat, fun facts

Impressions   What others have said

Invitation to the Readers

While researching this book, I have come across many wonderful establishments, the best of which I have included here. I'm sure that many of you will also come across appealing hotels, inns, restaurants, guesthouses, shops, and attractions. Please don't keep them to yourself. Share your experiences, especially if you want to comment on places that have been included in this edition that have changed for the worse. You can address your letters to:

Lisa Legarde
Frommer's Amsterdam, 8th Edition
c/o Macmillan Travel
15 Columbus Circle
New York, NY 10023

A Disclaimer

Readers are advised that prices fluctuate in the course of time and travel information changes under the impact of the varied and volatile factors that affect the travel industry. Neither the author nor the publisher can be held responsible for the experiences of readers while traveling. Readers are invited to write to the publisher with ideas, comments, and suggestions for future editions.

Safety Advisory

Whenever you're traveling in an unfamiliar city or country, stay alert. Be aware of your immediate surroundings. Wear a moneybelt and keep a close eye on your possessions. Be particularly careful with cameras, purses, and wallets—all favorite targets of thieves and pickpockets.

1

Introducing
Amsterdam

LIVE-AND-LET-LIVE, EASYGOING, LIBERAL, AND TOLERANT ARE SOME OF THE sobriquets most often applied to Amsterdam—and with good reason. For centuries Amsterdam has been a magnet for the oppressed and persecuted, particularly in the 17th century, when it became a haven for the Jews and Huguenots being driven from France and other Catholic countries. That tradition of tolerance has continued into the 20th century: In the 1960s the city became the hippie capital of Europe; in the 1990s Amsterdam and Holland have taken leading roles in liberalizing laws against homosexuality, even sanctioning gay marriages. Similar pragmatic liberal attitudes help explain the existence of Amsterdam's Red Light District, which is as much a part of the city that visitors come to see as are the Rijksmuseum, the Stedelijk, and the Anne Frankhuis.

This city will soon capture you in its spell—especially at night, when the more than 1,200 bridges spanning the nearly 200 canals are lit with a zillion tiny lights that give them a fairy-tale appearance, or in the morning, when the landscape slowly unfolds through a mysterious fog or mist to reveal its treasures. Besides the sights mentioned above and the many canals and bridges, Amsterdam offers such delights as the Vincent van Gogh Museum, the Museum Het Rembrandthuis, the Artis Zoo, the Albert Cuypstraat flea market, the floating flower market, antiquarian bookstores, and brown cafés and tasting rooms, as well as cafés and nightclubs providing a variety of entertainment.

Amsterdam, the kind of place that's comfortable in a domestic way, is perhaps best summed up in Henry James's description of the city as "perfect prose." It has been drawn to a human scale. Few skyscrapers mar the clarity of the sky; instead, narrow brick houses topped with plain or ornamental gables and keystones line the streets and canals. The populace walks or bicycles from place to place. Everything in Amsterdam will remind you of the atmosphere captured in those great 17th-century paintings of interiors.

Speaking of the populace, every Dutch person seems to speak at least four languages (including English), and all are quite friendly to visitors—if you plop yourself down in a brown café (the Dutch equivalent of a neighborhood bar) with nicotine-stained walls to enjoy a beer or a *jenever* (gin), you'll soon find yourself chatting with at least one amiable Amsterdammer.

Both the city and its inhabitants will make your trip to Amsterdam an extraordinary and rewarding experience.

1 History & People

Tucked into a corner between Germany and Belgium, Holland is the great river delta of the European continent and the place at which much of the melted snow of the Alps finally finds its way into the sea. It's a marshy country—there are nearly 1,100 square miles of water within Holland's borders, in the form of lakes, rivers, and canals—with a dense, sandy, and peatlike soil that tends to settle over

What's Special About Amsterdam

Canals

- Prinsengracht, Herengracht, and Keizersgracht, lined by stunning canal houses topped by step, bell, and other decorative gables.
- Smaller canals with colorful houseboats anchored along their banks.

Museums

- Rijksmuseum, with 200-plus rooms of incredible Dutch and other European masters, plus superb decorative arts and Asian art collections.
- Vincent van Gogh Museum, where you can trace the artistic and psychological development of this great impressionist.
- Stedelijk Museum of Modern Art, with its cache of modern artists.
- Anne Frankhuis, the World War II hideaway in which Anne Frank wrote her famous diary, a moving and eerily real experience.
- Museum Het Rembrandthuis, once the home of the city's greatest portrait painter, now an art museum.

After Dark

- Concertgebouw, for world-class performances in one of the most acoustically fine halls anywhere.
- The Red Light District, testament to the city's tolerance and pragmatism—not for everyone though.
- Jordaans, a lively former working-class area now filled with clubs, coffeehouses, and vibrant life.

Monuments

- *Homomonument*—in memory of those gays and lesbians killed during World War II.
- *The Dockworker*—a moving memorial to the February Strike against the deportation of Jews in World War II.

Shopping

- Kalverstraat, Amsterdam's main shopping street.
- Nieuwe Spieglstraat, hunting ground for fine antiques.
- Waterlooplein Flea Market and Albert Cuyp Markt, where you can find just about anything.

Architectural Highlights

- Bridges—more than 1,200 of them spanning the canals.
- Hotel Americain, with its extraordinary art nouveau interior.
- Striking buildings designed by Berlage and the Amsterdam school, such as the Amsterdam Stock Exchange.

time (it sinks an average of one meter, or 39 inches, every 1,000 years). As a result, approximately 50% of Holland now lies *below* sea level, protected from flooding only by sand dunes, dikes, and Dutch ingenuity.

The "Great Rivers"—the Rhine, the Waal, and the Maas (or Meuse, as it is known in France, where its headwaters lie)—divide the country along geographic and spiritual lines. The Dutch living in the lower land "above," or north of, the rivers have long been predominantly Calvinist, whereas the population of the higher lands "below," or south of, the rivers has been traditionally Catholic. Natural boundaries are also formed by the mountains—well, hills—of the southeast; the forest in the center of the country (the provinces of Utrecht and Gelderland); the islands and former islands along the coast of the North Sea (the province of Zeeland in the southwest and a string of small sandbar islands off the coast of the province of Friesland in the north); the polders, or reclaimed land, of the former Zuiderzee (the Zuider Sea, now a freshwater lake); and the flat farmland of the rest of the country (some of which is actually old and well-established polder land).

There are no dramatic canyons or towering peaks in the Netherlands: Its highest point wouldn't top the roof of a New York City skyscraper, and its average altitude is just 37 feet above sea level. This makes for few panoramic vantage points—most of the lakes and canals can't be seen until you're about to fall into them. Yet, as the famous Dutch landscape painters of the 17th century helped the world learn, the vistas in Holland are among the most beautiful anywhere: wide-angle dioramas of green pastures and floating clouds, with tiny houses, church spires, and grazing cattle silhouetted against the horizon.

Amsterdam is the major city of Holland, a tiny country that's barely half the size of the U.S. state of Maine. You can drive from one corner of the Netherlands to the other in an afternoon and travel from Amsterdam to the farthest point of the railway network in under $2^1/_2$ hours. The nation's 14,192 square miles are the most densely populated in the world, holding 14.5 million people, or approximately 1,000 per square mile.

Before going any further, let's clear up the matter of nomenclature: The Netherlands is the official name of the country, but Holland is the name by which the country has always been known.

History ——————————————————————————

Dateline

- **1275** Count Floris V grants Amsterdam freedom from tolls on travel and trade.
- **1300** Amsterdam receives charter.

➤

MOST PEOPLE'S KNOWLEDGE OF Dutch history is confined to the role Peter Minuit played in the purchase of Manhattan Island and the role Peter Stuyvesant played as governor of Nieuw Amsterdam, but a working knowledge of when, why, and how the Dutch city came to be will add interesting dimensions to any visit to Amsterdam.

HOLLAND'S BEGINNINGS   The earliest inhabitants of what is now Holland were three tribes that settled the marshy deltas of the "lowlands" sometime in the dawn of recorded history. They were the ferocious Belgae of the southern regions; the opportunistic Batavi, who settled in the area of the Great Rivers; and the fiercely independent Frisians, who took residence along the northern coast. The three tribes each posed a challenge to the Roman legions, who managed to get both the Belgae and the Batavi to knuckle under but never had their way with the indomitable Frisians. In A.D. 47, the Roman emperor Claudius I gave up the attempt to acquire the marshy northlands (to an Italian they must have seemed like worthless real estate anyway), settling for the River Rhine as the northern border of the Roman Empire.

The Frisians resisted the Romans and then the conquering hordes of Saxons and Franks through the next seven centuries—they even managed to greatly extend their territory. Not until the late 8th century did they surrender their independence, when the mighty Charlemagne, king of the Franks and emperor of the West, managed to force the Frisians to give up their pagan gods in exchange for Christianity.

EARLY AMSTERDAM   Sometime around 1100, almost 1,000 years after Holland was established during the 1st century A.D., some fishermen realized that the area that is now Amsterdam allowed them easy access to the lucrative fishing in both the river IJ and the Zuiderzee. They built huts there, and soon traders followed, distributing the catch to the more developed surrounding villages.

The marshy terrain left these early settlers at the mercy of tides and storms—many died or lost their homes as a result of flooding. Sometime around 1240 the Amstel River was dammed in an effort to control water flow over the land. This is the source of the city's original name, Amstelledamme, and to this day you can

Dateline

- **1323** Amsterdam declared a toll center for imported beer.
- **1334** Oude Kerk mentioned as Amsterdam's first parish church.
- **1345** "Miracle of the Host."
- **1350** Amsterdam becomes transit point for grain.
- **1367** Amsterdam joins German and Dutch towns in a treaty against the king of Denmark.
- **1400** Population between 4,400 and 5,000.
- **1514** Amsterdam the largest town in Holland with a population of 12,000.
- **1517** Martin Luther issues condemnation of Catholic church.
- **1530** Anabaptists develop significant following in Amsterdam.
- **1535** Anabaptists seize Amsterdam Town Hall.
- **1550** Education of public grows.
- **1560** Calvinism spreads.
- **1566** First Protestant services held in public; Catholic churches sacked.
- **1578** Amsterdam abandons cause of Philip II; Calvinists take over churches.

➤

watch the sluices on either side of the old dam being opened by hand when the canals get their nightly flushing.

There are few records of the village of Amstelledamme before 1275, when Count Floris V, becoming the first to officially recognize the town, granted toll privileges that allowed Amsterdammers to trade anywhere in Holland or Zeeland without having to pay tolls along the way. It wasn't until 1300 that the town was granted its charter.

PROSPERITY IN HOLLAND During the 14th and 15th centuries, Holland's position at the mouths of the great European rivers made it a focal point in the many shifts of feudal power. After numerous small-scale struggles for control, the House of Burgundy became the first major feudal power in the lowlands, consolidating its hold on the region by acquiring fiefdoms one by one through various means—marriage, inheritance, military force. Their day soon passed, however, as the Hapsburg emperor Maximilian I acquired the lowlands from the Burgundians by much the same means.

As these political struggles raged, the Dutch people were quietly making themselves wealthy. Always skillful traders—archaeological remains have made it clear that the Frisians made their living primarily as traders—the Dutch began to establish strong guilds of craftspeople and to put ships to sea for herring and salt. Albeit not without some squabbles, they opened up lucrative trade with the Baltics by joining the Hanseatic League.

These years were equally important to the city of Amsterdam. It began to rise to commercial prosperity in 1323, when Count Floris VI established Amsterdam as one of two toll points for the import of beer. During the Middle Ages, beer was a major commodity—practically everyone relied on it as a substitute for drinking water, much of which was contaminated. Later, Amsterdam was also granted toll rights on exported ale. Beer thus became a major component of Amsterdam's prosperity, and it continues to be today, as anyone who visits the city's famous Heineken Brewery will see.

CATHOLICISM During the Middle Ages Holland was a bastion of Catholicism, with powerful bishoprics in the cities of Utrecht and Maastricht and a holy shrine in the upstart town of Amstelledamme, which attracted its own share of pilgrims during the age of the Crusades. No one is sure when Amsterdam became an independent parish, but it is thought to have been around 1334, when the Oude Kerk (Old Church) is first mentioned in the city's records.

In 1342, Count Floris VI granted Amsterdam another charter, giving it more independence as well as definitive boundaries. As the town became more of a city and grew in prosperity, cloisters began to spring up within these boundaries. Eventually there were 18 of these *beguinages* in Amsterdam. The cloisters functioned as social-welfare agencies, providing care to the sick, orphaned, or poor and hospitality to travelers and pilgrims.

The many monasteries and nunneries helped attract people to the city. A few years later a major event, referred to as the "Miracle of the Host," made the city even more beguiling to the religious. It is said that on the Tuesday before Palm Sunday in 1345, a dying man sent for a priest to administer last rights to him. He was given the Host; a few hours later he vomited. The women who were caring for him threw his vomit on the fire, and the next day they found the unburnt Host amid the embers. Soon after, it was placed in a shrine built to commemorate this miracle; twice it was removed to be taken to another place of worship, but somehow it returned itself to the original shrine. During a procession to the Oude Kerk involving the same Host, many miracles were said to have happened. The bishop declared the whole thing a miracle the next year and had a chapel erected in place of the dying man's house.

Dateline

- **1876** Opening of North Sea Canal; opening of the country's first steam laundry.
- **1877** Municipal Sanitation Department set up.
- **1890** Privately owned utilities under control of the city.
- **1894** Social Democratic Labour party formed.
- **1897** July 21; Amsterdam's first automobile.
- **1910** Flushable water system set up.
- **1917** Public rioting due to food shortages.
- **1940** German troops invade and occupy Holland.
- **1941** "February Strike."
- **1945** March 10: Canadian troops liberate Amsterdam.
- **1951** *Dockworker* statue unveiled.
- **1966** Protests against Princess Beatrix's marriage to German Claus von Amsberg.
- **1975** Amsterdam's 700th anniversary; Dutch Guyana gains independence as Surinam; influx of immigrants to Amsterdam.
- **1978** First squatters occupy the old Handelsblad newspaper offices.
- **1980** Sixteen people squat at 72 Vondelstraat. Police remove them, but they return and

➤

Within a few years the place came to be known as the *Heilige Stede* ("Holy Place"). Today there is still an annual pilgrimage to the Holy Place.

THE REFORMATION The 16th century was a time when religion was often truly inseparable from power and politics, a time when kings still routinely considered themselves their kingdom's link with the divine and demanded that their subjects think as they thought. As the century that witnessed the Reformation, which began with Martin Luther nailing his 95 theses to the door of the Catholic church in Wittenberg, Germany, and eventually radiated Protestantism throughout the Christian world, it was also a time of tremendous religious ferment.

Nations throughout Europe wrestled with the notion of religious diversity. The result in Spain was the infamous Inquisition, which was designed to rid the realm of such "heretics" as Lutherans, Jews, and intellectuals. In Holland, ironically, the anti-Catholic, iconoclastic ideas of Protestantism took root in the Dutch psyche at the same time the Dutch provinces officially came under the rule of Charles V, the intensely Catholic king of Spain. Holland, and Amsterdam, became a pressure point and fulcrum for the shifting political scene that the Reformation occasioned everywhere in Europe.

Among the more radical Protestant sects were the Anabaptists, some of whom had left Germany in 1530 in hopes of finding a more tolerant climate in Amsterdam. The Anabaptists rejected the Catholic practices of infant baptism and celebrating saints' days and did not believe in the Trinity. They did believe in adult baptism. For the most part the Anabaptists gained their following from among the poor, and in general Amsterdam's Catholics tolerated the presence of Anabaptists in their city—until 1534. The previous year, a group of Anabaptists had successfully taken over the town hall in the Westphalian town of Münster, declaring it a New Jerusalem in anticipation of a Second Coming. When they attempted to reproduce this success in Amsterdam by seizing Amsterdam Town Hall, they found the city unwilling to go along—the leaders of the uprising were all executed.

The Anabaptists continued their agitation into the following year. On February 11, 1535, a so-called prophet, Hendrick Hendricksz, was preaching to a small group of men and women when he suddenly told them that the Lord had spoken to him and all present were damned to Hell. The congregation asked for forgiveness, which was immediately granted, but then Hendricksz went a bit mad, ripped off his clothes, threw them on the fire, and bade the others to do the same—which they did. Then they all ran naked through the city.

Even the landlady of the building in which they were holding their meeting ran with them. Ever since they have been referred to as the Naked Runners—Amsterdam's original streakers. The men were all executed, and the landlady was hung in the doorway of her building as an example to the public. In this, Amsterdam became like many communities in Europe, abandoning religious toleration in favor of religious repression.

About 20 years later a series of events changed the course of history in Holland and Amsterdam, turning the country toward a path that would make it a world-renowned symbol of religious, political, and intellectual tolerance. In 1555, Philip II, a great-grandson of Emperor Maximilian I, became king of Spain. An ardent Catholic, he was determined to defeat the Reformation and set out to hunt heretics everywhere throughout his empire. The Dutch resented Philip's intrusion into their affairs and began a resistance movement. Within 10 years a League of Protestant Nobles had been formed in the Netherlands by the taciturn but tactful William of Orange, count of Holland, known also as William the Silent. King Philip's response was to send the vicious duke of Alba to Holland. He was to function as an overseer, with the specific instruction to establish a Council of Blood to enforce the policy of "death to heretics."

The Dutch nobles fought back, though they had no army, no money to raise one, and little support from the Dutch cities—including Catholic Amsterdam, which was interested mostly in maintaining its prosperous trade. William of Orange and his brother John of Nassau managed to wage war on Spain despite all this, their only ally a ragtag "navy" of Protestant pirates called the Sea Beggars. They were helped when Spain levied a new tax on its Dutch "colony," an action so unpopular as to rally the majority of Dutch people—Protestant and Catholic alike—to the anti-Spanish cause.

A few towns, including Amsterdam, declined to join the fight against Alba, deeming resistance bad for business. These communities were spared destruction when the Spanish invaded Holland. The Spanish armies marched inexorably through Holland, besting the defenses of each city they laid siege to, with few exceptions. In an ingenious if desperate move, William of Orange saved the city of Leiden by flooding the province, allowing the Sea Beggars to sail their galleons right up to the city's walls. The attack surprised the Spaniards in the middle of dinner; they were promptly routed. A stew pot left behind became a national symbol of freedom for Holland, and its contents inspired the traditional Dutch dish called *hutspot.*

This sweet victory galvanized the Dutch in fighting for their independence. The Protestant merchants of Amsterdam turned out their Catholic city council. The Dutch nobles strengthened their commitment to one another in 1579 by signing the Union of Utrecht, in which they agreed to fight together in a united front. Although the union was devised solely to prosecute the battle against Spain, consolidation inevitably occurred, and by the turn of the 17th century what had once been the Spanish Netherlands became the Seven

United Provinces—Zeeland, Vriesland, Utrecht, Gelderland, Groningen (Overijsse), North Holland, and South Holland. The struggle with Spain would continue through the first half of the 17th century, but Holland's strength was growing, and a new, prosperous era was about to begin.

THE GOLDEN AGE Over the first 50 to 75 years of the 17th century the Dutch entrepreneurial gift would come into its legendary full flower. These years have since become known as the Golden Age—it seemed that every business venture the Dutch initiated during this time turned a profit, that each of the many expeditions to the unknown places of the world they mounted resulted in a new jewel in the Dutch colonial empire. Colonies and brisk trade were established to provide the luxury-hungry merchants at home with new delights, such as fresh ginger from Java, foxtails from America, fine porcelain from China, and flower bulbs from Turkey that produced big, bright, waxy flowers and grew like crazy in Holland's sandy soil—tulips. Holland was rich and Amsterdam was growing.

Until 1589 Amsterdam had always been just a bit behind its neighboring cities, despite having extended its trade routes to Russia, Scandinavia, and the Baltics. But in that year Amsterdam's biggest commercial rival, the Belgian port of Antwerp, was taken over by the Spanish and Amsterdam came to benefit. Many industrious Protestant and Jewish craftspeople fled from Antwerp to Amsterdam with the arrival of the Spanish, and they brought with them their merchant skills and their businesses—among them was the diamond industry, which has remained a famous and central part of the city's commerce.

Over the next 65 years Amsterdam grew into one of the world's great cities. The diamond industry flourished. The Dutch East India Company (Verenigde Oost Indische Compagnie) was set up in 1602 by businesspeople from each of the major cities in the Republic of the Seven Provinces and was granted a monopoly on trade in the East. The company's purpose was to mount safe, cost-effective exploratory voyages and trading ventures to the East Indies, and it was wildly successful. The East India Company established the Dutch presence in the Spice Islands (Indonesia), Goa, South Africa, and China. Great wealth flowed back to Amsterdam, and the merchants used it to build the canals and the impressive 17th-century architecture you can see today if you walk along the Golden Bend on the Herengracht.

In 1613 work on the three major canals (the Keizersgracht, Prinsengracht, and Herengracht) was begun. The large canals were to be connected by smaller transverse canals to make travel by water more convenient throughout Amsterdam. City planners decided it would be proper for the wealthy to live facing the major canals and to set aside the connecting canals for the middle and lower classes.

The growing city bustled in many other ways: A variety of churches and other houses of worship were built during this time, traders and craftspeople of all sorts began setting up protectionist guilds, and there was an increase in interest in the arts and sciences. Artists—including Rembrandt—were working overtime, commissioned by newly affluent merchants who had become obsessed with portraying themselves and surrounding themselves with beautiful images. It is thought that most Dutch homes had at least four paintings in them at that time.

Amsterdam's first school of higher education, the Athenaeum Illustre, was established in 1632. The Athenaeum Illustre was not a university, but it did raise the city's educational possibilities above the level offered before. In another attempt at public education, the Guild of Surgeons began giving anatomy demonstrations to both interested doctors and laypeople. Amsterdam expanded in trade, population, education, and cultural awareness.

The long war with Spain finally ended in 1648 after 80 years, and although the Nieuwe Amsterdam colony (present-day New York City) was lost to the English in 1664, the Dutch continued to grow wealthy from their Spice Islands holdings. The descendants of William of Orange had by then established a de facto monarchy, which was further strengthened when William III married into the English royal family. The ascension of William III and his wife, Mary, to the English throne in 1688 may have been the beginning of the end for the Dutch Republic, however. Wars, commercial failures, misguided political decisions, and bad morale were the hallmarks of the next century of Dutch history, which ended with the House of Orange in exile in England and an upstart Batavian Republic (allied with the brand-new French Republic) in power in the Netherlands.

THE 19TH CENTURY   When Napoléon gained power in France, he took Holland; and when he took Holland, he turned the town hall of Amsterdam into a palace and gave the Dutch the monarchy they had had in spirit for more than 200 years—he made his youngest brother, Louis Bonaparte, king of Holland. The French regime was short, but the taste of royalty was sweet. When the Dutch recalled the House of Orange in 1815, it was to fill the role of king in a constitutional monarchy. The monarch was yet another William of Orange; however, because his reign was to be a fresh start for the republic, the Dutch started numbering their Williams all over again (which makes for a very confusing history).

IMPRESSIONS

On a desolate marsh overhung by fogs and exhaling diseases, a marsh where there was neither wood nor stone, neither firm earth nor drinkable water, a marsh from which the ocean on one side and the Rhine on the other were with difficulty kept out by art, was to be found the most prosperous community in Europe. The wealth which was collected within five miles of the Stadhous of Amsterdam would purchase the fee-simple of Scotland.
—T. B. Macaulay, *History of England,* 1849–61

In the 1860s Amsterdam's economy grew strong again as the city worked to equip itself for modern trade. The first improvement was the building of a railway line between Haarlem and Amsterdam in 1839; the North Sea Canal, which ran from Amsterdam to IJmuiden and gave Amsterdam a better crack at German industrial trade, was built in 1876. Another major boon to the city was the building of the Suez Canal in 1869, which made travel to Asia easier.

For about two centuries after Amsterdam's Golden Age the city's population remained at a quarter of a million. Between 1850 and 1900, however, it jumped to half a million. As did most major cities during the Industrial Revolution, Amsterdam began to face issues of overpopulation. Housing was in short supply, the canals were increasingly befouled with sewage, and for many life in the city became increasingly nasty, brutish, and short.

THE WORLD WARS & THE GREAT DEPRESSION Holland maintained strict neutrality during World War I, but the war still had an impact on Amsterdam. While the wealthy exploited the situation by selling arms and other supplies, the city suffered from acute food shortages and the poor were constantly faced with starvation. In 1917 there were food riots; Amsterdam answered with soup kitchens and rationing. In the 1920s Amsterdam shared in the wealth as Europe's condition improved (particularly in 1924), but conditions were very bad during the 1930s, when the widespread unemployment brought on by the Great Depression caused the government to use the army in 1934 to control the unruly masses; during this time many poor Dutch families were forced to move to Germany, where jobs were easier to come by.

Amsterdam was just beginning to recover from the depression when the Germans invaded on May 10, 1940. Queen Wilhelmina—probably the most popular Dutch ruler since William the Silent, she was a tiny woman, whom Churchill once called "the only man in the Dutch government"—fled to England, where she stayed until 1945. An Austrian Nazi by the name of Arthur Seyss-Inquart was put in charge of the Netherlands.

As he did in most other cities, Hitler managed to gain a following in Amsterdam. However, there was resistance to Nazi treatment of Jews, gypsies, and homosexuals by the citizens of Amsterdam. In February of 1941 city workers organized a strike against the deportation of Jews. Today, in the Old Jewish Quarter, where many Jews lived until the war, you can see the statue, *The Dockworker*, that is a tribute to the February Strike (Amsterdam was the first city in the world to have a memorial to the quarter million gays and lesbians who were killed by Nazis during World War II—it's called *Homomonument*). Unfortunately, the strike did little good; by 1942 the Nazis had forced all Dutch Jews to move to three isolated areas in Amsterdam. Between July 1942 and September 1943 most of Amsterdam's Jews were sent to death camps. Of the 140,000 Jews in Amsterdam, 100,000 were killed.

In 1944 the citizens of Amsterdam were faced with what is today known as the Hunger Winter. Food supplies were practically non-existent, and many people were forced to steal or buy provisions on the Black Market. Often people made treks into the country to visit farms in hopes of getting milk and eggs, but even then they had to stand in line and were in danger of not getting back to the city before curfew.

On May 5, 1945, the ordeal was over—the Dutch celebrated in the wake of the Allies' liberation of the Netherlands.

PRESENT-DAY AMSTERDAM   After World War II Holland's colonies were liberated and the city began to grow and prosper again. In the 1960s Amsterdam was just as much a hotbed of radicalism as the United States. These radical politics, which began with "Happenings" staged by the small group known as the Provos, continued and intensified in the 1970s. In 1966 the Provos were behind the protests that marred the wedding of Princess Beatrix to German Claus von Amsberg—smoke bombs were thrown and fights occurred between protesters and police. The Provos formally disbanded in 1967, but much of their program was adopted by the Green Gnomes, or Kabouters. Although they won several seats on the municipal council, they, too, eventually faded.

Some of their members joined neighborhood groups to protest against specific local government plans. The scheme that provoked the greatest ire was a plan to build a subway through the Nieuwmarkt area. Demonstrations were launched in 1975, with the most dramatic confrontation between the police and the human barricades defending the housing that had been condemned taking place on Blue Monday, March 24. Thirty people were wounded and 47 arrested in a battle of tear gas and water cannon against paint cans and powder bombs. Despite the protests, the subway opened in 1980.

With the influx of immigrants from newly independent Surinam and other countries, shortage of decent affordable housing has continued to be a major issue; in fact, it was to spark the squatting movement that came to dominate the late 1970s and '80s. In 1978 the first squatters occupied the old Handelsblad newspaper office building, but it took a series of squat happenings to unify the squatters into a movement. The biggest confrontations came in 1980, first at the Vondelstraat squat in the heart of the museum area, when 500 police and army tanks evicted squatters. Riots followed, and 50 people were wounded and much damage was sustained. The second and larger disturbance occurred on Beatrix Coronation Day, when 200 buildings were occupied in 26 cities and in Amsterdam itself protesters battled the police and totally disrupted the festivities. Other squatting incidents occurred, though slowly both sides developed a more constructive dialogue.

Protests similar to those that had been started against the subway were launched against the proposals to build a new town hall and Muziektheater on Waterlooplein. Despite this Stop the Opera (Stopera) campaign, both buildings were completed in 1986.

The Provos and Green Gnomes (Kabouters) had long advocated specific environmental programs like banning all motor vehicles from the city and providing 20,000 bicycles for citizens' use. Some of their ideas came to fruition in 1992 when the populace voted to create a traffic-free zone in the city center.

Although the turbulent events of the 1970s and '80s seem distant today, the independent spirit and social conscience that fueled them remains, making the city still one of the most socially advanced in Europe today.

People

THE DUTCH CHARACTER It's not Holland that's extraordinary, it's the Dutch. Can you imagine Americans, for example, having the patience to fill acres and acres of land, seemingly by spoonfuls, knowing at the outset that the project might take centuries to complete? (It did.) Or Germans, sharing as they might the Dutch love of precision, devoting seven years to the building of a perpetually moving planetarium in a living room simply to educate their neighbors, as one Dutchman did in the 18th century? And who but the Dutch would have the ingenuity and audacity to tell rivers when and where to flow and birds where to fly, to turn inland cities into world ports, and to risk a fortune on a project whose margin for error was so small that misplacing any of a series of massive, deep-water pilings spread out over a 3-mile span by as little as 10 inches would have resulted in failure?

But these are collective traits and national accomplishments. You want to know what to expect from the person in the street and the person behind the shop counter. The most honest thing to say about the Dutch is that they can be the most infuriating—and the most endearing—people in the world. One minute they treat you like a naughty child (surely you've heard the expression about being talked to like a Dutch uncle) and the next they're ready for a laugh and a beer. They can be rude or cordial (it may depend on the weather), domineering or ever ready to please (it may depend on you). In a shop, they may get annoyed with you if you don't accept what they have, but they get mad at themselves if they don't have what you want.

The Dutch have a passion for detail that would boggle the mind of a statistician—and a sense of order and propriety that sends them into a tailspin if you show up at the railway station with your one-month rail pass issued on a *jaarkaart* (year card). They organize everything (people, land, flower beds), and they love to make

IMPRESSIONS

There is no people in the universe so free from low spirits or the affectation of them as the Dutch. They cannot endure anything that looks being pensive without a cause; and as for low spirits, they laugh at them.
—David Dalrymple, 1764

schedules and stick to them. They may allow you to indulge an occasional whim, though they haven't a clue about what it means to "play it by ear." They do love to quote homilies ("While the cat's away, the mouses [sic] will play," "Everybody talks about my drinking, but no one knows about my thirst," "In the concert of life, no one gets a program"), including a number that tend to suffer in translation ("Try to find it out with a wet thumb," "It fits like a hand shoe").

The Dutch aren't particularly emotional or hotheaded, but then they aren't shy about speaking their minds either. They are fiercely independent and yet are so tolerant of other people's problems and attitudes that their country nearly equals the United States as a traditional haven for the world's exiles and émigrés (you'll find Italian, Spanish, and French names in the telephone book that belong to families as Dutch as the van Dijks and van Delfts and whose roots in Holland go back several centuries). The uniquely Dutch combination of tolerance and individualism has from time to time allowed scandalous eyesores to develop: the nightly spectacle of hippies sleeping on Amsterdam's Dam Square in the 1960s; the riots that occurred within earshot of the pomp and pageantry of Beatrix's investiture as queen of the Netherlands; the uproar over the dubious decision of prominent Dutch cabinet ministers to pose nude in the chambers of Parliament for publication in the Dutch edition of *Playboy* magazine. This combination, however, has also been the source of both their strength as a nation and their successes in business over the centuries. Holland may be just half the size of the state of Maine, but it was a country rich enough to rule world commerce for a time in the 17th century, and today Holland is—in its careful, quiet way—rebuilding its position. Royal Dutch Shell Group (Shell Oil), Unilever (Lever Brothers), and the electronics firm Philips are all Dutch-based corporations and are all among the top 20 companies in the world in both size and annual sales. The Dutch have never been out to conquer the world on the battlefield—they've devoted their energy to conquering the sea. But you can bet your boots the Dutch will always be found where there's trading to be done and money to be made.

LANGUAGE   You may speak English in Amsterdam as freely as you do at home, particularly to anyone in the business of providing tourist services, whether cab driver, hotel receptionist, waiter or waitress, or shop assistant. English is Holland's second language and is taught in the schools from the early grades, with the result that nearly everyone speaks it fluently. Most Dutch today are also conversant in French or German, or both, and some speak Spanish as well.

If foreign languages interest you, however, Dutch should prove a fascinating study. It's a Germanic tongue that at first sounds like a close cousin to German because of the guttural, rolled "*s*" and "*sch*" sounds, and the abundance of the letters *k*, *v*, and *b* in the everyday vocabulary; but after a couple of days English-speakers may begin to hear words that sound familiar. In fact, Dutch is a bridge language between German and English; in the northern province of Friesland one can hear a Dutch regional language that's an even closer cousin to English.

2 Famous Amsterdammers

Karel Appel (b. 1921) This controversial postwar painter was born in Amsterdam. In 1950 he moved to Paris, where he was instrumental in founding COBRA (Copenhagen, Brussels, and Amsterdam), a group of now-famous artists. In 1954 Appel won the UNESCO Prize, and he also won the Guggenheim Prize in 1960. A great deal of his work is exhibited at the Stedelijk Museum; you can also go to the Café Roux in the Grand Amsterdam Hotel (formerly the Amsterdam City Hall) for a close-up view of a piece he did to pay a debt he owed the city. Apparently, the staff of that section of city hall were so repulsed by the mural that they covered it up—it was only recently rediscovered.

Hendrik Petrus Berlage (1856–1934) This Dutch architect advocated a return to simplicity of form and clarity of line and structure. His theories can be seen most clearly at work in the Amsterdam Stock Exchange (1898–1903) and the Diamond Workers' Union Building (1899–1900). He greatly influenced "modern" architecture, the Amsterdam school, and urban planning.

Willem Jansz Blaeu (1571–1638) A cartographer and printer, Blaeu founded a company in Amsterdam that was famous for marine publications, globes, and atlases, as well as for navigational and astronomical instruments. His son, Jan, published the 11-volume *Atlas Major* in 1663.

Anne Frank (1929–45) Anne is famous the world over for her diary, a profoundly moving record of an intelligent and vivacious teenager's struggle to cope with the horrific wartime realities slowly closing in around her. A German Jew living in Amsterdam, Anne and her family (as well as another family) went into hiding when the Nazis occupied Amsterdam. Cut off from other outlets for her energies, she began to keep a journal telling of her thoughts, feelings, and experiences as a Jew during Nazi times. The last entry was on August 1, 1944. Not long after that entry, she and her family were discovered and sent to concentration camps. Anne and her sister were sent to the Bergen-Belsen camp, where they died of typhus just a few short days before Allied forces liberated the camp. Otto Frank, Anne's father, was the only survivor of the Frank family, and it was he who first had Anne's diary published.

Piet Mondrian (1872–1944) This Dutch painter attended the academy in Amsterdam before moving on to Paris and later, New York. A leader of the De Stijl group of artists, Mondrian developed a geometric art style he called neoplasticism, which influenced the later Bauhaus movement and international style of architecture.

Rembrandt van Rijn   (1606–69) This painter, whose works hang in places of honor in the world's great museums, may be *the* most famous Amsterdammer, to both outsiders and today's Amsterdammers. Born in Leiden, Rembrandt moved to Amsterdam in 1632. When he first moved to Amsterdam he was in great demand as a portraitist. Later, however, as he began to refuse to compromise his artistic ideas, he began to lose popularity, and thus a number of his commissions. In 1639 he bought a home (now the Museum Het Rembrandthuis) on Jodenbreestraat in the Old Jewish Quarter. Not long after the purchase of his house he began to have financial difficulties. In 1642 his wife, Saskia, died, and one of his most famous paintings today, *The Night Watch,* was refused by those who had commissioned the painting. In 1656 Rembrandt declared bankruptcy, a financial state from which he would never recover. He is now buried in the Westerkerk.

Baruch Benedictus de Spinoza   (1632–77) A giant of philosophy who was thrown out of the Jewish community for his independent thinking, he spent his life writing compelling, philosophical works, the theories of which he tried to prove through mathematics. *Ethica,* his best-known work, proved ethical theories using mathematics. When he wasn't philosophizing and writing, he polished spectacles.

Joost van den Vondel   (1587–1679) Van den Vondel is one of the most famous Dutch poets and playwrights of Amsterdam's Golden Age. His best-known works are *Gijsbrecht van Aemstel* and *Lucifer.* He is the namesake of Amsterdam's Vondelpark.

3   Art & Architecture

Art

THE 17TH-CENTURY GOLDEN AGE   Although there were earlier Dutch artists, Dutch art came into its own during the 17th century, benefiting, like so many other aspects of Dutch society, from the wealth of the Golden Age. Many successful merchants began commissioning portraits as well as landscapes, still lifes, and domestic scenes—they wanted realism. The art of this period remains some of the greatest ever created in Holland, and Amsterdam was (and still is) a major art center.

While the roots of 17th-century Dutch realism are clearly found in the work of Belgian Jan van Eyck (1395–1441), another influence was the new "realism of light and dark," or *chiaroscuro,* which had first been introduced into art by Caravaggio (1573–1610), an Italian. Early 17th-century Utrecht artist **Gerrit van Honthorst** (1590–1656), who had studied in Rome with Caravaggio, introduced the technique into Holland. Best known for lively genre scenes such as *The Supper Party* (1620), which depicted ordinary people against a plain background, Honthorst often used multiple hidden light sources to heighten the dramatic contrast of lights and darks.

Among the great landscape artists of this period, **Jacob van Ruisdael** (1628–82) stands out. He painted cornfields, windmills, and forest scenes, as well as his famous views of Haarlem. In these paintings human figures rarely appear and vast skies filled with moody clouds cover two-thirds of the canvas.

Frans Hals (1581–1666), the undisputed leader of the Haarlem school (schools differed from city to city), was a great portrait painter whose relaxed, informal, and naturalistic portraits contrast strikingly with the traditional formal masks of Renaissance portraits. His light brush strokes help convey immediacy and intimacy, making his works perceptive psychological portraits. He also had a genius for comic characters, showing men and women as they are and a little less than they are, as in *Malle Babbe* (1650). As a stage designer of group portraits Hals's skill is almost unmatched—only Rembrandt outshines him in this. Although he carefully arranged and posed each group, balancing the directions of gesture and glance, his *alla prima* brushwork (direct laying down of pigment) makes these public images—such as *The Archers of St. Aidan* (1633)—seem spontaneous. It's worth taking a day trip to Haarlem just to visit the Frans Halsmuseum (see "The Historic Art Towns" in Chapter 10).

The greatest genius of the period was **Rembrandt van Rijn** (1606–69). One of his accomplishments was pushing the art of chiaroscuro to unprecedented heights. In his paintings the values of light and dark gradually and softly blend together; this may have diffused some of the drama of chiaroscuro, but a more truthful appearance is achieved. Rembrandt's art seemed capable of revealing the soul and inner life of his subjects, and to view his series of 60 self-portraits is to see a remarkable documentation of his own psychological evolution. The *Self-portrait with Saskia* shows him with his wife at a prosperous time when he was being commissioned by many wealthy merchants to do portraits. Later self-portraits are more psychologically complex, often depicting a careworn old man whose gaze is nonetheless sharp, compassionate, and wise.

Rembrandt's series of religious paintings and prints are intensely spiritual, but the figures are treated in very human terms; these works project a sense of contemplative stillness. His religious prints brought him much renown and were a major source of income. At the Museum Het Rembrandthuis in Amsterdam—which has been restored to very much the way it was when the master lived and worked there—you can see his self-portraits along with some 250 etchings.

In his group portraits—such as *The Night Watch* (1642), on view in the Rijksmuseum in Amsterdam—each individual portrait is done with care. Although art historians do not know how he proceeded, a long studio sitting may have been required of each man. The unrivaled harmony of light, color, and movement of these works is a marvel to be appreciated.

In his later years Rembrandt was at the height of his artistic powers, but his work was judged too personal and eccentric by his contemporaries. Some considered him a tasteless painter who was obsessed with the ugly and ignorant of color; this opinion prevailed until the 19th century, when Rembrandt's genius was reevaluated.

Jan Vermeer (1632–75) of Delft is perhaps the best known of the "little Dutch masters" who specialized in one genre of painting, such as portraiture. Although they confined their artistry within a narrow scope, these painters rendered their subjects with an exquisite care and faithfulness to their actual appearances.

Vermeer's work centers on the simple pleasures and activities of domestic life—a woman pouring milk or reading a letter—all of his simple figures positively glow with color and light. Vermeer placed the figure (usually just one, but sometimes two or more) at the center of his paintings against a background in which furnishings often provided the horizontal and vertical balance, giving the composition a feeling of stability and serenity. Art historians have determined that Vermeer used mirrors and the *camera obscura*, an early camera, as compositional aids. A master at lighting interior scenes and rendering true colors, he was able to create an illusion of three-dimensionality. As light—usually afternoon sunshine pouring in from an open window—moves across the picture plane, it caresses and modifies all the colors.

Jan Steen (1626–79) is another artist who painted marvelous interior scenes, often satirical and didactic in their intent. The allusions that much of the satire depends on may escape most of us today, but any viewer can appreciate the fine drawing, subtle color shading, and warm light that pervades such paintings as *Woman at Her Toilet* and *The Feast of St. Nicholas.*

VAN GOGH & THE TURN OF THE CENTURY If **Vincent van Gogh** (1853–90) had not failed as a missionary in the mining region of Belgium, he might not have turned to painting and become the greatest Dutch artist of the 19th century. *The Potato Eaters* (1885) was the anxious and sensitive van Gogh's first masterpiece. Dark and crudely painted, it depicts a group of peasants gathered around the table for their evening meal after a long day of manual labor—one is powerfully impressed with a sense of the hard, rough conditions of their lives. Gone are the beauty and serenity of traditional Dutch genre painting.

After the death of his father, Vincent traveled first to Antwerp and then to Paris to join his favorite brother, Theo. In Paris he discovered and adopted the brilliant color palette of the impressionists. Theo, an art dealer, introduced him to Gauguin, and they had many conversations on the expressive power of pure color. Van Gogh developed a thick, highly textured style of brushwork that complemented his intense color schemes.

In 1888 van Gogh traveled to Arles in Provence. He was dazzled by the Mediterranean sun, and his favorite color, yellow (it signified love to him), dominated such landscapes as *Wheatfield with a Reaper* (1889). Until his death two years later, van Gogh remained in the south of France painting at a frenetic pace, in between bouts of madness. In *The Night Café* (1888), the red walls and green ceiling of a billiard hall combine with a sickly yellow lamplight to charge the scene with an oppressive, almost nightmarish air. (With red and green, Vincent wrote, he tried to represent "those terrible things, men's passions.") We see the halos around the lights swirl as if we, like some of the patrons slumped over their tables, have had too much to drink. Perhaps van Gogh's best-known nightscape is *The Starry Night* (1889), with its whirling starlight—a turbulent universe filled with personal anxiety and fear.

The Vincent van Gogh Museum in Amsterdam has more than 200 of his paintings—including *The Sunflowers*—presented to Holland by Theo's wife and son with the provision that the canvases not leave Vincent's native land.

Before **Piet Mondrian** (1872–1944) became a master/originator of De Stijl (also called neoplasticism) he was a painter of windmills, cows, and meadows. He painted his expressionistic masterpiece, *The Red Tree* (1909)—which looks as though it is exploding on fire against a background of blue—at age 41, and it marks a turning point in his career as a contemporary painter. He had always said that when he had discovered his true personality he would drop one of the two *a*'s in his last name—it is this canvas that he first signed as Mondrian.

With his friend Theo van Doesburg, Mondrian began in 1917 a magazine entitled *De Stijl* (The Style), in which he expounded the principles of neoplasticism—a simplification of forms, reducing what is represented to a limited number of signs, or in other words, purified abstraction. In large part this movement was an outgrowth of and a reaction against the cubist work of Picasso and Braque, which Mondrian had seen while he lived in Paris from 1912 to 1914. To Mondrian and the poets, sculptors, and architects associated with De Stijl, abstraction was a moral necessity; to simplify vision would simplify life, and a universal plastic language would bring about a better world. For these reasons, the geometric painters of the De Stijl school attempted a "controllable precision." Their basic form was the rectangle—with horizontal and vertical accents at right angles. Their basic colors were the primaries—red, blue, and yellow—along with black and white. In works such as *Composition in Blue, Yellow, and Black* (1936), no part of the picture plane is more important than any other; with its design, Mondrian achieves an equilibrium but does not succumb to a mechanical uniformity.

Mondrian suppressed the use of curves and the color green in his later work because, he said, it reminded him of nature. Ironically, Mondrian's principal source of income for much of his life was painting flowers on porcelain. In 1940 Mondrian moved to New York City, which he loved, to escape the war in Europe. In the evenings he would take walks around the art deco Rockefeller Center; the geometry of the lighted windows reminded him of his paintings. Mondrian's last paintings were lively abstract representations of New York: *Broadway Boogie Woogie* (1942) and *Victory Boogie Woogie* (1943).

In the late 1940s **Karel Appel** (b. 1921), a Dutch abstract painter, sculptor, and graphic artist who helped found the experimental COBRA group, came on the scene. His work, including *Child and Beast II* (1951), has a childlike quality, employing bright colors and abstract shapes. He himself once said, "I paint like a barbarian in a barbarous age." He worked in Amsterdam for some time, and in order to pay debts to the city, he painted a mural in what used to be the Amsterdam Town Hall (and is now the Grand Amsterdam Hotel)— for years it was considered so revolting it was covered up. If you go to Café Roux (the café at the Grand Amsterdam), you can see it preserved behind glass.

Architecture

If you're interested in studying a bit of architecture, Amsterdam is a great place for it. You might think the canal houses in Amsterdam all look similar (they do for the most part, in terms of shape). However, if you look a little more closely you'll find that Amsterdam's buildings demonstrate a wonderful mix of architectural detail ranging from classical to Renaissance to modern.

EARLY AMSTERDAM   Amsterdam's very first houses were built of wood and had thatch roofs, for practical reasons. Wood was lighter than stone or brick, and therefore a timber house was less likely to sink into the marshy, constantly shifting ground. Even today, though foundations are much stronger than they were in the beginning, you'll see canal houses leaning precariously against one another as a result of the ground movement. (You might also see that the streets and sidewalks of Amsterdam are constantly being torn up, straightened out, and relaid for the same reason.) Houses were narrow but very deep and fairly tall. The gables were made of wood, and on each floor they projected out farther than the one below for drainage purposes.

In 1452 about three-quarters of Amsterdam was destroyed by fire. The side walls of new houses were then made of brick to prevent the spread of fire from one house to its very near neighbor. At the beginning of the 16th century (again to counter the threat of fire), thatch roofs began to disappear beneath a covering of clay and were eventually replaced with tiles. The houses, though now made of brick, looked exactly like the wood ones that came before.

In the 16th and 17th centuries the *strap and scroll* ornament became quite popular. A fluid form, the strap and scroll frames the top part of the facade and resembles curled leather. The *step gable,* a nonclassical element resembling a small staircase (with varying numbers of steps and varying step heights), was used on many of the buildings you'll see as you walk along the canals today. Often you'll find step gables of this period augmented by Renaissance features, such as vases and masks. A particular favorite of mine is the step gable with strap and scroll work because of the contrast between the angles of the steps and the fluidity of the straps.

Hendrik de Keyser (1565–1621), an architect who worked in Amsterdam at the height of the Renaissance, is known for using decorative, playful elements in a way that was practical to the structure. For instance, he combined hard yellow or white sandstone decorative features (like volutes, keystones, and masks) with soft red brick, creating a visually stimulating multicolored facade, while at the same time utilizing the sandstone as protection for the brick from rain erosion. **Philip** and **Justus Vingboons** were architects and brothers who also worked in the Renaissance style, and if you walk along the Herengracht, Keizersgracht, and Prinsengracht, you'll see many of the buildings they designed.

Many other buildings from the 17th century have typically classical elements, such as pilasters, entablatures, and pediments. These details give a sense of order and balance to their facades and move away from de Keyser's playful Renaissance style. The classical pediment, often used as a protective element against the rain, was typically used to shield windows and to cap gable ends. It was also during this time that a harder, brown brick came to be used as a replacement for the red brick used in the 16th century. Because classical elements tend to have straight lines and don't flow like the Renaissance elements did, the focus on the facade shifted to a more boxed-in, central location which eventually grew into the raised-neck gable (a tall, narrow, rectangular gable). It was during this classical period that fruits and flowers were used as ornamentation in the scrolls. Soon, the raised-neck gable gave way to the neck gable (which looks relatively the same, only shorter) with human and animal figures carved into the scrolls. **Jacob van Campen** (1595–1657), who built the Amsterdam Town Hall and the Dam, was probably the single most important architect of the classical period in Amsterdam architecture.

Around 1665 **Adriaan Dortsman** (1625–82), best known as an architect of the classic restrained Dutch style, began building homes with balconies and attics, leaving off the pilasters and festoons that had adorned facades earlier in the century. The emphasis had once again shifted, this time from ornamentation and decoration to utility of space and harmony of the features with the basic structure.

THE 18TH & 19TH CENTURIES   During the 18th century Amsterdam's population did not increase, so new housing wasn't needed. However, many people rebuilt the facades of their homes and incorporated some new styles that architects had been studying. **Daniel Marot,** a French architect who lived in Amsterdam from 1705 to 1717, is credited with introducing the "Louis" styles to Amsterdam, and they are common to buildings of the 18th century.

The heavy, baroque Louis XIV style was suitable for the neck gable, but the asymmetrical, rococo Louis XV style was better executed on a new gable type—the bell gable. Its name is description enough, although you might at first confuse it with the neck gable because if you look only at the outer lines of the top of the structure you'll frequently see the same basic triangular shape (due to the ornamentation of the neck gables); however, the bell gable is very clearly shaped like a bell.

There was virtually no population growth in the first half of the 19th century, and new housing development in Amsterdam remained at a standstill from the end of the 18th century to about 1860. During this period much of Amsterdam's architecture underwent a reversion to classicism, albeit in a more ornate manner. Many of the more ornate gables were replaced with straight cornices. However, in 1876, **Petrus Josephus Herbertus Cuypers** (1827–1921) came on the scene, quickly establishing himself as the most influential architect of the time. Perhaps best known for designing Centraal Station and the Rijksmuseum, he worked in a Neo-Gothic style using steep roofs and dormers and is considered to be the "grandfather of modern architecture." He ascribed to a theory known as "structural rationalism," which is Gothic in principle, and believed in utilizing ornamentation that is natural and organic to the basic form of the structure.

At the end of the century this heavily ornamented look was simplified by, among others, **Willem Kromhout** (1864–1940), who designed the Hotel Americain, which is worth a visit. **Hendrik Berlage** (1856–1934), said to be the "father of modern architecture," followed, and his Amsterdam Exchange and Diamond Worker's Trade Union buildings are two examples of a more refined Dutch style. Kromhout and Berlage's most important works were not built until the beginning of this century.

THE 20TH CENTURY   Between 1900 and 1940 many different styles of architecture were purveyed from the offices of various Amsterdam architects, but one style stands out above the others: the famous Amsterdam school, with Ed. Cuypers (nephew to P. J. H. Cuypers) at the helm. Architects P. L. Kramer, M. de Klerk, and J. M. van der Mey were employed by Cuypers at the beginning of the century and were all contributors to the Amsterdam school.

Some of Amsterdam's most "fantastic" buildings were designed by the members of the Amsterdam school; they succeeded in creating forms of brickwork that had henceforth existed only in the fantasies of earlier architects. These buildings are massive but somehow fluid and use such decorative features as stained glass, wrought iron, and corner towers.

Closer to the middle of the century the decorative brickwork features used by the Amsterdam school were abandoned because architects were more interested in creating an absolutely functional space, placing a premium on eliminating architectural flourishes that cluttered and detracted from the utility of a space. Lines were clean, straight, and sharp—not rounded and free-form. Up sprang high-rises constructed with concrete, steel, and glass. After World War II the focus on design shifted to suburban development and urban renewal. It was then that this "functionalism," just becoming popular before the war, really flourished. This architectural ideology is the basis for what we know as modern urban planning, with its sleek skyscrapers and high-rise office and apartment buildings.

4 Food & Drink

Meals

The first step in gaining an acquaintance with Dutch gastronomy is to forget that we use the word *entrée* to mean a main course; in Holland, an entrée is an appetizer, and main courses are listed separately as *vis* (fish) and *vlees* (meats) or, in a less pretentious restaurant, *dagschotels* (plates of the day). The other courses you will see on Dutch menus are *soepen* (soups), *warme* or *koude voorgrechten* (warm or cold appetizers), *groenten* (vegetables), *sla* (salad), *vruchten* (fruits), *nachgerechten* (desserts), *dranken* (beverages), and *wijn* (wine).

The next step is to understand that Dutch is a language of compound words, and just as Leiden Street becomes Leidsestraat—one word for two ideas—you'll notice on menus that beef steak becomes *biefstuk*, pork chop becomes *varkenscotelette*, and so on.

Similarly, you will find listings for *gehakte biefstuk* (chopped beef) or *gebrakken worst* (fried sausage). The clue is to look for the following key words and word endings as you scan a menu for basic information on the cuts of meat available and the modes of preparation of the dishes you are choosing among:

- For cuts of meat: *-stuk* (steak or, literally, piece), *-scotelet* or *-scotelette* (chop), *-kotelet* or *-kotelette* (cutlet).
- For modes of preparation: *gekookt* or *gekookete* (boiled), *gebakken* (fried), *gebraden* (roasted), *geroosteren* (broiled), *gerookte* (smoked).
- For meat cooked to your taste: *niet doorgebakken* (rare), *half doorgebakken* (medium), *goed doorgebakken* (well done).

Dining Customs

BREAKFAST The Dutch don't eat bacon and eggs or drink orange juice, but they eat nearly as much as we do in the morning. Dutch hotel restaurants serve the same kind of breakfast the Dutch make for themselves at home, with the cost sometimes incorporated in your room rate. Bring a good appetite to the table, however, because a typical Dutch morning begins with a selection of breads (often fresh from the *warme bakker*) and rusks (crunchy toasted rounds, like Zweiback), a platter of cheese and sliced meats (ham, roast beef, salami), butter and jam (and perhaps chocolate sprinkles, which are a favorite with Dutch children), and as much coffee (Dutch coffee is thicker and stronger than its American cousin, and is often served with a thick dairy product called *koffiemelk,* similar to condensed milk) or tea as you can drink. Plus, some hotels include a boiled egg, yogurt, a glass of fruit juice, or all three (if not offered or available on the buffet table, however, these extras tend to be expensive).

LUNCH & DINNER These are much the same as you'd find in the United States. For instance, the Dutch will often have a sandwich with meat and cheese or a hamburger for lunch, then a rela-tively early dinner consisting of meat, potatoes, and a vegetable.

The Cuisine

In your travels around Holland you may notice in restaurant windows a distinctive small sign with a soup tureen encircled with the words "NEERLANDS DIS." This is the tip-off you've found a restaurant that serves traditional Dutch and Dutch-regional special-ties at reasonable prices. There are 240 restaurants in this program around the country.

LUNCH & SNACK SPECIALTIES   Below are a number of dishes you may notice on lunch menus or may want to look for as typically Dutch choices for your midday meal:

Uitsmijter   An open-face sandwich consisting of a slice of bread (or two), buttered and topped with cold slices of ham or roast beef and one or two fried eggs.

Ertwensoep   Pea soup, thick and creamy and chock-full of chunks of ham, carrots, and potatoes—a meal by itself. (This is what the Dutch call a winter dish, so you may have trouble finding it on menus in summer.)

Croquetten   Fried croquettes of meat or cheese that may be quite gooey inside but are at their best when served piping hot with a blob of mustard for dunking.

Broodjes   Small sandwiches on round buttered rolls, made with ham, cheese, roast beef, salami, or other fillings. They're often or-dered in pairs and eaten standing up or perched at a narrow counter in a *broodjeswinkel,* or sandwich shop.

Tostis   Grilled ham-and-cheese sandwiches.

Pannekoeken & Poffertjes   Dutch pancakes that are the equiva-lent of French crêpes, served flat on a dinner plate and topped with plain sugar, confectioner's sugar, jam, syrup, hot apples, or—typically Dutch—hot ginger sauce. Less common are pannekoeken with meat.

Bitterballen   Fried potato balls, or croquettes, that are generally quite spicy.

Saucijzenbrood   A Dutch hot dog, except in this case the bun is flaky pastry and the hot dog is a spicy Dutch wurst, or sausage.

Bami/Nasi Goreng & Nasi Rames   Miniature versions of an In-donesian rijstaffel (see below) that are served in a bowl on a bed of either noodles or rice, with spiced meat and possibly a fried egg or stick of sateh (a grilled kebab) on top.

Nieuwe Haring   New herring, the fresh-caught fish that is eaten whole (or chopped if you're squeamish) with minced onion at stands all over town during summer; during the rest of the year it's eaten pickled.

DINNER SPECIALTIES With the exception of an exceptional taste treat—an Indonesian rijstaffel (see below)—the Dutch may seem to be less inventive in the area of native dinner specialties than they are for lunch and snacks. This is partly due to the fact that many traditional, typically Dutch dishes closely resemble dishes we know here at home, but mostly it's due to modern Holland's ongoing and ever-growing love affair with French cuisine. Here, however, are a few typically Dutch menu choices you may encounter, particularly in winter, when the stick-to-the-ribs nature of real Dutch cooking can be best appreciated:

Hutspot A stew made of ribs of beef, carrots, onions, and potatoes, often mashed together. This is a dish with historic significance, particularly for the people of Leiden: It's the Dutch version of the stew found in the boiling pots left behind after the Spaniards were routed from their city at the end of the long siege during the Eighty Years' War.

Zuurkool Met Spek en Wurst Sauerkraut with bacon and sausage.

Rolpens A combination of minced beef, fried apples, and red cabbage.

Krabbetjes Dutch spareribs, usually beef ribs rather than pork.

Capucijners Met Spek Marrow beans with bacon.

Stampot Cabbage with smoked sausage.

Hazepeper Jugged hare.

Gerookte Paling Smoked eel, a typically Dutch appetizer.

Gember Met Slagroom The typically Dutch sweet-and-sour dessert of tangy slices of fresh ginger, topped with whipped cream.

A SPECIAL DUTCH FEAST The Indonesian feast **rijstaffel** is Holland's favorite meal and has been ever since the Dutch East India Company captains introduced it to the wealthy burghers of Amsterdam in the 17th century. It's an acquired taste, and unless you already have a stomach for both Chinese and Indian cooking, you may not like much of what you eat. But to be in Holland and not at least try a rijstaffel is as much a pity as it would be to miss seeing Rembrandt's *The Night Watch* while you had the chance. Besides, with more than 20 different dishes on the table, you're bound to find a few you enjoy.

The basic concept of a rijstaffel is to eat a bit of this and a bit of that, blending the flavors and textures. A simple, unadorned bed of rice is the base and the mediator between spicy meats and bland vegetables or fruits, between sweet-and-sour tastes, soft-and-crunchy textures. Although a rijstaffel for one is possible, this feast is better shared by two or by a table full of people. In the case of a solitary diner or a couple, a 17-dish rijstaffel will be enough food; with four or more, order a 24- or 30-dish rijstaffel and you can experience the total taste treat.

Before you begin to imagine 30 dinner-size plates of food, it's important to mention that the dishes used to serve an Indonesian meal are small and the portions served are gauged by the number of people expected to share them. Remember, the idea is to have tastes of many things rather than a full meal of any single item. Also, there are no separate courses in an Indonesian rijstaffel (the name means "rice table"). Once your table has been set with a row of low, Sterno-powered plate warmers, all 17 or 24 or 30 dishes are served at one time, the sweets along with the sours and the spicy, so you're left to plot your own course through the extravaganza. (Beware, however, of one very appealing dish of sauce with small chunks of what looks to be bright-red onion—that is *sambal badjak*, or simply *sambal*, and it's hotter than hot!)

Among the customary dishes and ingredients of a rijstaffel are *loempia* (classic Chinese-style egg rolls); *satay*, or *sateh* (small kebabs of pork, grilled and served with a spicy peanut sauce); *perkedel* (meatballs); *gado-gado* (vegetables in peanut sauce); *daging smoor* (beef in soy sauce); *babi ketjap* (pork in soy sauce); *kroepak* (crunchy, puffy shrimp toast); *serundeng* (fried coconut); *roedjak manis* (fruit in sweet sauce); and *pisang goreng* (fried banana).

Drink

You know the old saying, "Wine is fine, but. . . ." Well, wine is fine for the Dutch, they like to have a glass or a bottle at dinner, but they don't usually sit around sipping wine in a bar.

Instead, the Dutch are most famous for their gin, or ***jenever,*** and their beer. You can get flavored jenever—from berry to lemon—and just like the cheese, you can get *oude* or *jong* jenever, and every bar has a wide selection of most or all of the above on its shelves. Now, as for **beer,** well, you can get the regular Heineken or Amstel—called *pils* in Amsterdam, or you could try something different as you make the rounds of the brown cafés (the world-renowned Dutch beer halls). I happen to like the *witte,* or white, beer, which is sweeter than pils. Or, on the opposite end of the spectrum, you can have a dark beer, like De Koninck or Duvel.

5 Recommended Books

Architecture

Hitchcock, Henry-Russel. *Netherlandish Scrolled Gables of the Sixteenth and Early Seventeenth Centuries,* New York University Press.

Kemme, Guus, ed. *Amsterdam Architecture: A Guide.* IDEA Books.

Polano, Sergio. *Hendrik Petrus Berlage.* Rizzoli International Publications.

Troy, Nancy. *The De Stijl Environment.* MIT Press.

de Wit, Wim. *The Amsterdam School.* MIT Press.

Art

Brown, Christopher. *Images of a Golden Past: Dutch Genre Painting of the 17th Century.* Abbeville.

————, and Peter C. Stanton. *Masters of SeventeenthCentury Dutch Landscape Painting.* University of Pennsylvania Press.

Clark, Kenneth. *An Introduction to Rembrandt.* Harper & Row.

Fuchs, R. H. *Dutch Painting.* Oxford University Press.

Wheelock, Arthur. *Vermeer.* Abrams.

History

Blok, Petrus, J. *History of the People of the Netherlands.* Putnam.

Boxer, C. R. *The Dutch Seaborne Empire 1600–1800.*

Carasso, Dedalo. *A Short History of Amsterdam.* Amsterdam Historical Museum.

Cotterell, Geoffrey. *Amsterdam: The Life of a City.* Little, Brown.

Geyl, Pieter. *The Netherlands in the 17th Century.*

————. *The Revolt of the Netherlands 1555–1609.* Barnes & Noble.

Huizinga, J. *Dutch Civilization in the 17th Century.*

Kistemaker, R., and R. Van Gelder. *Amsterdam. The Golden Age 1275–1795.*

Kossmann, E. H. *The Low Countries 1780–1940.* Oxford University Press.

Murray, J. J. *Amsterdam in the Age of Rembrandt.* Norman.

Parker, Geoffrey. *The Dutch Revolt.* Cornell University Press.

Schama, Simon. *The Embarrassment of Riches: An Interpretation of Dutch Culture in the Golden Age.* Knopf.

————. *Patriots and Liberators: Revolution in the Netherlands.* Knopf.

Vaan Loon, Hendrik. *The Golden Book of Dutch Navigators.* Ayer.

Nazi Occupation

Frank, Anne. *The Diary of Anne Frank.* Doubleday. For Grade 7 and up.

Janssen, Pierre. *A Moment of Silence,* translated by William R. Tyler. Macmillan. For Grade 5 and up.

2

Planning a Trip to Amsterdam

Aɴʏ ᴛʀɪᴘ ᴛᴏ ᴀ ꜰᴏʀᴇɪɢɴ ᴅᴇꜱᴛɪɴᴀᴛɪᴏɴ ꜱᴜᴄʜ ᴀꜱ Aᴍꜱᴛᴇʀᴅᴀᴍ ᴄᴀɴ ʙᴇᴄᴏᴍᴇ an ordeal if not properly planned. To really put your best foot forward, you'll want to know how much everything will cost; how you're going to get there; what documents, clothing, and other travel necessities you should bring along; and when you should go to best take advantage of special events in the city. Below you'll find all the information you'll need to help you plan your trip before you leave home.

A sound way to begin your preparations for a trip to **Amsterdam** would be to avail yourself of the **Amsterdam Culture Card,** which contains 25 coupons granting free entry or substantial discounts to the Rijksmuseum, the Stedelijk Museum of Modern Art, the Vincent van Gogh Museum, and several other attractions, excursions, and restaurants. It also offers reduced rates on the Museum Boat and the canal boats—all for only Dfl 29.90 ($15.73). For information or to order the card, contact your local Netherlands Board of Tourism or one of the tourist offices in Amsterdam.

1 Information, Entry Requirements, Customs & Money

SOURCES OF INFORMATION   Before leaving for Holland, you can obtain information on the country and its travel facilities by contacting the **Netherlands Board of Tourism,** which maintains offices in countries around the world. In the **United States,** you can reach them at 225 N. Michigan Ave., Chicago, IL 60601 (☎ **312/ 819-0300**). The following is a partial listing of offices in other countries: **Canada,** 25 Adelaide St. E., Toronto, ON M5C 1Y2 (☎ **416/ 363-1577**); **Australia,** 5 Elizabeth St., Sydney NSW 2000 (☎ **02/2476921**); **Belgium,** Ravensteinstraat 68, 1000 Brussels (☎ **2/511-8646**); **France,** 31/33 ave. des Champs-Elysées, 75008 Paris (☎ **1/42-25-41-25**); **Great Britain,** 25–28 Buckingham Gate, London SW1E 6LD (☎ **71/630-0451**); **Italy,** via Turati 8, 20122 Milan (☎ **02/65-75-301**); **Japan,** No. 10 Mori Bldg., 1-18-1 Toranomon, Minato-Ku, Tokyo (☎ **03/508-8015**); **Spain,** 55-4-G Gran Vía, 28013 Madrid (☎ **1/541-58-28**).

ENTRY REQUIREMENTS   Citizens of the United States, Canada, Australia, and New Zealand need only a valid passport for a visit to the Netherlands for stays of less than three months. If you are planning to stay longer, you should contact the **Bureau Vreemdelingenpolitie** at Waterlooplein 9 (☎ **559-91-91**) for further information.

CUSTOMS   Amsterdam Customs is a simple matter that operates essentially on the honor system. You're allowed to bring one carton of cigarettes and one liter of scotch, bourbon, or the like; there are no limitations on the amount of foreign currency you can bring into Holland, and you choose one of two Customs clearance aisles, red or green, depending on whether or not you have "goods to declare."

The Dutch Guilder

For American Readers At this writing $1 = approximately Dfl 1.90 (or Dfl 1 = 53¢), and this was the rate of exchange used to calculate the dollar values given in this guide (rounded to the nearest nickel).

For British Readers At this writing, £1 = approximately Dfl 2.80 (or Dfl 1 = 36 p), and this was the rate of exchange used to calculate the pound values in the table below.

Note International exchange rates fluctuate from time to time and may not be the same when you travel to the Netherlands. Therefore, this table should be used only as a guide.

Dfl	U.S.$	U.K.£	Dfl	U.S.$	U.K.£
.25	.15	.10	30	15.80	10.70
.50	.30	.20	35	18.45	12.50
.75	.40	.30	40	21.05	14.30
1	.55	.40	45	23.70	16.10
2	1.05	.70	50	26.30	17.85
3	1.60	1.10	60	31.60	21.40
4	2.10	1.45	70	36.80	25.00
5	2.65	1.80	80	42.10	28.60
6	3.15	2.15	90	47.35	32.15
7	3.70	2.50	100	52.35	35.70
8	4.20	2.85	125	65.80	44.60
9	4.75	3.20	150	78.90	53.60
10	5.30	3.60	175	92.10	62.50
15	7.90	5.35	200	105.30	71.40
20	10.60	7.15	250	131.60	89.30
25	13.15	8.40	300	157.90	107.15

One more thing: If you are carrying valuables with you, take the receipts along. When you return to the United States, these receipts will be proof that you owned such items before your trip to Amsterdam, and thus they will protect you against any unwarranted duty charges. (For more on Customs when you return to the United States, see "Customs" under "Fast Facts: Amsterdam" in Chapter 3.)

MONEY Dutch currency is based on the decimal system. Consequently, you will see prices written in the familiar format of 1.95, 3.50, 5.00, and so on, although the symbol preceding the figures will probably be an *f, fl,* or *Dfl* (a holdover from earlier days when the florin was coin of the realm). Today the **guilder** is the basic monetary unit in Holland, and there are 100 Dutch cents to each guilder. All Dutch banknotes have a bumpy patch on one corner; this is the bill's denomination in Braille as an aid to the blind. The table below lists the denominations of coins and frequently used banknotes along with their familiar names (for coins), identifying colors (for bills), and U.S. dollar and British pound equivalents. The U.S. denominations are based on the exchange rate at press time, about Dfl 1.90 for $1 U.S.

Dutch Currency

Dutch Coins				Bills			
Dfl	Name	U.S.$	U.K.£	Dfl	Color	U.S.$	U.K.£
0.05	stuiver	0.05	0.02	5	green	2.60	1.80
0.10	dubbeitie	0.10	0.05	10	blue	5.30	3.60
0.25	kwartje	0.15	0.10	25	red	13.15	8.90
1.00	guilder	0.55	0.40	50	yellow	26.30	17.85
2.50	rijksdaaier	1.30	0.90	100	brown	52.40	35.70
5.00	beatrix	2.60	1.80	1,000	green	523.60	357.10

Traveler's Checks   It's a good idea, for safety's sake either to carry most of your money in traveler's checks instead of cash or to use automated-teller machines (ATMs) or credit or charge cards. You will want to have about $100 in Dutch guilders with you when you arrive in Amsterdam to take care of expenses incurred during your

What Things Cost in Amsterdam	U.S.$
Taxi from the airport to the city center	28.90
Metro from Centraal Station to Waterlooplein	1.60
Local telephone call	0.15
Double room at the Amstel Hotel (expensive)	368.40
Double room at the Hotel Estherea (moderate)	152.65
Double room at Hotel Seven Bridges (inexpensive)	71.05
Dinner for one, without wine, at Dynasty (expensive)	42.10
Dinner for one, without wine, at Bodega Keyzer (moderate)	30.50
Dinner for one, without wine, at Haesje Claes (inexpensive)	18.40
Glass of beer	1.85
Coca-Cola	1.60
Cup of coffee	1.60
Roll of ASA 100 color film, 36 exposures	7.90
Admission to the Vincent van Gogh Museum	5.30
Movie ticket	10.55
Theater ticket to the Concertgebouw	18.00

first few days. Banks will give you a better rate of exchange than shops and hotels. Be sure to keep a record of the numbers of your traveler's checks in a separate place; replacement of lost checks will then be a simple matter.

Credit & Charge Cards   **Visa** is the most widely used card, along with **MasterCard** (known as **EuroCard** in Europe). **American Express** is often accepted, mostly in the middle- and upper-bracket category.

If you make a purchase with a credit or charge card, remember that credit- and charge-card companies compute the exchange rate on the date the charge is posted, not on the date you actually made the transaction.

You can also withdraw cash from bank automated-teller machines (ATMs) at many locations in Amsterdam. Check with your credit- or charge-card company before leaving home. Until banks start charging hefty transaction fees for the service, withdrawing cash from an ATM will probably secure you the most favorable rates of exchange. ATMs can be found at airports and railway stations as well as throughout the city. MasterCard/Cirrus operates 169,000 machines in 60 countries, and Visa/PLUS has 185,000 machines in 80 countries. Before leaving home ask your bank for the Visa Plus *ATM Locator Guide* and MasterCard's *ATM Travel Directory.*

2   When to Go

Climate

Although the temperature rarely dips below freezing in winter, remember that Amsterdam and much of Holland is below sea level, making fog, mist, and dampness your ever-present companions. This dampness can seem to cut through to your very bones so you'll want to layer yourself in Goretex or something similar in winter. In summer, the temperature rarely rises above 75°F, making for a pleasant, balmy urban climate. Expect some rain though. The average annual rainfall is 25 inches. Most of it falls from November through January, although substantial showers occur throughout the year.

Amsterdam's Average Monthly Temperature & Days of Rain

	Jan	Feb	Mar	Apr	May	June	July	Aug	Sept	Oct	Nov	Dec
Temp. (°F)	36	36	41	46	54	59	62	62	58	51	44	38
Days of rain	21	17	19	20	19	17	20	20	19	20	22	23

Holidays

A Dutch holiday can add a festive note to your trip, particularly if it involves a parade or special observance somewhere in the country. But you can expect banks, shops, and some museums to be closed on New Year's Day, Good Friday, Easter Sunday and Easter

Monday, Ascension Day, April 30 (the Queen's Birthday—the actual birthday of the former queen, Juliana, and the anniversary of the coronation of her daughter Beatrix), Whit Monday/Pentecost (a European religious holiday that usually falls in late May or early June), Christmas, and December 26.

Amsterdam Calendar of Events

The biggest and most exciting event in Holland is the **Elfstedentocht,** the eleven-town race in which skaters compete to complete the 125-mile course in the fastest time. The first race was run in 1909, and it has been run only 13 times since, the last in 1987. Perhaps the weather and ice conditions will allow the race to be held when you are visiting.

March

⊠ Stille Omgang

A silent procession held every year by Catholics to celebrate the "Miracle of the Host," which occurred in 1345; see "History" under "Geography, History, and People" in Chapter 1 for the full story.
Where: Along the Kalverstraat. The central meeting point is the Queen's Palace in Dam Square from midnight to 2:30am. **When:** Sunday closest to March 15; in 1995 it will be March 18–19. **How:** Contact Gezelschap voor de Stille Omgang, Zandvoorterweg 59, 2111 GS Aerdenhout (☎ **24-54-15**), for more information.

April

⊠ National Museum Weekend

A weekend during which many national museums offer free or reduced admission and have special exhibitions.
Where: Most museums in Amsterdam and 400 in Holland. **When:** April 22–23, 1995; April 20–21, 1996. **How:** Contact Stichting Museumjaarkaart, Groen-hazengracht 2c, 2311 VT Leiden (☎ **13-32-65**), for information.

• **Queen's Day (Koninginnedag).** This citywide celebration is, in fact, more like one big shopping day, so be prepared! April 30.

June

• **Kunst RAI.** An annual arts fair in which many Dutch art galleries participate. Each year the theme centers around a different country. Contact the Foundation Kunstbeurs, Prinsengracht 629, 1016 HV Amsterdam (☎ **020/620-12-60**), for further information and dates.

⭐ Holland Festival

Each year, the Dutch cities of Amsterdam, The Hague, Rotterdam, and Utrecht join forces to present a culture buff's smörgåsbord of music, opera, theater, film, and dance. The schedule includes all the major Dutch companies as well as visiting companies and soloists from around the world, and it's a marvel of planning. Although it would seem that a festival taking place in four cities at one time would be impossible to enjoy, Holland is a very compact nation, and the festival's organizers skillfully rotate performers among auditoriums in the four cities. Even for tourists, then, it's possible to see much of the festival's offerings. Don't wait until the last minute to plan for this event, however; it becomes more popular every year.

Where: Amsterdam, The Hague, Rotterdam, and Utrecht. **When:** Throughout June. **How:** For information on how to get tickets in advance, contact Holland Festival, kl Gartmanplantsoen 21, 1017 RP Amsterdam (☎ **020/627-65-66**).

- **World Roots Festival.** This festival features music and dance from all over the world. Workshops, films, and exhibitions are also offered. Contact Foundation Melkweg, Lijnbaansgracht 234a, 1017 PH Amsterdam (☎ **624-17-77**), for exact dates and information.

September

⭐ Bloemencorso

Every year for nearly half a century, Amsterdam has been the final destination for the Flower Parade that originates in Aalsmeer. The parade features a large number of floats that carry a variety of in-season flowers (don't expect to see tulips, however).

Where: The parade ends at the Dam but follows an established route from Aalsmeer to Amsterdam. **When:** First Saturday in September. **How:** Contact Stichting Bloemencorso, P.O. Box 332, 1430 AH Aalsmeer (☎ **02977-25100**), for parade times and route.

3 Health & Insurance

HEALTH PREPARATIONS   You will encounter few health problems traveling in Holland. The tap water is safe to drink, the milk is pasteurized, and health services are good. Occasionally the change in diet may cause some minor diarrhea, so you may want to take some antidiarrhea medicine along.

Pack all your vital medicine in your carry-on luggage and bring enough prescribed medications to sustain you during your stay.

Bring along copies of your prescriptions that are written in the generic—not brand-name—form. If you need a doctor, your hotel can recommend one or you can contact your embassy or consulate.

If you suffer from a chronic illness, talk to your doctor before taking the trip. For such conditions as epilepsy, diabetes, or a heart condition, wear a **Medic Alert Identification Tag.** The tag not only alerts any doctor to your condition but also provides the number of Medic Alert's 24-hour hotline so that a foreign doctor can obtain medical records for you. The cost of membership begins at $35. An annual fee of $15 will be charged after the first year's membership. Contact the Medic Alert Foundation, 2323 Colorado Ave., Turlock CA 95382-2018 (☎ toll free **800/432-5378**).

INSURANCE Before purchasing any additional insurance, check your homeowner's, automobile, and medical insurance policies as well as the insurance provided by credit-card companies and auto and travel clubs. You may have adequate off-premises theft coverage; your credit-card company may even provide flight cancellation coverage if the ticket is charged to the card. Remember, Medicare covers only U.S. citizens traveling in Mexico and Canada.

Also note that to submit any claim you must always have thorough documentation, including all receipts, police reports, medical records, and the like.

If you are prepaying for your vacation or are taking a charter or any other flight that has cancellation penalties, look into cancellation insurance.

The following companies will provide further information:

Travel Guard International, 1145 Clark St., Stevens Point, WI 54481 (☎ toll free **800/826-1300**), features comprehensive insurance programs that cover everything from trip cancellation, lost luggage, and medical coverage to emergency assistance and accidental death; it also offers a 24-hour worldwide emergency hotline. Premiums vary depending on the dollar amount and length of coverage you're seeking. For a comprehensive package covering a two-week tour costing $2,500 per person expect to pay between $125 and $175.

Travel Insured International, Inc., P.O. Box 280568, East Hartford, CT 06128-0568 (☎ toll free **800/243-3174**), exclusive agent for The Travelers Insurance Company of Hartford, offers illness and accident coverage. For lost or damaged luggage, $500 worth of coverage costs $20 for 6 to 10 days. You can also get trip-cancellation insurance.

Mutual of Omaha (Tele-Trip), 3201 Farnam St., Omaha, NE 68131 (☎ **402/345-2400** or toll free **800/228-9792**), offers trip-cancellation insurance, lost or stolen luggage coverage, the standard accident coverage, and some other policies. Call to find out the premiums; the average cost is about $14 per day.

Wallach & Company, 107 W. Federal St. (P.O. Box 480), Suite 13, Middleburg, VA 22117-0480 (☎ **703/687-3166,** or toll free **800/237-6615**; fax 703/687-3172), offers a policy called HealthCare Abroad, good for 10 to 90 days, that costs $3 per day, including accident and sickness coverage to the tune of $100,000. Medical evacuation is also included, along with a $25,000 accidental death or dismemberment compensation. Trip cancellation and lost or stolen luggage can also be written into this policy at a nominal cost.

Access America, 6600 W. Broad St., Richmond, VA 23230 (☎ toll free **800/284-8300**), has a 24-hour "hotline" in case of an emergency and offers medical coverage for 9 to 15 days costing $49 for $10,000 worth. If you want medical plus trip cancellation, the charge is $111 for 5 to 15 days.

4   What to Pack

Lest you be led astray by the limited fluctuations in temperature, here are a few tips that will help ensure your comfort in Amsterdam, particularly if your visit is to be in fall or winter or during one of the region's less predictable seasons, such as tulip time.

First, invest in a fold-up umbrella and hope you never have to use it; likewise, carry a raincoat (with a wool liner for winter).

Second, pack a sweater or two (even in July) and be prepared to layer your clothing at any time of year. It's always simpler to add a cardigan over a summer dress or to eliminate a jacket under your raincoat than it is to swelter in long sleeves beneath the July sun or to shed a bulky winter coat on the first balmy days of spring, which can arrive as early as February in Holland.

Third, bring warm socks (one pair may be enough for summer) because damp ground and moist air have a way of carrying the cold right to your bones on a sunless day.

Fourth, and finally, leave your thin-soled shoes or boots at home— you may be unfazed by the damp, but you'll quickly sour on the city if your shoes aren't up to the challenge of the cobblestone streets.

5   Getting There

By Plane

THE MAJOR AIRLINES • **From North America   KLM** (☎ toll free **800/777-5553** in the U.S., **800/361-5330** in Canada, **800/366-9041** in Toronto), the Dutch airline, offers more flights to Holland from more cities around the world than any other airline, including service twice daily from New York City; daily from Chicago, Los Angeles, Houston, and Toronto; and two to six times each week from Anchorage, Atlanta, Baltimore, and Orlando in the United States, and from Calgary, Halifax, Montréal, Ottawa, and Vancouver in Canada.

Also offering a comprehensive schedule of services between North America and Amsterdam is **Martinair** (☎ toll free **800/FON-HOLLAND** or **800/366-4655** in the U.S. and Canada). Gateways are New York City (Kennedy and Newark airports), Baltimore, Tampa, Miami, Detroit, Minneapolis/St. Paul, Seattle, Los Angeles, San Francisco, and Toronto. Flights are offered May to

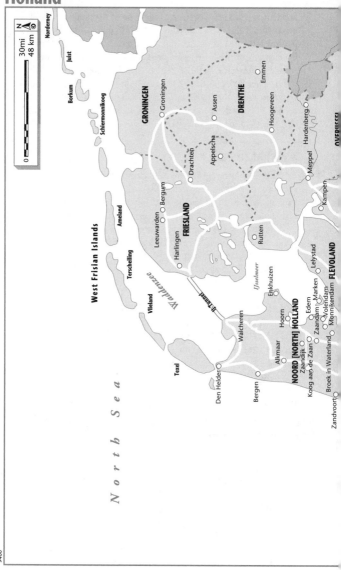

September only (except services from Tampa and Miami, which are offered year-round) and are available only one or two days each week, but the good news is that fares are discounted compared to the larger, more well-known airlines.

Other airlines flying directly to Holland from North America are **Canadian Airlines International** (☎ toll free **800/426-7000**), **Japan Airlines** (☎ toll free **800/525-3663**), **Northwest Airlines**

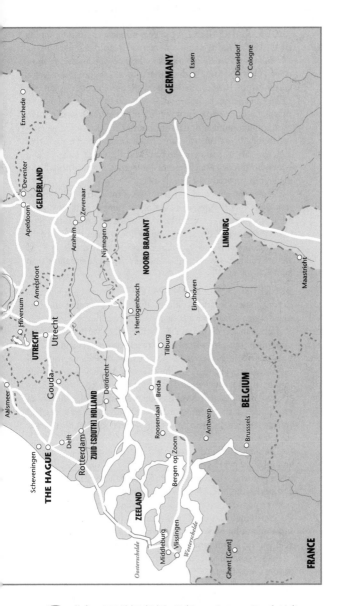

(☎ toll free **800/447-4747**), **Pakistan International Airlines**
(☎ **212/370-9158**), **Royal Jordanian** (☎ **212/949-0050**),
TWA (☎ toll free **800/221-2000**).

• **From the United Kingdom**   Airlines flying to Amsterdam from
Great Britain include **British Airways** (☎ **081/897-4000** in Lon-
don), **British Midlands** (☎ **0345/554-555** in London), and **Air
U.K.** (☎ **0345/666-777** in London).

REGULAR AIRFARES Advance planning and precision timing are the keys to saving money on international airfares; flexibility in scheduling and the ability to stick to the dates you reserve are also a help. The lowest fares in the business these days are called APEX (advance-purchase excursion) fares. Requirements vary among airlines, but generally these fares require you to reserve and pick up tickets at least seven days in advance and to stay abroad a minimum or maximum number of days (or both); they also might obligate you to additional charges for cancellations or changes of flight. These fares also vary by season of the year, with the lowest prices offered November through March (except during the Christmas period) and the highest between June and October.

To give you an idea of costs, in 1994 a round-trip APEX ticket from New York to Amsterdam during the summer peak travel periods was priced at $713 on KLM, $598 on Martinair; from the West Coast the same tickets were $805 and $778. On the other end of the spectrum, if you wanted to splurge, business-class service on KLM will set you back over $2,740 from the East Coast and more than $4,045 from the West Coast.

BUCKET SHOPS/CONSOLIDATORS These companies act as clearinghouses for blocks of tickets that airlines discount and consign during normally slow periods of air travel.

Tickets are usually priced 20% to 35% below the full fare. Terms of payment can vary—anything between last-minute and 45 days prior to departure. Tickets can be purchased through regular travel agents, who usually mark up the ticket 8% to 10%, maybe more, thereby greatly reducing your discount. A survey conducted of flyers who use consolidators voiced only one major complaint: Use of such a ticket doesn't qualify you for an advance seat assignment, and you are therefore likely to be assigned a "poor seat" on the plane at the last minute.

The survey revealed that most flyers estimated their savings at around $200 per ticket off the regular price. Nearly a third of the passengers reported savings of up to $300 off the regular price. But— and here's the hitch—many people who booked consolidator tickets reported no savings at all, as the airlines will sometimes match the consolidator fare by announcing a promotional fare. The situation is a bit tricky and calls for some careful investigation on your part to determine just how much you are saving.

Bucket shops abound from coast to coast. Look also for their ads in your local newspaper's travel section—they're usually very small and a single column in width. Here's one recommendation:

Travel Avenue, 10 S. Riverside Plaza, Suite 1404, Chicago, IL 60606-3807 (☎ **312/876-1116** or toll free **800/333-3335**), is a national agency with headquarters in Chicago. Its tickets are often cheaper than those of most shops because it charges the customer only a $25 fee on international tickets, rather than taking the usual 10% commission from an airline. Travel Avenue rebates most of that back to the customer—hence the lower fares.

Since dealing with unknown bucket shops might be a little risky, it's wise to call the Better Business Bureau in your area to see if complaints have been filed against the company from which you plan to purchase a fare.

CHARTER FLIGHTS Strictly speaking, a charter flight is an aircraft reserved months in advance for a one-time-only transit to some predetermined point. Before paying for a charter, check the restrictions on your ticket or contract. You may be asked to purchase a tour package and pay far in advance. You'll pay a stiff penalty (or forfeit the ticket entirely) if you cancel. Charters are sometimes canceled when the plane doesn't fill up. In some cases, the charter-ticket seller will offer you an insurance policy for your own legitimate cancellation (hospital confinement or death in the family, for example).

There is no way to predict whether a proposed flight to Amsterdam will cost less on a charter or from a bucket shop. You have to investigate at the time of your trip.

One company arranging charters is the **Council on International Educational Exchange (CIEE) (Council Travel),** 205 E. 42nd St., New York, NY 10017 (☎ **212/661-1414**), the travel division of CIEE. It offers the budget traveler a full range of affordable services on travel, work, and study abroad.

One of the biggest New York charter operators is **Travac,** 989 Sixth Ave., New York, NY 10018 (☎ **212/563-3303** or toll free **800/TRAV-800**), which operates charters from New York to London and other continental destinations, such as Paris.

REBATORS To confuse the situation even more, rebators also compete in the low-cost air-travel market. These outfits pass along to the passenger part of their commission, although many of them assess a fee for their services. Most rebators offer discounts that range from 10% to 25% (but this could vary from place to place), plus a $20 handling charge. They are not the same as travel agents, although they sometimes offer similar services, including discounted land arrangements and car rentals.

Rebators include **Travel Avenue,** 10 S. Riverside Plaza, Suite 1404, Chicago, IL 60606-3807 (☎ **312/876-1116** or toll free **800/ 333-3335**); **The Smart Traveler,** 3111 SW 27th Ave., Miami, FL 33133 (☎ **305/448-3338** or toll free **800/448-3338**); **Blitz Travel,** 8918 Manchester Rd., St. Louis, MO 63144 (☎ **314/961-2700**); and **Travel Management International (TMI),** 18 Prescott St., Suite 4, Cambridge, MA 02138 (☎ **617/661-8187** or toll free **800/245-3672**).

STANDBYS A favorite of spontaneous travelers with absolutely no scheduled demands on their time, standby fares leave your departure to the whims of fortune, and the hopes that a last-minute seat will become available. Most airlines don't offer standbys, although some seats are available to London and to Vienna. These fares are generally offered from April to November only.

GOING AS A COURIER This cost-cutting technique may not be for everybody. You travel as a passenger and courier, and for this service you'll secure a greatly discounted airfare or sometimes even a free ticket.

You're allowed one piece of carry-on luggage only; your baggage allowance is used by the courier firm to transport its cargo (which, by the way, is perfectly legal—often documents). As a courier, you don't actually handle the merchandise you're "transporting" to Europe, you just carry a manifest to present to Customs. Upon arrival, an employee of the courier service will reclaim the company's cargo. (Incidentally, you fly alone, so don't plan to travel with anybody.)

Most courier services operate from Los Angeles or New York, but some operate out of other cities, such as Chicago or Miami. Courier services are often listed in the *Yellow Pages* or in advertisements in travel sections or newspapers. For a start, check **Halbert Express,** 147-05 176th St., Jamaica, NY 11434 (☎ **718/656-8189** from 10am to 3pm daily); or **Now Voyager,** 74 Varick St., Suite 307, New York, NY 10013 (☎ **212/431-1616** daily from 11:30am to 6pm; at other times you'll get a recorded message announcing last-minute special round-trips).

By Train

Rail service to Amsterdam from other cities in the Netherlands and elsewhere in Europe is frequent, fast, and inexpensive. The **Eurailpass** allows unlimited first-class travel on the rail systems of 15 countries at a cost of $498 for 15 days, $648 for 21 days, $798 for 1 month, $1,098 for 2 months, and $1,398 for 3 months. The **Eurail Youth Pass** is available to those under 26 years of age at a cost of $578 for 1 month and $678 for 2 months. Both the Eurailpass and the Eurail Youth Pass must be purchased *before leaving the United States* and are available through travel agents.

There are rail connections to Amsterdam from France, Germany, Spain, Switzerland, Italy, and Austria, and you can book in advance through any of the Netherlands Board of Tourism offices (see "Sources of Information" at the beginning of this chapter). International trains include the Amsterdam/Brussels/Paris Express, and connections can be made in Brussels to the North Express, the Oostende-Vienna Express, the Oostende-Moscow Express, and the Trans-Europe Express.

At press time, the cost of a one-way second-class ticket to Amsterdam from Paris was $76; from Copenhagen, $133; from London, $94; from Vienna, $182; from Brussels, $32; from Rome, $232; and from Venice, $196. Be forewarned, however, that this information should be used only as a general guide.

Britain and the continent are now connected via the 50-km-long Channel tunnel (or Chunnel). The travel time between Paris and London is about three hours. At present two round trips are made daily from London to Paris and from London to Brussels; by late 1995 there should be departures about every hour. Fares as of late 1994 are $154 one way for unrestricted first class, $123 one way for unrestricted standard class, and $75 for nonrefundable restricted second class (tickets must be purchased 14 days in advance). For more information, in Folkestone, England, call **0233/617-575;** in Brussels, Belgium, call **02/219-2640;** in Paris, France, call **1/051-22-122.** In the United States, call Brit Rail for all train and Hovercraft information at toll free **800/677-8585.** For Hovercraft service information you can also call **0304/240-241** in the United Kingdom.

By Bus

There is coach service between London and Amsterdam (via ferry), with two departures daily in the summer. Travel time is just over 12 hours. For full details, contact **National Express** (☎ **071/730-0202,** or **084/358-1333** in the U.K.). For service to Holland from most European centers, inquire at bus stations in your city of departure for schedules and booking.

By Car

Holland is crisscrossed by a network of major highways connecting its cities with those in other European countries. Distances between destinations are relatively short, road conditions are excellent, service stations are plentiful, and highways are plainly signposted. The major highway to Amsterdam is the A4 motorway, which also runs to The Hague and Rotterdam.

The drawback of driving into Amsterdam lies in the monumental traffic jam you're likely to encounter coming into the city—traffic congestion is at an all-time high. If you must drive into the city, do yourself a favor and get the car stowed away in a garage, then walk or use public transportation within the city (see "Getting Around" in Chapter 3).

By Ship

If you're one of the lucky few whose "ship has come in," as the saying goes, there's just no more romantic and relaxing way to travel to Europe than by cruise ship. Cunard's *Queen Elizabeth 2* is currently the only liner offering regular transatlantic service between New York and Europe. The *QE2* takes five days to complete its crossing, and Cunard offers packages that allow you to travel one way by air and one way by ship—and you truly haven't known luxury until you've spent five days in surroundings such as those offered by the Cunard flagship. Contact a travel agent or **Cunard Line Limited,** 555 Fifth Ave., New York, NY 10017 (☎ **212/880-7500,** or toll free **800/221-4770**).

The *QE2* docks in Southampton, England. There's excellent Sealink car-ferry service for foot passengers as well as cars between London (via train to Harwich) and the Hook of Holland, where trains will carry you on to Amsterdam, with both day and night crossings. In the United States, detailed information is available on this and other channel crossings from Brit Rail Travel International, Inc. (☎ **212/575-2667**).

3

Getting to Know Amsterdam

Nот so long ago Amsterdam was a simple little city, notable for its hundreds of arching bridges, thousands of historic gabled houses, and many canals—more than Venice has in fact. It seemed to have survived intact from its moment of glory in the 17th century. It was a quiet, unhurried, provincial sort of town, and it was very, very clean. But, as is inevitable, Amsterdam grew and changed. Amsterdam today is a sophisticated city with a busy harbor and is circled by industrial towers, multistory apartment communities, and elevated highways—all the hallmarks of a modern urban center.

There are still a few housewives who wash their steps each morning, and most shopkeepers do their best to keep their portals tidy, but graffiti, miscellaneous grime, and other ubiquitous aspects of city life are in evidence in Amsterdam as much as in any other urban center. There are days when the water in the city's canals resembles the famous Dutch pea soup. Fortunately, it's easy to overlook these things, as the historic heart of the city is still there to charm us with its tree-lined canals, gabled houses, and pretty bridges. The Dutch National Monument Care Office has exercised great foresight in working to preserve the feel of the 17th century along the canals. There are still traces of yesteryear in the street life, too: You'll see barrel organs and bicycles, antiques shops and herring stands. In addition to the palpable sense of history a trip to Amsterdam will occasion, there are other lures—great museums, fine dining, and a diverse nightlife scene.

1 Orientation

Arriving

BY PLANE   The Netherlands has only one airport that handles international arrivals and departures—**Schiphol Airport.** It's one of the easiest airports in the world to figure out. After you deplane, moving sidewalks will take you to the main terminal building, where you pass through Customs.

Getting to & from the Airport   The **KLM Hotel Shuttle** offers two different routes into the city and directly serves a total of 11 hotels—the Hotel Pulitzer, Grand Hotel Krasnapolsky, Holiday Inn Crowne Plaza, Hotel Renaissance, Victoria Hotel, Golden Tulip Barbizon Palace, Hotel Ibis, Hilton Hotel, Golden Tulip Barbizon Centre, Parkhotel, Apollo Hotel, and Hilton Hotel. (Most of these are reviewed in Chapter 4.) The fare for the KLM Hotel Shuttle is Dfl 17.50 ($9.20) one-way; no reservations are needed and buses leave from a spot in front of the Arrivals Hall at the airport. Check at the KLM Hotel Desk for information—if you're not staying at one of the above hotels, their clerks can tell you which KLM Hotel Shuttle stop is closest to your chosen lodgings.

Another option is to head for the **trains** at Schiphol Airport's train station. To get there, find the escalator in "Welcomer's Hall" and follow the signs from there—it's a small hike, but there are moving sidewalks, including one that climbs an incline.

Once there, make sure you get the right train. The VVV Amsterdam Tourist Office (with its excellent hotel reservations service), the hotels near Centraal Station and Dam Square, and along the canals near the Center, and other hostelries along the major tram routes are all served by NS Schiphollijn. It departs the airport for Centraal Station approximately every 30 minutes. The fare is Dfl 5.50 ($2.90) and the trip takes about 20 minutes.

If you're staying at a hotel near Leidseplein, Rembrandtsplein, in the Museumkwartier, or in Amsterdam South, a better bet for you is an alternate route to Amsterdam Zuid ("South") Station at Minervalaan. After changing at Minervalaan for Leidseplein or the Museumkwartier take Tram 4. Then for Rembrandtsplein take Tram 5 from RAI Congress Centre station. The fare is Dfl 5.50 ($2.90) and travel time from the airport is about 10 minutes.

As is true anywhere in the world, **taxis** are the expensive way to travel, but they're the preferred choice if your luggage is burdensome or if there are two or more people to share the cost. You'll find taxi stands at both ends of the sidewalk that runs in front of the Arrivals Hall. Taxis operating from the airport are all metered and charge Dfl 5.80 ($3.05) when you get in plus Dfl 2.80 ($1.50) per kilometer. Expect to pay Dfl 60 ($31.50) to the city and Dfl 55 ($28.95) for a trip to hotels in Amsterdam South and about Dfl 15 ($7.90) for rides within the city. But remember, in Holland a service charge—or tip— is already included in the price shown on the meter.

BY TRAIN International trains arrive at **Centraal Station,** built on an artificial island along the river IJ. The building itself is an ornate architectural wonder. Centraal Station is the flashpoint for a lot of activity: it is at the hub of the city's concentric rings of streets and canals, it's the originating point for most of the city's trams; it houses an office of the GWK Bureau de Change, where you can exchange traveler's checks and U.S. dollars (see "Currency Exchange" under "Fast Facts" later in this chapter); and it is a main departure point for canal-boat tours.

Luggage deposit costs from Dfl 4 to 6 ($1.90 to $3.15) per day if you use a standard locker, Dfl 10 ($5.30) if you leave your suitcase or knapsack with a porter.

Just across the street is the main VVV tourist office (see "Tourist Information," below, for details). To get to your hotel by tram, consult one of the **GVB/Amsterdam Municipal Transport** ticket booths, located in front of the station building, for fare information and schedules. Or you can head for the **taxi stand** in front of the station. (Details on transportation within the city can be found under "Getting Around," below.)

BY BUS International coaches arrive at the main bus terminal opposite Centraal Station.

Tourist Information

Few countries in the world are more organized in their approach to tourism or more meticulous in their attention to detailed travel information than Holland, where every province and municipality has its own tourist organization and even small towns have information offices with someone on duty who speaks several languages. These amazing Dutch tourist offices are uniformly named throughout the country with the tongue-twister **Vereniging Voor Vreemdelingen-verkeer,** or Association for Tourist Traffic, but, thankfully, even the Dutch refer to them simply as the **VVV** (pronounced "vay-vay-vay"). These tourist information offices exist in profusion throughout the country; to find them, look for the "VVV," often enclosed in a triangle, on small blue-and-white roadside signs.

In Amsterdam, the focal point of the system is the **Main VVV Amsterdam Tourist Office** at 10 Stationsplein, across from Centraal Station (☎ **06/340-34-066**); a subsidiary office is located at 1 Leidseplein. The Stationsplein office is open April to October, daily from 9am to 11pm; November to March, daily from 9am to 5pm. At Leidseplein it's open April to October, daily from 12:30 to 5:30pm; call for hours during the rest of the year.

The **Amsterdam Uit Buro (AUB) Ticketstop,** Leidseplein 26, can also give you information regarding cultural events, but you should make a reservation before you go (☎ **621-12-11** on Monday through Saturday from 10am to 6pm).

City Layout

Amsterdammers will tell you it's easy to find your way around their city. However, when each resident offers you a different pet theory of how best to maintain your sense of direction, you'll begin to sense that the city's layout can be confusing. Some of the natives' theories actually do work—if you try to "think in circles," "follow the canals" (the one I use most), or "watch the way the trams go," you might be able to spend fewer minutes a day consulting a map or trying to figure out where you are and which way to walk to find the Rijksmuseum, a restaurant, or your hotel. The maps in this book will help you understand Amsterdam's basic pattern of waterways and the relationships between the major squares or landmarks and the major connecting thoroughfares. Once you get the hang of the necklace pattern of the five major canals and become familiar with the names (or series of names) of each of the five principal roads leading into the Center, all you need to do as you walk along is to keep track of whether you're walking toward or away from Dam Square, the heart of the city, or simply circling around it.

MAIN ARTERIES & STREETS   There are three major squares in Amsterdam that will be "hubs" of your visit to the city:

Dam Square is the heart of the city and the site of the dam across the Amstel River that gave the city its original name, Amstelledamme. Today it is encircled by the Koninklijk Paleis (Royal Palace), the

Nieuwe Kerk (New Church), several department stores, hotels, and restaurants; it's also the site of the National War Monument.

Leidseplein, with the streets around it, is the Times Square of Amsterdam. It bustles and glitters with restaurants, nightclubs, discos, performance centers, and movie theaters.

Muntplein is essentially a transportation hub—one of the busiest in the city—identified by the Mint Tower, one of the original fortress towers of the city (topped by a distinctive crown ornament dating from 1620).

FINDING AN ADDRESS   Of all the frustrations of travel, one of the worst is to be given a name and street address for a terrific little restaurant or a swell new shop and then have no clue where "Reestraat 8a" or some such address might be—or even in which section of town to look. For this reason, wherever possible in the following chapters, I've made an attempt to locate the addresses given, either by naming a nearby square or major thoroughfare ("near the Muntplein," "just east of Vijzelstraat") or by naming the adjacent canals ("between the Prinsengracht and the Keizersgracht"). You'll also see references to addresses that are "above" or "below" a major thoroughfare or "beyond" a canal; these directions refer to the fact that addresses along the canals in Amsterdam are numbered (as you look at the map) from left to right, low to high, and on streets leading away from Centraal Station and out from the Center, from top to bottom, low to high. Similarly, "inside" and "outside" in reference to a canal means "on the side of the canal toward the Center" and "on the side of the canal away from the Center," respectively. Got it?

Now, all you need to know is that in Dutch *-straat* means street, *-gracht* means canal, *-plein* means square, and *-laan* means boulevard, all of which are used as suffixes attached directly to the name of the thoroughfare (for example, Princes' Canal becomes Prinsengracht, one word).

STREET MAPS   The VVV has several maps and guides available, but the most detailed and helpful maps of Amsterdam—as well as the rest of Holland—are those published by **Surrland/N.V. Falkplan** of The Hague; the best and handiest map they produce is a small and easy-to-unfold version of their large city map, entitled *This Is Amsterdam* and available at the VVV offices. It sells for Dfl 4.50 ($2.40) and shows every street and jog, gives tram routes and tram stops, pinpoints churches and many museums, locates address numbers, and tells you which are one-way streets, bridges, or canals.

NEIGHBORHOODS IN BRIEF

The city of Amsterdam can be divided into six major touristic neighborhoods:

The Center   The oldest part of the city, around Dam Square and the Centraal Railway Station, includes the major downtown shopping areas and such attractions as the Royal Palace, the Amsterdam Historical Museum, Madame Tussaud's in Amsterdam, and the canal-boat piers.

Amsterdam Orientation

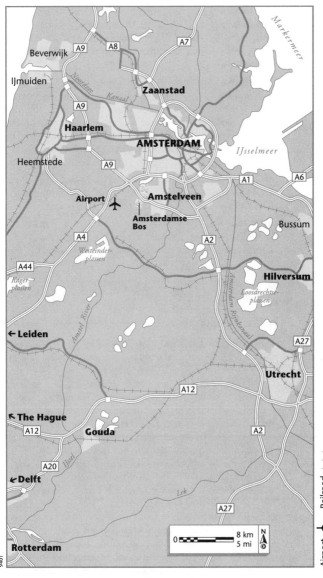

The Canal Area The semicircular, multistrand "necklace" of waterways built around the old part of the city during the 17th century includes elegant gabled houses, many restaurants, antiques shops, and small hotels, plus such sightseeing attractions as the Anne Frankhuis and the canal-house museums.

The Jordaan This nest of small streets and canals lies west of the Center, beyond the major canals. Once a working-class neighborhood, it's fast becoming a fashionable residential area—like New York City's SoHo—with a growing number of upscale boutiques and restaurants.

The Museumplein Area A gracious residential area surrounds the three major museums of art—the Rijksmuseum, the Vincent van Gogh Museum, and the Stedelijk Museum of Modern Art—and includes Vondelpark, the famous Concertgebouw concert hall, many restaurants and small hotels, and Amsterdam's most elegant shopping streets (P. C. Hooftstraat and Van Baerlestraat).

Amsterdam South The most prestigious modern residential area of Amsterdam is the site of a number of hotels, particularly along the Apollolaan, a wide boulevard that the locals have nicknamed the Gold Coast.

Amsterdam East Amsterdam East is another residential area on the far bank of the Amstel River, the location of such sightseeing attractions as the maritime and tropical museums, and also Artis, the local zoo.

2   Getting Around

By Public Transportation

FARE INFORMATION & DISCOUNT PASSES There are 11 fare zones for the buses and trams in Amsterdam, although tourists rarely travel beyond Zone 1. There are several types of tickets you can buy that are valid on buses, trams, the Metro, and the Light Rail, no matter how many times you get on and off or transfer between lines within the standard ticket's one-hour validity period. A single ticket costs Dfl 3 ($1.60). A **day ticket,** which is valid for the entire day of purchase and also the night following, can be purchased from any bus or tram driver, conductor, or ticket dispenser for Dfl 12 ($6.30). Also available are a **two-day ticket** at Dfl 16 ($8.40) and a **three-day ticket** at Dfl 19.75 ($10.40) both of which have to be purchased at the GVB/Amsterdam Municipal Transport ticket booths (Stationsplein in front of Centraal Station). They also sell the day ticket for Dfl 12 ($6.30).

A simpler solution is to buy a *strippenkaart,* or strip card, from the tram driver. You can buy an eight-ride strip card for Dfl 12 ($6.30), but then it's up to you to use the validating machine aboard the tram each time you ride until you've used up your allotment of trips. It's easy to use: Just fold at the line and punch in. And here's a budget tip: These are also available at the GVB ticket office in front of Centraal Station, where you pay the same Dfl 12 ($6.30) that you'd pay for a day ticket, and receive a strip ticket good for 15 rides instead of 8. Also note that you can buy strip cards at railway stations and post offices.

BY METRO & LIGHT RAIL   It's not much in comparison with the labyrinthine systems of Paris, London, and New York City, but Amsterdam does have one subway line and one light rail line that brings people in from the suburbs. You may want to take it simply as a sightseeing excursion.

BY BUS & TRAM   Half the fun of Amsterdam is walking along the canals. The other half is riding the trams that click and clang along every major street. There are 16 routes throughout the city, 10 of which begin and end at Centraal Station (so you know you can always get back to that central point if you get lost and have to start over again). The map in this chapter shows the routes you're likely to take and the trams to take to get to major sights and museums. Some tram shelters have large maps posted that show the entire tram and bus system, and all stops have small signs that list the stops yet to be made by the trams or buses that can be boarded at that location (a good way to check to be sure you're waiting on the right side of the street for the direction you want to go). If you need it, however, a detailed tram map is available from the VVV or at the offices of GVB/Amsterdam Municipal Transport, Stationsplein, or call the transportation information number (☎ **06/9292**) on Monday through Saturday from 7am to 10pm and Sunday from 8am to 10pm at a charge of 50¢ per minute.

Here's how the trams work: You board from the front for your first trip of the day and buy a ticket from the driver (on Lines 4 and 13, board at the rear and buy your ticket from the conductor). On Line 5 you can only purchase a ticket from the ticket dispenser with day tickets, one-hour tickets, and one-, two-, three-, and four-zone tickets. On subsequent rides within the time limitations of your ticket, you board at any door along the length of the tram simply by pushing the *deur open* ("door open") button on the outside of the car; getting off, you also have to push a *deur open* button. Tram doors in Holland don't open by themselves but do close automatically, and they do it quite quickly, so either step lively or keep one foot on the bottom step to prevent the door from closing until you—and your luggage—are off the tram. Another tip: Be sure to keep your ticket with you until it's no longer valid and be sure to use the ticket-validating machines located in the middle and rear of the tram. Dutch trams operate essentially on the honor system, but an inspector—in uniform or plain clothes—may ask to see your ticket, and the fine for not having it is Dfl 60 ($31.60), plus the ticket price.

By Taxi

In Amsterdam, unlike in a city such as New York, you can't simply hail a cab. You must call **Blokband Taxi** (☎ **677-77-77**) or find one of half a dozen or so **taxi stands** sprinkled around the city, generally near the luxury hotels or at major squares such as Dam Square, Centraal Station, Spui, Rembrandtsplein, Westermarktand, and Leidseplein. Taxis are metered, and fares—which include the tip—begin at Dfl 5.80 ($3) when you get in and run up at the rate of Dfl 2.80 ($1.50) per kilometer.

For a **water taxi,** call **622-21-81.**

By Car

Please, *don't rent a car* to get around Amsterdam: You will regret both the expense and the hassle. The city is a jumble of one-way streets, narrow bridges, and no-parking zones. In addition, it's not uncommon to hear that an automobile—apparently left parked with the handbrake carelessly unengaged—has rolled through a flimsy foot-high railing and into a canal. Spare yourself such anxiety!

Outside of the city, driving is another story. You may well want to rent a car for a foray into the Dutch countryside. For information on car and camper rentals, see "Excursions Orientation" at the beginning of Chapter 10.

By Bicycle

Instead of renting a car, follow the Dutch example and rent a bicycle while you're in Amsterdam. Sunday, when the city is quiet, is a particularly good day to pedal through the park and to practice riding on cobblestones and dealing with trams before venturing forth into the fray of an Amsterdam rush hour. Bike-rental rates average Dfl 10 to 12 ($5.30 to $6.30) per day or Dfl 50 to 60 ($26.30 to $31.60) per week, with a deposit required.

Mac Bike, Nieuwe Uilenburgerstraat 116 (☎ **620-09-85**), is conveniently located near the Muziektheater; they also rent tandem bicycles and 6-speed touring bikes if you have a notion to see Holland under your own power. Mac Bike Too is their second shop; it's only a five-minute walk from the Leidseplein, at Marnixstraat 220 (☎ **626-69-64**).

Bike City, Bloemgracht 70 (☎ **626-37-21**), near the Anne Frankhuis, also rents bikes and provides maps and suggested routes both inside and outside the city. They will also store and maintain your own bike, if you wish.

By Water Bicycle

Try Amsterdam's newest summer frolic—rent a water bicycle to pedal along the canals; they seat two or four and cost Dfl 19.50 ($10.30) for a one-hour jaunt for two; a four-passenger water bicycle is Dfl 29.50 ($15.50) per hour. Moorings are at Centraal Station, Leidseplein, Westerkerk near the Anne Frankhuis, Stadhouderskade, between the Rijksmuseum and the Heineken Brewery Museum, and at Toronto Bridge on the Keizersgracht, near Leidsestraat.

Bikes can be rented daily from 9am to 11pm (to 7pm in the spring and fall) from **Canal Bike** (☎ **626-55-74**). Or if you want to pedal along the Amstel River, **Roëll** (☎ **692-91-24**) has a mooring on the Mauritskade, near the Amstel Hotel; rates are Dfl 19.50 ($10.30) per hour for two people and Dfl 29.50 ($15.50) per hour for four.

Fast Facts: Amsterdam

American Express   Offices in Amsterdam are at Damrak 66 (☎ **520-77-77**) and Van Baerlestraat 38 (☎ **671-41-41**).

Area Code   When calling Amsterdam from the United States, first dial **31** (the country code for Holland), then **20** (the city code for Amsterdam), plus the number listed in this book. You will note that the phone numbers for accommodations begin with **020**. If you are already in Holland, you need to dial this code before the phone number; however, if you are calling from the United States, dial **20** as stated above.

Babysitters   Should you need to employ a babysitter during your stay in Amsterdam, ask your hotel manager or desk clerk.

Banks   The major Dutch banks with offices in Amsterdam are ABN Bank, Amro Bank, Centrumbank, Rabobank, GWK-Grenswisselkantoren, and NMB. Also, many major American and international banks maintain branches in Amsterdam, including Citibank and Chase Manhattan Overseas. Regular banking hours in Amsterdam are Monday through Friday from 9am to 5pm, until 7pm on Thursday evenings.

Bookstores   See Chapter 8 for listings of bookstores that sell primarily English books.

Car Rentals   See "Getting Around" earlier in this chapter.

Climate   See "When to Go" in Chapter 2.

Crime   See "Safety," below.

Currency Exchange   By far the smartest place to change your money in Amsterdam is at the VVV Tourist Office, or if you carry American Express traveler's checks, at American Express, Damrak 66 (☎ **520-77-77**; open Monday through Friday from 9am to 5pm), where there is no commission charge, so you save the customary bank service charges.

Another possibility is to go to one of the 75 GWK Bureau de Change locations throughout Amsterdam that allow you to exchange cash and traveler's checks for a minimum fee. They have 24-hour service at the Schiphol Airport and Centraal Station. GWK charges a flat rate of Dfl 2.50 ($1.30) per transaction for cash, traveler's checks, or credit cards up to an amount of Dfl 50 ($26.30), Dfl 4.50 ($2.40) up to Dfl 150 ($78.95), with 3% for higher amounts. They also do money transfers via Western Union.

A word of caution: Before you change money or sign over your traveler's checks, be sure you ask not only what exchange rate you will get but also what service charge will be added. Some exchange services in Amsterdam have been known to lure the gullible with a generous exchange rate and then clobber them with an exorbitant fee.

Customs   Citizens of the United States, regardless of age, may bring in foreign goods up to the value of $400 duty free if they have been out of the country more than 48 hours and have not claimed these exemptions within a 30-day period. There's a 10% duty on the next $1,000 and 12% for everything over $1,400. Restrictions within those allowances are 200 cigarettes, 100 non-Cuban cigars, and one bottle of perfume that is also trademarked in the United States. Only those meats, fruits, plants, soil, or other agricultural items certified for entry into the United States may be imported. Special restrictions apply for military personnel and to the importation of antiques, automobiles, and motorcycles, and the U.S. Customs Service will furnish details if you write them at Box 1301, Constitution Avenue, Washington, DC 20044.

You may mail purchases valued at up to $50 back to the United States provided they don't exceed one a day to any one addressee. Be sure to label such packages "Gift—Under $50."

Dentist/Doctor   In addition to the regular listings of all doctors and dentists to be found in the Amsterdam telephone directory, should you or anyone in your party need medical or dental service during the night or over the weekend, the Central Medical Service can be reached by calling **664-21-11.**

Directory Assistance   For telephone numbers throughout Holland, call **06/8008**; for directory assistance elsewhere, call **06/0418.** English is spoken.

Drugstores   In Holland there are two different kinds of drugstores: one for prescriptions (*apothek*) and one for such items as toothpaste, deodorant, and razor blades (*drogerijen*).

Among the apotheken conveniently located in the Center and canal areas are Dam, Damstraat 2 (☎ **624-43-31**); Koek, Vijzelgracht 19 (☎ **623-59-49**); Proton, Utrechtsestraat 86 (☎ **624-43-33**); Schaeffen es van Tijen, Vijzelgracht 19 (☎ **623-43-21**); and Het Witte Kruis, Rozengracht 57 (☎ **623-10-51**). Among those located in the museum area and Amsterdam South are Apollo, Beethovenstraat 19 (☎ **662-81-08**); De Lairesse, De Lairessestraat 42 (☎ **662-10-22**); Schaffers, Ferdinand Bolstraat 11 (☎ **662-22-40**).

Electricity   Before you weigh down your luggage with all your favorite appliances, note that Holland runs on 220 volts of electricity (we use 110 volts in North America). Thus you'll need to take with you one of the small voltage transformers now available in drug and appliance stores or by mail order, which plug into the round-holed European electrical outlet and convert the Dutch voltage from 220V down to 110V for any small appliance up to 1,500 watts (but check your appliances to be sure they don't exceed this limit).

Another tip: Even if you have appliances that are engineered to operate on either 110V or 220V with the flip of a switch, you still will want to buy a plug adapter before leaving home, as these are not sold in Holland.

Embassies/Consulates All embassies are located in Den Hague, the governmental capital city, but many nations also have consulates in Amsterdam. The Consulate of the **United States** is at Museumplein 19 (☎ **664-56-61**); the American Embassy is located at Lange Voorhout 102, Den Hague (☎ **070/362-49-11**). The Consulate-General of the **United Kingdom** is at Koningslaan 44 (☎ **676-43-43**).

Citizens of other English-speaking countries should contact their embassies in Den Hague: The Embassy of **Australia** is at Carnegielaan 14, Den Hague (☎ **070/310-82-00**); The Embassy of **Canada** is located at Sophialaan 7, Den Hague (☎ **070/361-41-11**); and the Embassy of **New Zealand** is at Mauritskade 25, Den Hague (☎ **070/346-93-24**).

Emergencies The equivalent to our **911** in Amsterdam is **06-11**. Of course, like **911**, you should use this number only in an emergency to call the police, fire department, or ambulance.

Eyeglasses Aside from the Pearle Express center on Kalverstraat (which you should probably only try if it's an emergency and you happen to be right there), there are many places around town. Here are two suggestions: Eye Society, Cornelis Schuytstraat 48 (☎ **664-53-59**); and Eyes, Weteringschans 165 (☎ **620-69-11**).

Hairdressers/Barbers In addition to the beauty and barbershops conveniently located in such major hotels as the Hilton, Renaissance, and Okura, the most stylish hairdressers of Amsterdam are located among the shops on P. C. Hoofstraat and on the Rokin.

Holidays See "When to Go" in Chapter 2.

Hospitals Hospitals located in the neighborhoods of Amsterdam convenient to the hotels listed in this book are Onze Lieve Vrouwe Gasthuis, le Oosterparkstraat 179 (☎ **599-91-11**); in Amsterdam East; and Boerhaave Kliniek, Tenierstraat 1 (☎ **679-35-35**), in the Amsterdam South and museum areas.

Information See "Tourist Information" under "Orientation," earlier in this chapter.

Laundry/Dry Cleaning Clean Brothers Launderettes have several locations throughout Amsterdam, among them Kerkstraat 56 and Westerstraat 26 (☎ **618-36-37** for both locations). Cleancenter, Ferdinand Bolstraat 7–9 (☎ **662-71-67**), and Wassalon Java, Javastraat 23 (☎ **668-24-83**), are two others. For dry cleaning, you might try Weerd van Der at Vaartstraat 64–68 (☎ **662-56-16**).

Newspapers/Magazines You'll find every English-language magazine or newspaper you can think of in either W. H. Smith at Kalverstraat 152 (☎ **638-38-21**) American Book Center at Kalverstraat 185 (☎ **625-55-37**), or in the Centraal Station.

Photographic Needs For one-hour photograph developing, you'll find conveniently located drop-off stations on the Rokin, near

Centraal Station, and on Kalverstraat. Swank Shot Studios is a good bet, and it's located at Spui 4 (☎ **623-69-26**) and Rokin 22 (☎ **624-40-00**).

Police See "Emergencies," above.

Post Office The main post office/PTT is at Singel 250, behind the Royal Palace at Dam Square, at the corner of Radhuisstraat (☎ **555-89-11**), open Monday through Friday from 8:30am to 6pm (on Thursday to 8:30pm) and on Saturday from 9am to noon. Airmail to the United States or Canada is Dfl 0.90 (47¢) for a postcard, Dfl 1.60 (85¢) for a letter weighing 10 grams (a third of an ounce); cards and letters to Europe cost Dfl 0.70 (37¢) and Dfl 0.90 (47¢).

To mail a large package, go to the post office at Oosterdijkskade, a large building to the right as you face Centraal Station. Also, hotels in Amsterdam generally keep a supply of stamps to sell to guests.

Radio There aren't very many local radio stations, but they broadcast a varied program.

Religious Services Of the more than 30 churches and synagogues in Amsterdam, among those that regularly provide services in English are the churches of the Begijnhof (the English Reformed Church, or Presbyterian), Begijnhof 48 (☎ **624-96-65**); the Anglican Church, Groenburgwal (☎ **624-88-77**); and St. John and St. Ursula, Begijnhof 30 (☎ **622-19-18**).

Safety Whenever you're traveling in an unfamiliar city or country, stay alert. Be aware of your immediate surroundings. Wear a moneybelt and don't sling your camera or purse over your shoulder. This will minimize the possibility of your becoming a victim of crime. It's your responsibility to be aware and be alert even in tourist areas.

Note: I have received a couple of letters from readers who were held up at gunpoint in Amsterdam. So be aware. The city may appear safe and nonviolent, but there are dangerous areas, especially in and around the Red Light District. Also, theft frequently occurs on public transportation, so watch out on streetcars, buses, or sightseeing boats.

Shoe Repairs Schoenreparatie 2000, at Kerkstraat 72 (☎ **623-51-37**), is a good place to have your shoes repaired.

Taxes In Holland tourists can shop tax free. The shops that offer tax-free shopping will advertise with a sign in the window, and they will provide you with the form you need to recover the value-added tax (VAT) when you leave the country.

Taxis See "Getting Around" earlier in this chapter.

Telephone/Telex/Fax The Dutch telephone system, one of the best in Europe, operates essentially the same way ours does in North America. There is a sustained dial tone and a beep-beep sound for a busy signal; plus there are standardized area codes (called *netnummers* in Dutch) that are used throughout the country to facilitate direct dialing—including overseas direct dialing—augmented in some outlying areas with local access codes. None of this is troublesome as long as you realize that when you're dialing a complicated long-distance number it works better if you allow time between codes and numbers (you'll hear an acknowledging "beep" tone). And don't forget, when calling locally you won't need to use the area codes shown here for phone numbers in every city other than Amsterdam; you may, however, need to use an area code to call from a small town into the nearest big town, even if the distance is only a few kilometers (Westkapelle to Vlissingen in Zeeland, for example).

Although you'll pay more for calls placed through your hotel switchboard or those you direct dial from your room phone, a guideline to the *basic* cost of international telephoning from Holland to the United States (except Alaska and Hawaii) is Dfl 2.80 ($1.45) per minute during business hours, Dfl 2.50 ($1.15) on nights and weekends. The international access code is 09 followed by 1, the U.S. area code, and the number.

A one-minute call within Europe costs Dfl 2 ($1.05) between 8am and 8pm and Dfl 1.50 (80¢) during other hours.

To operate a Dutch public telephone you need a Dfl 0.25 (15¢) coin, called a *kwartje,* which is inserted in a slot on the side of the phone box. Until your call is connected, the coin will show through a glass panel below the dial; when your call is answered, the kwartje drops and you can begin to talk. Should there be no answer, push the plunger marked *geld retour* and the kwartje comes back to you. For long calls, or long-distance calls, insert several kwartjes before you begin; as you talk, coins will drop automatically, as needed; excess coins will be returned when you hang up. Newer phones show a digital reading of your deposit (0.25, 1.00, or whatever); as you talk, the amount shown decreases to let you know when it's time to add more coins. And don't forget to add coins—when you're out of money, you're out of conversation; Dutch phones disconnect without a moment's grace.

A better option is to purchase a plastic phone card at a post office for Dfl 25 ($13.15). These are good for 115 units of phone time and can be used in every second green phone booth in town.

Calling home from Europe used to be complicated, expensive, and inefficient. Now, thanks to AT&T's **USADIRECT,** it's easy to call home, even if you're not an AT&T user in the United States. It's also cheaper in many cases. Here's the way it works: In Holland you can use any phone—in your hotel room, at a friend's home or office, at a public booth—and all you do is dial the number below; you'll be connected immediately and directly to a U.S.-based telephone operator, who then puts your call through (collect, person to person, or with an AT&T Card, station to station) to any number (except toll-free 800 numbers) in any of the 48 contiguous states. Call them for rates and reduced time periods. The USADIRECT number from any phone in Holland is

06/022-9111. A similar service is MCI Call USA; the number is **06/022-9122.**

Television   If the hotel you're staying in has cable television, you'll be able to watch both BBC 1 and BBC 2, as well as the local stations. CNN is also broadcast 24 hours a day.

Time   Holland is on Greenwich mean time plus one hour in winter, two hours in summer, this means you should set your watch ahead by five to nine hours, depending on the season of the year and your North American time zone.

Tipping   The Dutch government requires that all taxes and service charges be included in the published prices of hotels, restaurants, cafés, discos, nightclubs, beauty/barbershops, and sightseeing companies. Even taxi fare includes taxes and a standard 15% tip.

To be absolutely sure in a restaurant, for example, that tax and service are included, look for the words *"inclusif BTW en service"* (BTW is the abbreviation for the Dutch words that mean value-added tax)—or ask: The Dutch are so accustomed to having these charges included that many restaurants have stopped spelling it out.

To handle the matter of tipping as the Dutch do, leave any small change up to the next guilder, or in the case of a large tab, up to the next 5 or 10 guilders—if the dinner check is Dfl 77 ($40.50), for example, leave Dfl 80 ($42.10) or Dfl 85 ($44.75) and call it square.

Transit Information   For information regarding the tram, bus, and metro, call **06/9292** Monday through Saturday from 6am to midnight, and Sunday from 7am to midnight.

3   Networks & Resources

FOR STUDENTS   Since the main university has moved outside the city of Amsterdam, it's no longer convenient to students in the city as a resource. Students do tend to congregate in the cafeteria-style Atrium restaurant, at Grimburgwal 237. It's open daily from noon to 7pm.

If you're interested in cultural events and are under 26, go by the AUB (Leidseplein at Marnixstraat), and pick up a CJP (Cultural Youth Pass), which will grant you free admission to most museums and discounts on most cultural events. It's open Monday through Saturday from 10am to 6pm.

FOR GAY MEN & LESBIANS   You shouldn't have any trouble finding information about gay or lesbian bars or clubs in Amsterdam because they're extremely well publicized. However, if you do have trouble or you're just interested in meeting some people, you should stop by **COC,** Rozenstraat 14 (☎ **626-30-87**). There's a coffee shop, pub, and disco on the premises.

The **Gay and Lesbian Switchboard** (☎ **623-65-65**), open daily from 10am to 10pm, can provide you with all kinds of information—as well as advice.

The tourist office (VVV at Centraal Station) publishes the *Use It* guide, which has listings of all kinds of gay and lesbian establishments. Also see "Gay and Lesbian Bars" under "The Bar Scene" in Chapter 9.

FOR WOMEN   Amsterdam is very much a center of women's activism, and there are many women's centers around the city. **Vrouwenhuis,** at Nieuwe Herengracht 95 (☎ **625-20-66**), is open on Monday, Tuesday, and Thursday from 11am to 4pm.

4

Amsterdam Accommodations

Your choice of hotel in Amsterdam should be the beginning of a great time in a great town. Hotels, like people, have personalities that may or may not jibe with your own. To avoid any mismatches, this chapter first tries to help you find the hotels that fit your budget and then tries to impart a sense of the particular style and ambience of each. It is a select group of hotels, chosen on the basis of firsthand inspection.

Hotel Orientation

CHOOSING YOUR HOTEL For most people, the first consideration in choosing a hotel is money: How much does a particular hotel cost, and is it worth it? The hotels listed in this chapter have been divided into the following price categories: very expensive, expensive, moderate, inexpensive, and budget. The cost of a double room with bath now averages $125 per night, but don't despair if you wish to spend less than that. The Dutch determination to provide quality service and good value never slackens, and most Amsterdam hotels, whatever their cost, are still spotlessly clean and tidily furnished, and in many cases they've been recently renovated or redecorated.

The next consideration is location: How close is a hotel to sights, restaurants, shops, or the transportation facilities to get to them, and what sort of neighborhood is it situated in? Unfortunately, there are neighborhoods in Amsterdam that you probably won't want to stay in; these might include a few places known to be the haunts of drug or sex peddlers. Amsterdammers accept such phenomena as facts of life, but although you'll probably venture into Amsterdam's shady corners in daylight or as an evening lark, there's no reason to spend your nights in a less-than-desirable location or worry about getting back to your room. The hotels described here, then, are all decent hotels in decent neighborhoods.

STANDARD AMENITIES Most Americans take their standards on the important matter of plumbing for granted. When we travel most of us would be sorely put out if we had to accept a hotel room without a private bath, which until recently was quite common all around Europe. Although Amsterdam's canal houses and older buildings have posed a major obstacle to attempts to modernize plumbing, most Amsterdam hoteliers have shown persistence and creativity in finding ways to provide private facilities. (One particularly ingenious Dutch solution you may encounter is referred to as a shower/toilet—it's a combination shower stall and water closet, fully tiled, that surely results in a lot of soggy toilet paper!) Since we're used to private baths in every price range of hotel here at home, only those hotels whose rooms all, or nearly all, have private facilities are listed here, even in the budget category. Only rates that apply to rooms with bath are given in listings or used to determine a hotel's price category. The term *bath*, by the way, is used whether the bathing facilities are a tub, tub/shower combination, shower stall, or one of those silly little shower/toilets (that's not a knock; it's a warning, so you won't laugh when you see one).

Holland is one of the few non-English-speaking countries you can visit and get as much out of your hotel-room TV as you might at home. Dutch channels show a number of American programs and air them in English with Dutch subtitles—"L.A. Law" and "Roseanne" are big hits. That's only the Dutch channels, however, if you flip the dial and get a Belgian or German station, you may have the pleasure of watching "Simon & Simon" or "Jake and the Fatman" speak German or Flemish. Another plus of television in Amsterdam is that cable TV is firmly entrenched in Holland and, as fast as they tore up the cobblestones, Dutch hotels—even some of the smaller ones—got hookups. That may add BBC, CNN, MTV, Sky, and other wonders of space-age media to the menu.

THE RATES & WHAT THEY INCLUDE   In the following pages, the hotels of Amsterdam are grouped by price, with specific rates given. **Very Expensive** hotels cost Dfl 400 ($210.50) and up for a double room with bath; **Expensive** hotels cost Dfl 300 to 400 ($157.90 to $210.50); **Moderate** hotels cost Dfl 200 to 300 ($105.30 to $157.90); **Inexpensive** hotels cost Dfl 100 to 200 ($52.65 to $105.30); and **Budget** hotels cost less than Dfl 100 ($52.65). All prices include applicable taxes, a 15% service charge, and breakfast in some cases; where breakfast is not included in the room rate, expect to pay Dfl 28 ($14.75) and up for a Dutch or American breakfast.

To protect your budget against surprises, assume that every room rate quoted here will have increased from 5% to 15% or more for each year after the copyright date of this book.

TIPPING   The standard 15% service charge that is included in hotel rates in Holland eliminates the need to tip under normal circumstances. Tip if you wish for a long stay or extra service, but don't worry about not tipping if that's your style. The Dutch accept tips but don't expect them (and it's an important distinction if you've ever been hassled by a bellboy who lit every lamp in your room until he heard the rattle of spare change).

RESERVATIONS   Although Amsterdam has more than 25,000 hotel beds, an advance reservation is always advised. A travel agent knows whom to call to book the larger hotels described here or—if you have plenty of time—you can reserve for yourself by calling or faxing the numbers given (see "Area Code" under "Fast Facts: Amsterdam" before dialing) or by writing to the addresses given (use the postal codes; they are the Dutch ZIP Codes and are customarily written *before* the city name: For example, 1001 AS Amsterdam, Netherlands). Or to book for all of Holland, contact the free hotel-booking service of the Dutch hotel industry: **NRC/Netherlands Reservations Centre,** P.O. Box 404, 2260 AK Leidschendam (☎ **070/320-25-00**; fax 070/320-26-11).

Should you arrive in Amsterdam without an advance reservation, the **VVV Amsterdam Tourist Office** is well organized to help you for the moderate charge of Dfl 5 ($2.60), plus a refundable room deposit of Dfl 5 ($2.60). This is a nice reassurance if you prefer to freelance your itinerary, but at certain busy periods of the year—such as tulip time—you have to expect to take potluck.

1   Overlooking the Amstel River

Very Expensive

⭐ **Amstel Hotel,** Professor Tulpplein 1, 1018 GX Amsterdam, Netherlands. ☎ **020/622-60-60.** Fax 020/622-58-08. 79 suites. A/C MINIBAR TV TEL

Rates: Dfl 700–1,400 ($368.40–$736.80) suite for one or two. AE, DC, EU, MC, V.

No book about Amsterdam would be complete without including the luxurious and stately Amstel, the grande dame of Dutch hotels since its 1867 opening. After being closed for a $40-million renovation, the Amstel is again open, offering the ultimate in luxury. This is where royalty sleeps and where a superstar performing at the nearby Théâtre Carré can hide from eager fans. Though it's in Amsterdam near the Torontobrug, the hotel looks as if it belongs in Paris, with its mansard roof and wrought-iron window guards, while in the rooms is all the elegance of an English country home.

Each of the luxurious suites and executive rooms has a VCR and stereo sound system (for which the guests are given their favorite compact discs). The marble bath have a separate lavatory and shower. Personalized notepaper awaits every guest. In the tradition of all members of the Inter-Continental hotel chain, each guest's personal preferences are noted down so their next visit will be just as wonderful as their first.

Dining/Entertainment: La Rive is the Amstel's famous restaurant, which was recently assigned a Michelin star. The breakfast, lunch, and dinner menus are à la carte.

Services: Room service, valet laundry, limousine service (on request).

Facilities: Fully equipped health center (with heated pool, Jacuzzi, sauna, weight room, Turkish bath); professional masseurs, personal trainer, beauty specialists guests' disposal.

Hôtel de l'Europe, Nieuwe Doelenstraat 2–8, 1012 CP Amsterdam, Netherlands. ☎ **020/623-48-36.** Fax 020/624-29-62. 101 rms and suites. A/C MINIBAR TV TEL

Rates (including continental breakfast): Dfl 395–495 ($207.80–$260.50) single; Dfl 495–770 ($260.50–$405.30) double: Dfl 845–1,370 ($444.70–$721.10) suite. Additional person Dfl 80 ($42.10) extra. AE, EU, MC, V. **Parking:** Dfl 3.50 ($1.80) per hour.

Almost as elegant, old, and prestigious as the Amstel (above) is the Hôtel de l'Europe, which offers a decidedly more central location, at Muntplein. Built in 1895, the de l'Europe has a grand style and a sense of ease. Rooms and bath are spacious and bright, furnished with classic good taste. Some rooms have minibalconies overlooking the river, and all boast marble baths.

Dining/Entertainment: The Hôtel de l'Europe's formal dining room is the Restaurant Excelsior (see Chapter 5 for details), which serves breakfast, lunch, and dinner daily. In Restaurant Le Relais (see Chapter 5 for more information) you'll find less formal surroundings for light lunches or dinners. Le Bar and La Terrasse (summer only) serve drinks and hors d'oeuvres daily from 11am to 1am.

Services: Room service.

Facilities: Indoor pool, sauna, health club, massage.

Moderate

Bridge Hotel, Amstel 107–111, 1018 EM Amsterdam, Netherlands. ☎ **020/623-70-68.** Fax 020/624-15-65. 26 rms. TEL

Rates (including breakfast): Dfl 120–140 ($63.15–$73.70) single; Dfl 150–175 ($78.95–$92.10) double. Children under 4 stay free in parents' room. Additional person Dfl 55 ($28.95) extra. AE, DC, MC, V.

Not far from the Amstel (above), the tiny and tastefully done Bridge Hotel (formerly the Mikado), near the Théâre Carré, probably offers its guests more space per guilder than any other hotel in Amsterdam. The rooms seem like studio apartments, with couches, coffee tables, and easy chairs arranged in lounge areas in such a way that there's plenty of room left between them and the beds for you to do your morning calisthenics. There's also a sauna and an Italian restaurant.

2 In the Center

Very Expensive

Amsterdam Renaissance Hotel, Kattengat 1, 1012 SZ Amsterdam, Netherlands. ☎ **020/621-22-23.** Fax 020/627-52-45. 432 rms and suites. A/C MINIBAR TV TEL **Transportation:** KLM Hotel Shuttle service from Schiphol Airport.

Rates: Dfl 332 ($174.75) single; Dfl 395 ($207.90) double; Dfl 850 ($447.35) suite. Children under 12 stay free in parents' room. Additional person Dfl 65 ($34.20) extra. AE, DC, EU, MC, V. **Parking:** Dfl 5 ($3.30) per hour, Dfl 45 ($30) per day.

The Amsterdam Renaissance is a small city within a city. Located at the top of Spuistraat in an area of old warehouses, the hotel has inspired a renaissance in its neighborhood. Built around an open central courtyard, the six-story hotel is artfully designed to blend with the gabled facades nearby. Plus there's a restored 17th-century church that's been converted into a conference room seating 700. The influence of antiquity stops at the front door, however; the Renaissance is supermodern, totally computerized, and all-American, offering big beds and color TVs with closed-circuit feature films; in the suites, bathtubs measure two meters (78 inches) square. You'll also find electronic security and message-retrieval systems.

Dining/Entertainment: Your choices include the Cupola Café, Patio Lounge, Brasserie Noblesse, and Boston Nightclub.

Facilities: Shopping arcade, airline ticket office, health club.

Golden Tulip Barbizon Palace Hotel, Prins Hendrikkade 59–72, 1012 AD Amsterdam, Netherlands. ☎ **020/556-45-64.** Fax 020/524-33-53. 263 rms. A/C MINIBAR TV TEL

Transportation: KLM Hotel Shuttle service from Schiphol Airport.

Rates: Dfl 360–450 ($189.50–$236.80) single; Dfl 390–510 ($205.25–$268.40) double. AE, DC, EU, MC, V.

This sparkling-new establishment meets every criterion for the ideal Amsterdam hotel: elegance, luxury, and a five-star rating. Built alongside a row of traditional canal houses, the hotel is fully modern and efficient inside; it's also centrally located within walking distance of Centraal Station and Dam Square.

The Barbizon Palace has every facility and amenity possible. A Roman Forum may come to mind as you step into the hotel; the lobby is a long promenade of highly polished black and white marble floor tiles, with a massive skylight arching above.

Dining/Entertainment: Large faux-marble columns define the spaces for the lobby's Café Barbizon. Also opening onto this grand lobby is the award-winning Restaurant Vermeer, featuring the artist's paintings.

Facilities: Fully staffed health center (including health bar, sun room, massage, sauna, Turkish bath, power-training equipment), lobby shops.

★ **The Grand Amsterdam,** Oude Zijds Voorburgwal 197, 1012 EX Amsterdam, Netherlands. ☎ **020/555-31-11** or toll free **800/637-7200** in the U.S. and Canada. Fax 020/555-32-22. 166 rms and apartments A/C MINIBAR TV TEL

Rates: Dfl 525 ($276.30) single; Dfl 625 ($328.95) double; Dfl 725–2,000 ($381.60–$1,052.65) AE, DC, EU, MC, V.

In a building that was once a nunnery, a royal "guesthouse," and the town hall, the Grand Amsterdam is indeed one of the grandest hotels in Amsterdam. To reach the lobby, you'll walk through a fountained courtyard, then through the brass-and-wood revolving door. There are fresh flower arrangements on all the tables in the lobby and lounge area, where tea is served in the afternoon. The black-and-white marble floors are covered with Oriental rugs.

The guest rooms are done in coral and teal, and each has king-size or double bed or two twin beds. Most have couches and armchairs; all have a personal safe and a voice-mail answering system for the telephone. All the baths come equipped with hair dryers and the standard amenities.

Dining/Entertainment: The plush hotel restaurant, done in deep red with plaid upholstery and wood furnishings, has a full bar and serves an elegant lunch and dinner. You can also have lunch or dinner at Café Roux, where you'll see an original Karel Appel mural (see Chapter 5 for full details).

Accommodations in Central Amsterdam

American Hotel 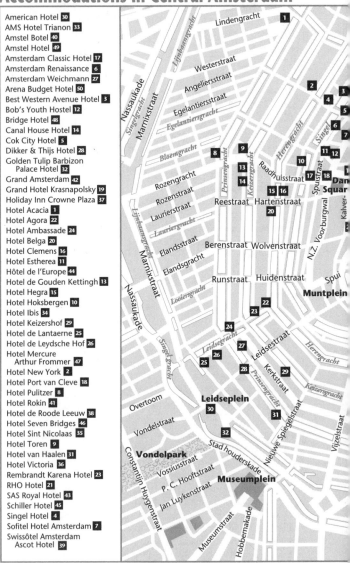30
AMS Hotel Trianon 33
Amstel Botel 40
Amstel Hotel 49
Amsterdam Classic Hotel 17
Amsterdam Renaissance 6
Amsterdam Weichmann 27
Arena Budget Hotel 50
Best Western Avenue Hotel 3
Bob's Youth Hostel 12
Bridge Hotel 48
Canal House Hotel 14
Cok City Hotel 5
Dikker & Thijs Hotel 28
Golden Tulip Barbizon
    Palace Hotel 32
Grand Amsterdam 42
Grand Hotel Krasnapolsky 19
Holiday Inn Crowne Plaza 37
Hotel Acacia 1
Hotel Agora 22
Hotel Ambassade 24
Hotel Belga 20
Hotel Clemens 16
Hotel Estherea 11
Hôtel de l'Europe 44
Hotel de Gouden Kettingh 13
Hotel Hegra 15
Hotel Hoksbergen 10
Hotel Ibis 34
Hotel Keizershof 29
Hotel de Lantaerne 25
Hotel de Leydsche Hof 26
Hotel Mercure
    Arthur Frommer 47
Hotel New York 2
Hotel Port van Cleve 18
Hotel Pulitzer 8
Hotel Rokin 41
Hotel de Roode Leeuw 38
Hotel Seven Bridges 46
Hotel Sint Nicolaas 35
Hotel Toren 9
Hotel van Haalen 31
Hotel Victoria 36
Rembrandt Karena Hotel 23
RHO Hotel 21
SAS Royal Hotel 43
Schiller Hotel 45
Singel Hotel 4
Sofitel Hotel Amsterdam 7
Swissôtel Amsterdam
    Ascot Hotel 39

9402

Services: 24-hour room service.

Facilities: Pool, Jacuzzi, sauna, Turkish bath, massage, solarium.

Grand Hotel Krasnapolsky, Dam 9, 1012 JS Amsterdam,
Netherlands. ☎ **020/554-91-11.** Fax 020/122-86-07.
420 rms, 5 suites. A/C MINIBAR TV TEL

Rates (including breakfast): Dfl 410 ($215.80) single; Dfl 485 ($255.25)
double; Dfl 665–1,050 ($350–$552.65) suite. Children under 6 stay free

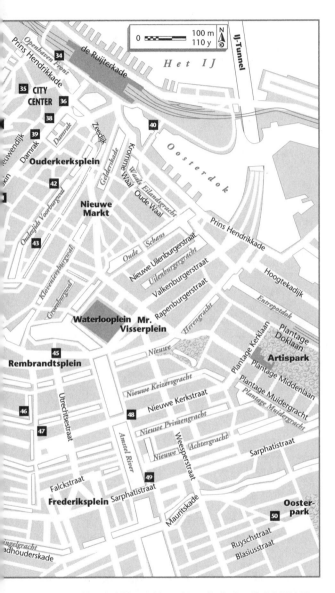

in parents' room; children 6–12 are charged half price. AE, DC, EU, MC, V. **Parking:** Dfl 4.50 ($2.65) per hour.

One of Amsterdam's landmark hotels, the Grand Hotel Krasnapolsky faces the Royal Palace. It began life as the Wintertuin ("Winter Garden") restaurant, where Victorian ladies and gentlemen sipped wine and nibbled pancakes beneath the hanging plants and lofty skylight ceiling—and today the restaurant still dominates the hotel's ground floor. Founded in 1866 by a Polish tailor turned entrepreneur, the original 100 hotel rooms were opened with parquet floors, central heating, and electric lights—the first hotel in Holland to have them (Krasnapolsky also headed a company called First Amsterdam Electric Company). Over the past century the "Kras," as it's known locally, has spread over three buildings on several different levels. The sizes and shapes of the rooms vary, with some tastefully converted into individually decorated, miniapartments (all unique, all chic, each with its own doorbell).

Dining/Entertainment: There's a unique range of restaurant choices. La Brasserie specializes in French cuisine, while Edo is a culinary challenge in that it maintains high standards of both French and Japanese cuisines. The Lido is the newest casino in town and is open to hotel guests and the public.

Services: Business center.

Holiday Inn Crowne Plaza, Nieuwe Zijds Voorburgwal 5, 1012 RC Amsterdam, Netherlands. ☎ **020/620-05-00.** Fax 020/620-11-73. 270 rms. A/C MINIBAR TEL **Transportation:** KLM Hotel Shuttle service from Schiphol Airport.
Rates: Dfl 395–425 ($207.90–$223.70) single; Dfl 495–545 ($260.50–$286.85) double. AE, DC, MC, V.

A red-coated footman greets you at the door when you arrive at the Holiday Inn Crowne Plaza, and he sets the tone for everything else you will discover about this fine hotel. Relaxed luxury is perhaps the best way to describe the Crowne Plaza. All the services and amenities (each room comes equipped with a hair dryer and trouser press) you expect of its status as a first-class hotel are here; so, too, is attention to detail. This is an ideal hotel for tourists and expense-account travelers alike.

Dining/Entertainment: There are various restaurants and a brasserie in the hotel.

Services: 24-hour room service.

Facilities: Indoor pool, whirlpool, sauna/solarium.

★ **SAS Royal Hotel,** Rusland 17, 1012 CK Amsterdam, Netherlands. ☎ **020/623-12-31.** Fax 020/520-82-00. 247 rms and suites. A/C MINIBAR TV TEL
Rates: Dfl 350–460 ($184.20–$242.10) single; Dfl 420–530 ($221.05–$278.95) double; Dfl 650–750 ($342.10–$394.75) suite. AE, EU, MC, V. **Parking:** Dfl 40 ($21.05) per day.

The SAS Royal, which opened in 1990, has an atrium lobby—the only one of its kind in the city. Also of interest in the lobby is the facade of a 1650 house that was once a rectory. Because of Amsterdam's historic preservation laws, SAS wasn't allowed to knock the old building down, so they built around it and incorporated it into the new building. If you go up the stairs to the left at the back of the lobby, you'll be soothed by the sound of running water (it's a romantic spot in the evening).

Basically, the hotel offers four types of rooms. The first, of course, is Dutch: decorated with colors typical to a Dutch home and filled with Dutch furnishings. The other rooms are done in either a Scandinavian, an Oriental, or an art deco theme. There's a writing desk and queen-size, king-size, or twin beds in each room. The telephones have a voice-mail system, and the minibars are called "Robo" bars—instead of having someone come into your room every day or even twice a day to check the minibar, the "Robo" bar records what you use with a built-in computer device. All the rooms also have a trouser press.

Dining/Entertainment: De Palmboom is an all-day brasserie serving light meals and salads. There's also an à la carte restaurant that features fish and beef specialties. The Pastorie is the bar (housed in the old vicarage).

Services: 24-hour room service, 24-hour concierge service.

Facilities: Shoe-shine machines, fitness center, solarium, sauna.

Swissôtel Amsterdam Ascot Hotel, Damrak 95–98, 1012 LP Amsterdam, Netherlands. ☎ **020/626-00-66.** Fax 020/627-09-82. 109 rms and 3 suites. A/C MINIBAR TV TEL **Transportation:** KLM Hotel Shuttle service from Schiphol Airport stops nearby.
Rates: Dfl 265–395 ($139.50–$207.90) single; Dfl 325–450 ($171.05–$236.85) double; Dfl 550 ($289.50) suite. Children under 12 stay free in parents' room. Additional person Dfl 75 ($39.50) extra. AE, MC, V. **Parking:** Dfl 40 ($21.05) per day.

If you like to stay at elegant, small hotels wherever you travel in Europe, you'll be pleased by the Swissôtel Amsterdam Ascot. Opened in 1987, this hotel, like so many in Amsterdam, was built anew within the walls of a group of traditional canal-house buildings. The location is superb, just footsteps off Dam Square and directly across from De Bijenkorf department store. The service is personal and thoughtful, guest rooms are large and quiet (thanks to double-glazed windows), and the baths are fully tiled in marble. You'll have to go elsewhere to find a health club or a hairdresser. But aren't these all the reasons why you choose a hotel such as this one?

Dining/Entertainment: Le Bistro (see Chapter 5 for details) has the ambience of an intimate bistro.

Services: 24-hour room service.

Facilities: Newsstand, souvenir shop, jewelry shop.

Expensive

Hotel Victoria, Damrak 1–6, 1012 LG Amsterdam, Netherlands. ☎ **020/623-42-55.** Fax 020/625-29-97. 320 rms and suites. A/C MINIBAR TV TEL **Transportation:** KLM Hotel Shuttle service from Schiphol Airport.
Rates: Dfl 340 ($178.95) single; Dfl 405 ($213.15) double; Dfl 560–660 ($289.45–$347.35) suite. Additional person Dfl 60 ($31.55) extra. AE, DC, MC, V. **Parking:** Dfl 32.50 ($17.10) per day.

You can survive in Amsterdam without taking taxis if you stay at Hotel Victoria. This is as close as you can be to Stationsplein, where most of the trams begin and end their routes; it's also as close as you can be to Centraal Station, where you can board a train to other parts of Holland or Europe, and to Schiphol Airport (in fact, the hotel provides complimentary first-class train travel to and from the airport). For years the Victoria has been a turreted landmark at the head of the Damrak, overlooking the canal-boat piers and the gaggle of bicycles usually parked in the square. There is a neon-lit mood to the Damrak beyond the hotel, but the Victoria maintains its inherent elegance and pizzazz. Its original spacious rooms were recently redecorated and refurnished, and the windows have been replaced with double-glazed panes. The hotel also doubled its size with the new Garden Wing. All the rooms have trouser presses, radios, remote-control TVs, and hairdryers in the bath. The idea of its new owners is to give you a five-star hotel at four-star rates. All this and location, too!

Dining/Entertainment: The Seasons Garden Restaurant has a Swedish atmosphere, in which you can enjoy an elegant dinner or a quick lunch. The Tasman Bar is a nice place to have a cocktail.

Services: Business center with secretarial services; free first-class train travel to and from airport.

Facilities: Fitness club, Turkish bath, solarium.

Sofitel Hotel Amsterdam, Nieuwe Zijds Voorburgwal 67, 1012 RE Amsterdam, Netherlands. ☎ **020/627-59-00.** Fax 020/523-89-32. 148 rms. A/C TV TEL

Rates (including breakfast): Dfl 260–380 ($136.85–$200) single; Dfl 310–480 ($163.15–$252.65) double. AE, DC, EU, MC, V.

Another hotel built within the walls of historic buildings is the Sofitel Hotel Amsterdam. The fun place here is the bar, which is a replica of a lounge car on the old *Orient Express:* the same paneling, the same plush red-upholstered armchairs (they're still made in France), the same panoramic windows, and the same characteristic Victorian logo of Wagon-Lits emblazoned on the walls, both inside and out. Beyond the bar, however, the Sofitel is a mix of styles: art deco here, beamed and cozy there, with a plaid carpet to catch your eye in the lobby. But somehow—probably because they're French—it all works and welcomes you to a pleasant hotel in a great location, just a quick walk from Dam Square or the canal area and within easy reach of Centraal Station. Among the amenities are a small and private fitness room with a sauna (get the key at the desk).

Moderate

Amsterdam Classic Hotel, Gravenstraat 14–16, 1012 NM Amsterdam, Netherlands. ☎ **020/623-37-16.** Fax 020/638-11-56. 33 rms. TV TEL

Rates (including breakfast): Dfl 140–190 ($73.70–$100) single; Dfl 180–235 ($94.75–$123.70) double. Children 12 and under stay free in parents' room. Additional person Dfl 50 ($26.30) extra. AE, DC, MC, V. **Parking:** Available nearby for Dfl 30 ($15.80) per night.

This hotel is another example of putting an old Amsterdam building to good use housing tourists. This time the old building, behind the Nieuwe Kerk, was a distillery—and a magnificent building it is! Its granite details accentuate the brickwork and massive curve-topped doors with elaborate hinges. Inside, the rooms are all you'll want: modern, bright, comfortable, and attractively priced. There is a hotel bar.

⭐ **Best Western Avenue Hotel**, Nieuwe Zijds Voorburgwal 27, 1012 RD Amsterdam, Netherlands. ☎ **020/623-83-07.** Fax 020/638-39-46. 50 rms. TV TEL

Rates (including breakfast): Dfl 150 ($78.95) single; Dfl 200–240 ($105.25–$126.30) double. Additional person Dfl 50 ($26.30) extra. AE, DC, MC, V. **Parking:** Available nearby for Dfl 30 ($15.90) per day.

One of the nicest surprises you can treat yourself to in Amsterdam these days is to book a room at the Avenue Hotel, about two minutes from Centraal Station. It has all the style of its neighbor, the Holiday Inn Crowne Plaza (above), at less than half the price. And while the rooms aren't huge, they're bright and have clean furnishings. They also have good-sized baths, some with double sinks and all with hairdryers. A full Dutch breakfast of breads, cheeses, meats, and fruit is served every morning. The hotel has an elevator, a bar, and room service.

Cok City Hotel, Nieuwe Zijds Voorburgwal 50, 1012 SC Amsterdam, Netherlands. ☎ **020/422-00-11.** Fax 020/422-03-57. 106 rms. TV **Transportation:** Tram 1, 2, 5, 13, or 17 from Centraal Station (one stop).

Rates (including breakfast): Dfl 170 ($89.75) single; Dfl 220 ($115.80) double; Dfl 260 ($136.85) triple. AE, MC, V.

This new six-floor hotel is only five minutes' walk from the Centraal Station and Dam Square. The comfortable modern rooms are brightly decorated in different colors and come equipped with full baths, color TVs, trouser presses, hairdryers, and safes. Added conveniences include food, beverage, and ice dispensers on every floor, as well as rooms equipped for ironing. Several shops that stay open 24 hours are located on the ground floor. The buffet breakfast features eggs, cereals, and fruit.

Hotel Ibis, Stationsplein 49, 1012 AB Amsterdam, Netherlands. ☎ **020/638-99-99.** Fax 020/620-01-56. 177 rms. TV TEL

Rates: Dfl 175 ($92.10) single or double; Dfl 340 ($178.95) family room with four beds. AE, DC, MC, V. **Parking:** Dfl 45 ($23.70) in nearby garage.

This hotel is on your right as you exit the Centraal Station. You can't miss the red-and-green floral logo and the 27 flags waving above the door. Rooms are modern, with soundproof windows. The hotel's restaurant features three daily menus priced from Dfl 29 ($15.25).

Hotel New York, Herengracht 13, 1015 BA Amsterdam, Netherlands.
☎ **020/624-30-66.** Fax 020/620-32-30. 18 rms. TV TEL

Rates (including breakfast): Dfl 150–175 ($78.95–$92.10) single; Dfl 200–225 ($105.25–$131.55) double or twin; Dfl 275 ($144.75) triple. AE, DC, MC, V.

The New York, 10 minutes' walk from the Centraal Station, is on one of the city's most picturesque canals overlooking the famous Milkmaid's Bridge. Three historic 17th-century buildings have been joined to create the hotel, which has a certain charm, partly provided by its French manager, Philippe. The guest rooms are spacious and furnished in a modern style. Additional facilities and services include a cocktail lounge, a bar, and same-day laundry service. Breakfast consists of cheese, ham, raisin bread, juice, and a boiled egg (you may have it delivered to your room). Note that this four-floor hotel has no elevator.

Hotel Port van Cleve, Nieuwe Zijds Voorburgwal 178–180, 1012 SJ Amsterdam, Netherlands. ☎ **020/624-48-60.** Fax 020/622-02-40. 99 rms. TV TEL **Transportation:** Tram 1, 2, 5, or 11 from Centraal Station (two stops).

Rates (including breakfast): Dfl 182 ($95.80) single; Dfl 283 ($148.95) double; Dfl 440 ($231.60) suite. Extra person Dfl 83 ($43.70). AE, DC, DISC, MC, V.

Located near the Royal Palace next to Magna Plaza, a huge shopping center, the Port van Cleve is one of the city's oldest hotels. Over the last hundred years it has accommodated many famous guests. The ornamental facade, complete with turrets and alcoves, is original; the interior has been completely modernized, and the rooms have been furnished very comfortably.

Hotel de Roode Leeuw, Damrak 95, 1012 LP Amsterdam, Netherlands. ☎ **020/555-06-66.** Fax 020/620-47-16. 80 rms. A/C MINIBAR TV TEL **Transportation:** Tram 4, 9, 16, or 24 from Centraal Station (one step).

Rates (including breakfast): Dfl 199 ($104.75) single; Dfl 295 ($155.25) double; Dfl 360 ($189.45) triple. Extra person Dfl 60 ($31.55) AE, DC, MC, V.

Only 400 yards from the Centraal Station near Dam Square, this hotel possesses an 18th-century facade; however, its rooms are supermodern, featuring thick carpets, ample wardrobe space, tea- and coffee-making facilities, and hairdryers. The Brasserie serves typical Dutch cuisine and daily two-course menus for Dfl 42.50 ($22.35). The latter offer such dishes as braised beef with red cabbage and boiled potatoes followed by hot stewed pears topped with whipped cream. The glassed-in heated terrace overlooking Dam Square is a pleasant relaxing spot for a beer (open daily from 11am to 11:30pm).

★ **Hotel Seven Bridges**, Reguliersgracht 31, 1017 LK Amsterdam, Netherlands. ☎ **020/623-13-29.** 11 rms (6 with bath).

$ **Rates** (including full breakfast): Dfl 100 ($52.65) single without bath, Dfl 160 ($84.20) single with bath; Dfl 135 ($71.05) double without bath, Dfl 210 ($110.50) double with bath. AE, MC, V.

The owners, Pierre Keulers and Gunter Glaner, have transformed the Seven Bridges into one of Amsterdam's true gems. Each room is individual. There are antique furnishings, as well as posters of impressionist art on the walls. The biggest room, able to accommodate up to four, is on the first landing, and it has a huge bathroom with wood paneling (somewhat similar to a sauna), double sinks, a fair-sized shower (with a curtain), and a separate area for the lavatory. The room itself is enormous, with high ceilings, a huge mirror over the fireplace (not working), a wicker table and chairs, and a lovely array of green plants. There are some attic rooms with sloped ceilings and exposed wood beams, plus big, bright basement rooms done almost entirely in white. The attic and basement rooms are the ones that have shared baths, but that's certainly no drawback. Eight rooms have TVs.

Every morning, at your requested time, Pierre or Gunter will bring breakfast to your door. You'll have your choice of coffee or tea, plus juice, and on your tray you'll find a variety of breads, meats, and cheeses. You can eat at your leisure, have time to shower, and then head out for a day of sightseeing feeling well rested and satiated. Pierre and Gunter are also quite willing to help you plan your day, so don't be afraid to ask.

Hotel Vondel, Vondelstraat 28, 1054 GE Amsterdam, Netherlands. ☎ **020/612-01-20.** Fax 020/685-43-21. 28 rms. MINIBAR TV TEL **Transportation:** Tram 1, 2, 5, or 11 from Centraal Station to Leidseplein (six stops).

Rates (including breakfast): Dfl 175 ($92.10) single; Dfl 195–300 ($102.65–$157.90) double; Dfl 350 ($184.20) triple; Dfl 400 ($210.50) quad. AE, DC, MC, V.

Named after the famous 17th-century Dutch poet Joost Van den Vondel, this five-floor hotel opened in late 1993 and has since become one of the leading three-star hotels in Amsterdam. Each room is named after one of Vondel's poems, like Lucifer or Solomon. Three of the rooms (all with soundproof windows) are on the first floor and are ideal for disabled travelers. The furniture is solid, the rooms are spacious, and the service is good. The buffet breakfast includes fresh fruit, a choice of cereals, cold meats, and 12 brands of tea. This is a comfortable place, conveniently located for the museum area and Leidseplein.

RHO Hotel, Nes 11–13, 1012 KC Amsterdam, Netherlands. ☎ **020/620-73-71.** Fax 020/620-78-26. 80 rms. TV TEL **Rates** (including breakfast): Dfl 90–125 ($47.35–$65.80) single; Dfl 140–220 ($73.70–$115.80) double. AE, MC, V.

Once you find it, you'll bless the easy convenience of RHO Hotel. Located just off Dam Square, the RHO is housed in a building that once was the offices of a gold company and before that housed a theater in the space that now holds the reception desk and breakfast area. There's an elevator and a restaurant, the rooms have been recently renovated, and the price is right. Finally, the location is one of the best in town.

Inexpensive

The Amstel Botel, Oosterdokskade 2–4, 1011 AE Amsterdam, Netherlands. ☎ **020/626-42-47.** Fax 020/639-19-52. 176 cabins (352 beds). TV TEL **Transportation:** Turn left out of the Centraal Station, pass the bike rental, and you can't miss it floating in front of you.

Rates (including buffet breakfast): Dfl 120 ($63.15) single; Dfl 140 ($73.70) double; Dfl 190 ($100) triple. AE, MC, V. **Parking:** Free.

This is a boat-hotel moored 250 yards away from the Centraal Station. Aboard you'll find 176 cabins spread out over four decks connected by elevator. The boat was built in 1993 to serve as a hotel. It's become very popular since it opened because of its central location, adventurous quality, and comfort at reasonable rates.

Hotel Belga, Hartenstraat 8, 1016 CB Amsterdam, Netherlands. ☎ **020/624-90-80.** Fax 020/623-68-62. 10 rms (6 with shower and toilet). **Transportation:** Tram 1, 2, 5, 13, or 17.

Rates (including breakfast): Dfl 100 ($52.65) double with wash basin; Dfl 150 ($78.95) double with shower and toilet; Dfl 187.50 ($98.70) triples with shower and toilet; Dfl 225 ($118.40) quads with shower and toilet. No single rooms. Extra 10-minute showers one guilder (50¢). AE, V.

This basic hotel near Dam Square and Westerkirk is popular with backpackers who pay only $26 per person for a five-bedded room. Daniel and Ellen, a Dutch/Israeli couple, have been the friendly hosts here since 1991. You'll find no frills here, but it's clean and centrally located.

Hotel Clemens, Raadhuisstraat 39, 1016 DC Amsterdam, Netherlands. ☎ **020/624-60-89.** 9 rms without bath. **Transportation:** Tram 13 or 17 from Centraal Station (three stops).

Rates (including breakfast): Dfl 50 ($26.30) single; Dfl 90 ($47.40) double; Dfl 40 ($21.05) per person for three- to five-bedded room. AE, DC, MC, V.

Right in the center of Amsterdam, this hotel is only a 5-minute walk from Dam Square, a 10-minute walk from Centraal Station, and a 2-minute walk from the Anne Frankhuis. Spread over four floors, it's located in one of those typical Dutch buildings with the reception and breakfast room up one flight of steep stairs. Owner Mr. Gijeleveld, nicknamed Ge, who has been in the hotel business since 1950, makes his guests feel at home. He speaks perfect English and seems to know more about Amsterdam than the tourist office. One of his hobbies is collecting plates, and 150 of them decorate the breakfast room. Try to book room 7 or 8, each with a balcony facing the Westerkirk. Small pets are allowed. This hotel is ideal for small groups, since three of the rooms can hold up to five beds each.

Hotel Piet Hein, Vossiusstraat 52, 1071 AK Amsterdam, Netherlands. ☎ **020/662-72-05.** Fax 020/662-15-26. 40 rms. TV TEL **Transportation:** Tram 2 or 5 from Centraal Station to Paulus Potterstraat (nine stops).

Rates (including breakfast) Dfl 95–125 ($50–$65.80) single; Dfl 145–175 ($76.15–$92.10) double; Dfl 205–225 ($107.90–$118.40) triple. AE, DC, MC, V.

Facing Vondelpark, near the most important museums, the appealing Hotel Piet Hein is one of the best-kept establishments in town. It's located in a dream villa and named after a Dutch folktale hero. The rooms are spacious and well furnished, and the staff is charming and professional. Half the rooms overlook the park, and two second-floor double rooms feature semicircular balconies. The lower-priced rooms are in the annex behind the hotel.

Hotel Rokin, Rokin 73, 1012 Amsterdam, Netherlands. ☎ **020/626-74-56.** Fax 020/625-64-53. 44 rms (35 with shower and toilet).

Rates (including continental breakfast): Dfl 80 ($42.10) single without shower; Dfl 125 ($65.75) single with shower and toilet, Dfl 98 ($51.55) double without shower; Dfl 140 ($73.70) double with shower and toilet; Dfl 195 ($102.65) triple with shower; Dfl 260 ($136.85) quad with shower; Dfl 60 ($31.55) per bed in room with seven beds. AE, MC, V.

A standard hotel that's 10 minutes' walk from Centraal Station and 2 minutes' walk from Dam Square, the Rokin is ideal for single or small family groups. Three hundred years ago Rokin was a canal, and the building was originally a warehouse where barges unloaded their merchandise.

Hotel Sint Nicolaas, Spuistraat 1A, 1012 SP Amsterdam, Netherlands. ☎ **020/626-13-84.** Fax 020/623-09-79. 24 rms. **Transportation:** From Centraal Station turn right and enter Spuistraat; the hotel is the prominent corner house with the dark facade.

Rates (including breakfast): Dfl 110 ($57.90) single; Dfl 140 ($73.70) double; Dfl 190 ($100) triple; Dfl 220 ($115.80) quad. AE, DC, MC, V.

Named after Amsterdam's patron saint, this hotel is conveniently near the Centraal Station. It's a typical family hotel with an easygoing atmosphere, and children are welcome. Originally the building was occupied by a factory that manufactured ropes and carpets from sisal imported from the then Dutch colonies. It was converted into a hotel in 1980. The rather basic furnishings are more than compensated for by the ideal location and the Mesker family's friendliness. There are no TVs in the rooms, but there's one in the guest lounge. Note that there's no elevator to the rooms, which are spread over four floors.

3 At Leidseplein

Very Expensive

American Hotel, Leidsekade 97, 1017 PN Amsterdam, Netherlands. ☎ **020/624-53-22.** Fax 020/625-32-36. 188 rms. MINIBAR TV TEL **Transportation:** KLM Hotel Shuttle service stops nearby.

Rates: Dfl 295–355 ($155.25–$186.85) single; Dfl 425–475 ($223.70–$250) double. Additional person Dfl 75 ($39.45) extra. AE, DC, MC, V.

One of the most fascinating buildings on Amsterdam's long list of monuments is the art nouveau, Neo-Gothic, castlelike American Hotel, which has been both a prominent landmark and a popular meeting place for Amsterdammers since the turn of the century. While the exterior of the American must always remain an architectural treasure (and curiosity) of turrets, arches, and balconies, in accordance with the regulations of the National Monument Care Office, the interior of the hotel (except that of the café, which is also protected) is modern and chic. The location is one of the best in town.

Dining/Entertainment: See the entry for the famous Café Americain in the Chapter 5.

Services: 24-hour room service, dry cleaning.

Facilities: Gift shop, fitness center.

Amsterdam Marriott Hotel, Stadhouderskade 21, 1054 ES Amsterdam, Netherlands. ☎ **020/607-55-55.** Fax 020/607-55-11. 393 rms. A/C MINIBAR TV TEL **Transportation:** KLM Hotel Shuttle service stops nearby.

Rates: Dfl 375–425 ($197.35–$223.70) single or double. AE, DC, MC, V.

This is one of the busiest hotels in Amsterdam. One reason for the Marriott's popularity is its location: Walk out the front door and you're at Leidseplein, with its restaurants, cafés, discos, nightclubs, movie houses, and the Stadschouwburg Theater; and beyond that is Leidsestraat, the shopping street that leads directly to the center. Turn right as you leave the hotel and you're at the Rijksmuseum or the elegant shopping street, P. C. Hoofstraat.

A less obvious advantage of the Marriott may be its pride in its polished service. The decor and the lineup of amenities are predictably Marriott, but among the extras you find are color TVs with two closed-circuit channels for feature films, heat lamps in the baths, and double-glazed windows that really do block out the street noise of the Marriott's busy location.

Dining/Entertainment: There's a bar, coffee shop, and full-service restaurant.

Services: 24-hour room service, laundry/dry cleaning.

Facilities: Gift shop.

Golden Tulip Barbizon Centre, Stadhouderskade 7, 1054 ES Amsterdam, Netherlands. ☎ **020/685-13-51.** Fax 020/685-16-11. 235 rms. A/C TV TEL **Transportation:** KLM Hotel Shuttle service from Schiphol Airport.

Rates: Dfl 370 ($194.75) single; Dfl 425 ($223.70) double; Dfl 570–975 ($300–$513.15) suite. Children under 12 stay free in parents' room. Additional person Dfl 85 ($44.75) extra. AE, DC, EU, MC, V.

This hotel has been totally rebuilt and redecorated with elegance and style. For longtime visitors to Amsterdam it's a pleasure to see what has happened here. To explain briefly, the building was built in 1927 as a YMCA to house athletes for the 1928 Amsterdam Olympic Games; later it became a hotel. But no matter how many times the hotel got a facelift, it always seemed dormlike and dull. Not now! Thanks to millions of guilders and lots of encouragement from its Golden Tulip owners, the Barbizon Centre is gracious, attractive, and imaginatively arranged. The color schemes here were developed with an eye to the colors found in the paintings of the late 19th-century Barbizon school of landscape painting—restful yet distinctive tones.

By way of welcome and convenience, guest rooms offer such courteous touches as peek holes in the door and computerized locks, windows that open, phones on extra-long cords, an extra phone at your desk, TVs that can be turned off from bed, a radio in the bath, a hair dryer tucked in a drawer, and a room safe you program yourself.

Dining/Entertainment: The hotel's Barbizon Restaurant was named one of Holland's 100 best by *Avante Garde* magazine. Café Barbizon offers light meals, and the Bar & Lounge is open for cocktails in the evening.

Services: 24-hour room service.

Facilities: Staffed health spa and adjoining bar, men's and women's hairdressing salon.

Inexpensive

Hotel Parkzicht, Roemer Visscherstraat 33, 1054 EW Amsterdam, Netherlands. ☎ **020/618-19-54.** Fax 020/618-08-97. 14 rms (11 with shower and toilet). **Transportation:** Tram 2 or 5 from Centraal Station to Paulus Potterstraat (nine stops).

Rates (including breakfast): Dfl 60 ($31.55) single without shower; Dfl 90 ($47.35) single with shower and toilet; Dfl 130 ($68.40) double with shower; Dfl 180 ($94.75) triple with shower and toilet; Dfl 210 ($110.50) quad with shower and toilet. AE, MC, V.

Owned and managed by Mr. Cornelissen since 1970, this hotel features large rooms with brass beds, old Dutch furniture, occasional fireplaces, and baths as large as the bedrooms. Many of the guests who stay here are English speaking—Australians, Americans, New Zealanders, and Brits. Try to book one of the large apartmentlike doubles on the second floor (no. 5 or 6), overlooking Vondelpark.

Budget

Hotel de Leydsche Hof, Leidsegracht 14, 1016 CR Amsterdam, Netherlands. ☎ **020/623-21-48.** 10 rms (4 with bath).

Rates: Dfl 85–95 ($44.75–$50) single or double. No credit cards.

Along the Leidsegracht canal, just off the Herengracht, is the Hotel de Leydsche Hof. Run by an ex-KLM purser, its greatest advantage may be its location. The accommodations are very basic, and the owners no longer serve breakfast, but there are many cafés in the immediate area.

4 | Along the Canals

Expensive

 Dikker & Thijs Hotel, Prinsengracht 444, 1017 KE Amsterdam, Netherlands. ☎ **020/626-77-21.** Fax 020/625-89-86. 25 rms. MINIBAR TV TEL

Rates: Dfl 250–280 ($131.55–$147.35) single; Dfl 315–365 ($165.80–$192.10) double. Children stay free in parents' room. AE, EU, DC, MC. **Parking:** Dfl 25 ($12.10) per day.

On the Prinsengracht, at the intersection of the lively Leidsestraat, is this small and homey hotel offering few services and no lobby area other than a small check-in desk. Upstairs, the guest rooms are clustered in groups of two or four around small lobbies, which furthers an impression of the Dikker & Thijs as more an apartment building than a hotel. Welcoming touches are flowers in the rooms, a subtle but elegantly modern art deco decor, and double-glazed windows to eliminate the noise of Leidsestraat during shopping hours.

 Hotel Pulitzer, Prinsengracht 315–331, 1016 GZ Amsterdam, Netherlands. ☎ **020/523-52-35.** Fax 020/627-67-53. 231 rms, 10 suites. MINIBAR TV TEL **Transportation:** KLM Hotel Shuttle service from Schiphol Airport.

Rates: Dfl 395–455 ($207.90–$239.45) single; Dfl 455–525 ($239.45–$276.30) double; Dfl 1,050 ($552.65) suite. Additional person Dfl 70 ($36.85) extra. AE, DC, MC, V. **Parking:** Valet parking Dfl 33 ($17.35) per day.

Before this hotel opened near Westermarkt, the only way a tourist could stay overnight in a gabled canal house was to forgo the expectation of first-class accommodations. The Pulitzer, however, is an all-new, top-service hotel that was built within the old and historic walls of 24 different canal houses. The houses, most of which are between 200 and 400 years old, adjoin one another, side by side and garden to garden, in a U shape that faces two canals and one small side street. From the outside, the Pulitzer blends inconspicuously with its neighborhood. You walk between two houses to enter the lobby or climb the steps of a former merchant's house to enter the ever-crowded and cheerful bar. And if you stay in a deluxe duplex room, you may even get a key to your own canalside door. With the exception of the bare beams or brick walls here and there, the devotion to history stops at the Pulitzer's many thresholds. Essentially this is a hotel designed to please business travelers, so rooms are spacious and modern. A recent expansion and redecoration has also made the Pulitzer quite chic, and some new rooms contain elaborate baths done *entirely* in gray marble.

Dining/Entertainment: On the premises are a restaurant, bar, and coffee shop.

Services: 24-hour room service, photo-developing service, laundry service.

Moderate

Amsterdam Wiechmann Hotel, Prinsengracht 328–330, 1016 HX
Amsterdam, Netherlands. ☎ **020/626-33-21.** Fax 020/626-89-62.
38 rms. TEL

Rates (including breakfast): Dfl 135–150 ($71.05–$78.95) single; Dfl
225–250 ($118.40–$131.55) double. No credit cards. **Parking:** Dfl 25
($13.15) per day in nearby garage.

It takes only a moment to feel at home in the antique-adorned lobby
of the Amsterdam Wiechmann. Owned by American T. Boddy and
his Dutch wife, Nicky, for a number of years, the Wiechmann is a
comfortable, casual sort of place, in spite of the suit of armor you
encounter just inside the front door. Besides, the location is one of
the best you'll find in this or any price range: Five minutes in one
direction is the Kalverstraat shopping street; five minutes in the other,
Leidseplein. Most of the rooms are standard, with twin beds or double
beds. The furnishings are elegant, and Oriental rugs grace many of
the floors in the public spaces. The higher-priced doubles have antique furnishings and TVs, and many have a view of the two canals.
The breakfast room has hardwood floors, lots of greenery, and white
linen cloths on the tables. There is a lounge and bar.

Canal House Hotel, Keizersgracht 148, 1015 CX Amsterdam,
Netherlands. ☎ **020/622-51-82.** Fax 020/624-13-17. 26 rms. TEL

Rates (including breakfast): Dfl 190 ($100) single; Dfl 210 ($110.50)
double. AE, DC, EU, V.

A contemporary approach to reestablishing the elegant canal-house
atmosphere has been taken by the American owner of the Canal
House Hotel. This small hotel below Raadhuistraat is in three adjoining houses that date from 1630; they were gutted and rebuilt to
provide private baths and filled with antiques, quilts, and Chinese
rugs. Fortunately, it's blessed with an elevator, plus a manageable
staircase (that still has its beautifully carved old balustrade), and overlooking the back garden (illuminated at night), a magnificently
elegant breakfast room that seems to have been untouched since the
17th century. Plus, on the parlor floor the owner has created a cozy
Victorian-era saloon. It is, as the owners have worked to create, a
home away from home.

$ Hotel Acacia, Lindengracht 251, 1015 KH, Amsterdam,
Netherlands. ☎ **020/622-14-60.** Fax 020/638-07-48. 14 rms and
studios. TEL **Bus:** 18 to Nieuwe Willemsstraat.

Rates (including breakfast): Dfl 120–210 ($63.15–$110.50) single or
double. V.

Not exactly located on one of the major canals, but in the Jordaan
and facing a small canal, just a block from the Prinsengracht, the
Acacia is shaped "like a piece of cake." It is a clean, well-kept hotel
run by Hans and Marlene van Vliet, a friendly young couple who
have worked hard to make their hotel feel like a home away from
home. The rooms are simple but clean and quite comfortable. They

all have writing tables, but none has a TV (there's a TV downstairs if you really can't live without it).

Breakfast is served downstairs in the triangular breakfast room. With windows on both sides and a nice view of the canal, it's a lovely way to start the morning. You'll be given some meat, cheese, and a boiled egg, along with your choice of coffee or tea every morning. It's a great place—and a real bargain.

Hotel Agora, Singel 462, 1017 AW Amsterdam, Netherlands. ☎ **020/627-22-00.** Fax 020/627-22-02. 14 rms (11 with bath). TV TEL

Rates (including breakfast): Dfl 115 ($60.50) single; Dfl 125 ($65.80) double without bath, Dfl 220 ($115.80) double with bath. Children 6 and under are charged Dfl 25 ($13.15). Additional person Dfl 40 ($21.05) extra. AE, DC, MC, V.

Up-to-date chic and old-fashioned friendliness are the keynotes of the Agora, which also enjoys one of the most convenient locations in town (one block from the Flower Market in one direction, one block from Spui in the other). Although housed in a canal house built in 1735, the Agora has a style that's distinctively eclectic. Furniture from the 1930s and 1940s mixes with fine mahogany antiques. Bursting bouquets greet you as you enter, and a distinctive color scheme creates an effect of peacefulness and drama at the same time. Before opening their doors, owners Yvo and Els rebuilt and repainted the entire building to create a completely new and modern small hotel that they describe, rightly, as comfortable. Somewhere they also managed to find an abundance of overstuffed furniture; nearly every room has a puffy armchair you can sink into after a wearying day of sightseeing.

Hotel Ambassade, Herengracht 335–353, 1016 AZ Amsterdam, Netherlands. ☎ **020/626-23-33.** Fax 020/624-53-21. 52 rms and suites. TV TEL

Rates (including breakfast): Dfl 225 ($118.40) single; Dfl 275 ($144.75) double; Dfl 425 ($223.70) suite. Additional person Dfl 60 ($31.55) extra. AE, DC, EU, MC, V. **Parking:** Dfl 35 ($18.40) per day in nearby parking lot.

More than any other hotel in Amsterdam, the Ambassade re-creates the feeling of living in an elegant canal house. The pity is that you may have to take the good with the bad and cope with a typically Dutch steep and skinny staircase to get to the sleeping quarters; but for the nimble footed or the lucky ones with rooms in the new wing the rewards are a spacious room with large multipane windows overlooking the canal below Koningsplein. Everyone who stays at the Ambassade enjoys the view each morning with breakfast in the bilevel chandeliered breakfast room or each evening in the adjoining parlor, with its Persian rugs and grandfather clock ticking away. When you look through the floor-to-ceiling windows at the Ambassade's elegant neighbors across the canal, you really feel that you're in the home of a rich 17th-century merchant—because you are! This location is the "Golden Bend," which has been the most fashionable address in Amsterdam for centuries.

Hotel Estherea, Singel 303–309, 1012 WJ Amsterdam, Netherlands. ☎ **020/624-51-46.** Fax 020/623-90-01. 73 rms. TV TEL

Rates (including breakfast): Dfl 240 ($126.30) single; Dfl 290–340 ($152.65–$178.95) double. Children 12 and under stay free in parents' room. Additional person Dfl 50 ($26.30) extra. AE, DC, EU, JCB, MC, V. **Parking:** Dfl 35 ($18.40) per day nearby.

The Estherea has been owned by the same family since its beginnings and is built within the walls of neighboring canal houses. It offers the blessed advantage of an elevator, a rarity in these old Amsterdam homes. In the 1930s the owners spent a lot of money on wood paneling and built-ins in this hotel; owners of recent years have had the good sense to leave all of it in place. While it will look dated to some, the wood bedsteads and dresser-desks in fact lend warmth to the recently renovated and upgraded rooms. The room sizes vary according to their location in the canal houses. Most of the rooms will accommodate up to two, but there are a few rooms with Murphy beds, which make them ideal for families.

Hotel Mercure Arthur Frommer, Noorderstraat 46, 1017 TV Amsterdam, Netherlands. ☎ **020/622-03-28.** Fax 020/620-32-08. 90 rms. MINIBAR TV TEL

Rates: Dfl 150–225 ($78.95–$118.40) single; Dfl 150–255 ($78.95–$134.20) double; Dfl 180–285 ($94.75–$150) triple. Dutch breakfast Dfl 20 ($10.50) extra. AE, DC, EURO, V. **Parking:** Free.

The Mercure (once owned by Arthur Frommer) is tucked away in the canal area near Vijzelstraat, with its entrance opening onto a small courtyard off a side street that runs like an alleyway behind the Prinsengracht. It's worth finding. New French owners have recently finished a top-to-bottom renovation that included a light and airy decor in soft seashore colors and brand-new blue-and-white tile baths. There's a small, cozy bar in the hotel.

Rembrandt Karena Hotel, Herengracht 225, 1016 BJ Amsterdam, Netherlands. ☎ **020/622-17-27.** Fax 020/625-06-30. 111 rms. TV TEL

Rates: Dfl 245 ($128.95) single; Dfl 315 ($165.80) double; Dfl 400 ($210.55) executive room. Children 14 and under stay free in parents' room. Additional person Dfl 65 ($34.20) extra. AE, DC, MC, V. **Parking:** Nearby lot.

Following the example of the Hotel Pulitzer, the British-owned Rembrandt Karena was built anew within old walls. In this case the structures are a wide 18th-century building on one canal above Raadhuistraat and four small 16th-century houses directly behind on the Singel canal. The look of the place is best described as basic, but rooms tend to be large (in all sizes and shapes) and fully equipped (down to the trouser press); some still have their old fireplaces (not working) with elegant wood or marble mantels. And as you walk around, occasionally you see an old beam or pass through a former foyer on the way to your room.

Inexpensive

Hotel de Gouden Kettingh, Keizersgracht 268, 1016 BJ
Amsterdam, Netherlands. ☎ **020/624-82-87.** Fax 020/624-28-94.
24 rms (18 with shower and toilet).

Rates (including breakfast): Dfl 75 ($39.45) single without shower; Dfl
100 ($52.65) single with shower; Dfl 110 ($57.90) double with shower,
Dfl 150 ($78.95) double with shower and toilet, Dfl 180 ($94.75) double
with tub and toilet. Additional person Dfl 30 ($15.80) extra. AE, DC,
MC, V.

This charming small hotel overlooking a canal was built in 1650 as
a residence for a wealthy merchant. Its name refers to a gruesome
story from that era, which you can read on a sheet given to every guest
on arrival. Most of the rather tiny rooms have beamed ceilings; six
of them face the canal. When you're having breakfast try to sit at the
two window tables so you can watch the boats and barges glide by.
The manageress, Wilma Strok, who speaks flawless English, is
extremely helpful.

Hotel Hegra, Herengracht 269, 1016 BJ Amsterdam, Netherlands.
☎ **020/623-78-77.** Fax 020/623-81-59. 15 rms (9 with shower).
Transportation: Tram 1 or 2 from Centraal Station to Dam Square
(three stops); turn into Radhuisstraat and then left into Herengracht.

Rates (including breakfast): Dfl 65 ($34.20) single without shower; Dfl
95 ($50) double without shower, Dfl 130 ($68.40) double without
shower, Dfl 145 ($76.30) double with shower. Additional person Dfl 50
($26.30) extra. AE, DC, MC, V.

Housed in a 17th-century building five minutes' walk from Dam
Square, this cozy little hotel has been under the same management
for two generations. Robert, the present owner, is extremely helpful
and friendly. The rooms are small but tastefully furnished and have
beamed ceilings. Note that there is no elevator.

Hotel Hoksbergen, Singel 301, 1012 WA Amsterdam, Netherlands.
☎ **020/626-60-43.** Fax 020/638-34-79. 14 rms. TV TEL

Rates (including breakfast): Dfl 130 ($68.40) single; Dfl 155 ($81.55)
double; Dfl 195 ($102.65) triple. Children under 4 stay free in parents'
room. Additional person Dfl 25 ($13.15) extra. AE, DC, EU, MC, V.
Parking: Dfl 27 ($14.20) per night at a nearby lot.

On the Singel, this inexpensive hotel is not flashy or elegant, but it's
bright and fresh, which makes it appealing to the budget conscious
who don't want to swap creature comforts for guilders. Its central
location makes it easy to get to all the surrounding sights and attractions. This place really is a bargain.

Hotel Keizershof, Keizersgracht 618, 1017 ER Amsterdam,
Netherlands. ☎ **020/622-28-55.** Fax 020/624-84-12. 4 rms
(2 with shower). **Transportation:** Tram 16 from Centraal Station
to Keizersgracht (four stops); it's two minutes from here.

Rates (including breakfast): Dfl 60 ($31.55) single without shower; Dfl
125 ($65.80) double without shower, Dfl 130 ($68.40) double with
shower. No credit cards.

This hotel in an old canal house is managed by genial Mrs. de Vries and her son. The four rooms are named after movie stars, and there are several other touches that make a stay here memorable. From the street-level entrance a wooden spiral staircase built from a ship's mast leads to the beamed rooms. Note that there's no elevator. Because it's so small you'll need to book well in advance.

Hotel de Lantaerne, Leidsegracht 111, 1017 ND Amsterdam, Netherlands. ☎ **020/623-22-21.** Fax 020/623-26-83. 24 rms (11 with bath).

Rates (including buffet breakfast): Dfl 70–85 ($36.85–$44.75) single without bath, Dfl 95 ($50) single with bath; Dfl 100–110 ($52.65–$57.90) double without bath, Dfl 135 ($71.05) double with bath. AE, V.

Not far from the Leidseplein is the Hotel de Lantaerne. It's small and inexpensive, perfect for long stays because it feels like home— for a couple of reasons. For one, not only are the standard rooms perfectly comfortable, but there are four studios that have kitchenettes, color TVs, and minirefrigerators—it's perfect if you're doing Amsterdam on a budget and would like to cook some of your own meals. The other thing that makes this place homey is the breakfast room. It's bright and airy, with an exposed beam ceiling, large windows, and red- and white-checked tablecloths.

Hotel Prinsenhof, Prinsengracht 810, 1017 SL Amsterdam, Netherlands. ☎ **020/623-17-72.** Fax 020/638-33-68. 10 rms (4 with bath). **Transportation:** Tram 4 to Prinsengracht.

Rates (including breakfast): Dfl 85 ($44.75) single without bath; Dfl 120–125 ($63.15–$65.80) double without bath; Dfl 160–165 ($84.25–$86.85) double with bath; Dfl 180 ($94.75) triple without bath; Dfl 215 ($113.15) triple with bath; Dfl 295 ($155.25) quad with bath. No credit cards.

A good choice for all age groups, the Prinsenhof is located near the Amstel River in a modernized canal house. Most of the guest rooms are large, with beamed ceilings. The front rooms look out onto the Prinsengracht, where colorful small houseboats are docked. Breakfast is served in an attractive blue-and-white dining room. The new owner, Mr. Ives Molin, takes pride in the quality of his hotel and will make you feel at home. A pulley will haul your bags to the upper floors (there's no elevator).

Hotel Toren, Keizersgracht 164, 1015 CZ Amsterdam, Netherlands. ☎ **020/622-60-33.** Fax 020/626-97-05. 43 rms. TEL

Rates (including breakfast): Dfl 135–195 ($71.05–$102.65) single; Dfl 150–245 ($78.95–$128.95) double. AE, DC, MC, V.

The Toren is a sprawling enterprise that encompasses two buildings, separated by neighboring houses. With so many rooms, it's a better bet than most canal-house hotels during the tourist seasons in Amsterdam. Clean, attractive, and well maintained, the Toren promises private facilities with every room, although you need to know that in a few cases that means a private bath located off the public hall (with your own private key, however).

There's a bridal suite here, complete with a blue canopy and a Jacuzzi. There's also a special little private guesthouse off the garden that's done up in Laura Ashley prints. All this and a canal-side location, too!

Hotel van Haalen, Prinsengracht 520, 1017 KJ Amsterdam, Netherlands. ☎ **020/626-43-34.** 20 rms (10 with bath). TEL

Rates (including breakfast): Dfl 75 ($39.45) single without bath, Dfl 105 ($55.25) single with bath; Dfl 110 ($57.90) double without bath, Dfl 165 ($86.40) double with bath. No credit cards. **Parking:** Private.

If you're looking for a canal hotel decorated with the dark woods and bric-a-brac you associate with Old Holland, you'll like the Hotel van Haalen. You'll also like the friendly owners, who've done a lot of work around the place, including building the platform beds. Location is another advantage: The van Haalen is in between the antiques shopping street Nieuwe Spiegelstraat and the bustling Leidsestraat shopping street.

Hotel Waterfront, Singel 458, 1017 AW Amsterdam, Netherlands. ☎ **020/623-97-75.** Fax 020/620-74-91. 10 rms, 4 studios. TV TEL
Transportation: Tram 1, 2, 5, or 11 from Centraal Station to Koningsplein (four stops).

Rates (including breakfast): Dfl 160 ($84.20) single; Dfl 175–185 ($92.10–$97.35) double; Dfl 215–235 ($113.15–$123.70). AE, DC, MC, V.

Housed in a quaint-looking narrow building with glassed-in verandas and a roof balcony overlooking the Singel canal, Hotel Waterfront is a good choice for longer-staying readers. The rooms have modern furniture, and the studios are equipped with kitchenette, fridge, pots and pans, and silverware. The street-level breakfast room with white-rattan chairs and tables looks out onto the canal.

Singel Hotel, Singel 13, 1012 VC Amsterdam, Netherlands. ☎ **020/626-31-08.** Fax 020/620-37-77. 32 rms. TV TEL
Rates (including breakfast): Dfl 135–160 ($71.05–$84.20) single; Dfl 185–210 ($97.35–$110.80) double. Additional person Dfl 50 ($26.30) extra. AE, DC, MC, V. **Parking:** Dfl 40 ($21.05) per day.

Style marries tradition in the elegant little Singel, near the head of the Brouwersgracht. If you stay here, you'll find it in one of the most pleasant, convenient locations in Amsterdam. The decor is bright and welcoming, and the rooms are spacious for a small hotel. There is an elevator, and with the recent addition of 10 rooms, a renovation, and all-new furnishings, you won't be disappointed.

5 At Rembrandtsplein

Expensive

Schiller Hotel, Rembrandtsplein 26–36, 1017 CV Amsterdam, Netherlands. ☎ **020/623-16-60.** Fax 020/624-00-98. 95 rms. TV TEL

Rates: Dfl 245 ($128.95) single; Dfl 315 ($165.80) double. AE, DC, MC, V.

Even more exciting to visit than a new hotel is the Schiller, an old hotel made new again—and made new in a way that enhances, rather than ignores, a unique heritage. The Schiller was built by a painter of the same name during the 1890s. His outpourings of artistic expression, in the form of 600 portraits, landscapes, and still lifes, are displayed in the halls, rooms, stairwells, and public areas; and although it's doubtful that any will ever grace the galleries of the Rijksmuseum, their presence fills this hotel with a unique sense of vitality, creativity, and personality. Equally bright and cheerful in their way, the rooms have been totally renovated, refurnished, and reappointed with such thoughtful amenities as pants presses for men's trousers and, in specially designated ladies' rooms, coffee makers and wall-mounted hair dryers.

But perhaps the happiest outcome of the revitalization of the Schiller (for so many years a fashionable tea-time gathering place for the inhabitants of the gabled canal houses nearby) is the new life it brings to the hotel's gracious oak-paneled dining room and to the Schiller Cafe, one of Amsterdam's few permanent, and perfectly situated, sidewalk cafés.

6   Near the Museumplein

Moderate

AMS Hotel Beethoven, 43 Beethovenstraat, 1077 HN Amsterdam, Netherlands. ☎ **020/664-48-16.** Fax 020/662-12-40. 55 rms. TEL

Rates (including breakfast): Dfl 190–240 ($100 to $126.30) single; Dfl 280 ($147.35) double. Additional person Dfl 65 ($34.20) extra. AE, DC, MC, V.

If you like to stay in a neighborhood atmosphere wherever you travel, make note of the AMS Hotel Beethoven. It's located in the heart of one of Amsterdam's most desirable areas, on one of its most beautiful shopping streets. The Beethoven has been treated to a top-to-bottom redecoration that includes the addition of personal safes in all the rooms. Plus, to the delight of local people as well as hotel guests, the Beethoven also gained an attractive restaurant, Brasserie Beethoven, that has a year-round sidewalk café.

Delphi Hotel, Apollolaan 101–105, 1077 AN Amsterdam, Netherlands. ☎ **020/679-51-52.** Fax 020/675-29-41. 50 rms and suites. TV TEL

Rates (including breakfast): Dfl 145–175 ($76.30–$92.10) single; Dfl 205–255 ($107.90–$134.20) double; Dfl 325 ($171.05) suite. AE, DC, EU, V. **Parking:** Free.

The Delphi offers a quiet, residential location just west of Beethovenstraat and the museum district. The atmosphere is friendly, and rooms have a contemporary style.

Accommodations in the
Museumplein Area & Amsterdam South

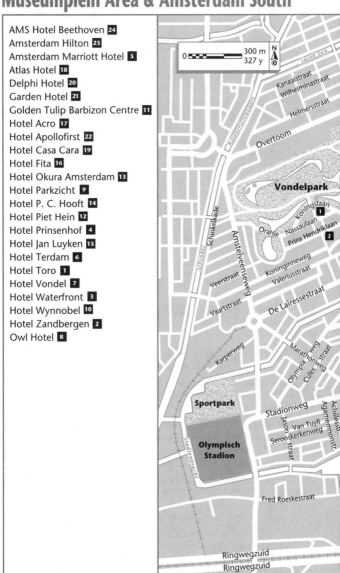

AMS Hotel Beethoven **24**
Amsterdam Hilton **23**
Amsterdam Marriott Hotel **5**
Atlas Hotel **18**
Delphi Hotel **20**
Garden Hotel **21**
Golden Tulip Barbizon Centre **11**
Hotel Acro **17**
Hotel Apollofirst **22**
Hotel Casa Cara **19**
Hotel Fita **16**
Hotel Okura Amsterdam **13**
Hotel Parkzicht **9**
Hotel P. C. Hooft **14**
Hotel Piet Hein **12**
Hotel Prinsenhof **4**
Hotel Jan Luyken **15**
Hotel Terdam **6**
Hotel Toro **1**
Hotel Vondel **7**
Hotel Waterfront **3**
Hotel Wynnobel **10**
Hotel Zandbergen **2**
Owl Hotel **8**

9403

Hotel Acro, Jan Luykenstraat 44, 1071 CR Amsterdam, Netherlands.
☎ **020/662-55-38.** Fax 020/675-08-11. 44 rms. TV TEL
 Rates (including breakfast): Dfl 75–128 ($39.45–$65.80) single; Dfl 90–
180 ($47.35–$94.75) double; Dfl 120–200 ($63.15–$105.25) triple;
Dfl 170–240 ($89.45–$126.30) quad. AE, DC, MC, V.

Young travelers might try the Acro, near Vondelpark and close to the museums. The hotel is modern and clean with its light blue-gray decor (walls, bedspreads, and furniture in the rooms are done in this color scheme). Included in the rates is a full Dutch breakfast, and you can help yourself to lunch and dinner at an extra cost. All rooms have showers; most rooms have two twin beds, but some of them

Railroad ┼┼┼┼┼

have four beds. The price is right and the rooms are neat—the Acro is definitely worth the money.

Hotel Apollofirst, Apollolaan 123, 1077 AP Amsterdam, Netherlands. ☎ **020/673-03-33.** Fax 020/675-03-48. 38 rms. TEL

Rates (including breakfast): Dfl 215–260 ($113.15–$189.45) single; Dfl 285–330 ($150–$173.70) double. AE, DC, MC, V.

The small and very elegant Apollofirst, near Memlingstraat, advertises itself as the "best quarters in town in the town's best quarter." Their boast may be debatable, but all the accommodations of this intimate hotel are quiet, spacious, and grandly furnished. Baths are fully tiled, and rooms at the back of the hotel overlook the well-kept gardens of the hotel and its neighbors, as well as the summer terrace where guests can have a snack or a cocktail. The small restaurant offers an international menu and cabaret on weekends.

Hotel Fita, Jan Luykenstraat 37, 1071 CL Amsterdam, Netherlands. ☎ **020/679-09-76.** Fax 020/664-39-69. 16 rms. TV TEL

Directions: Tram 1 or 5 from Centraal Station to Van Baerlestraat.

Rates (including breakfast): Dfl 130 ($68.40) single; Dfl 170–225 ($89.45–$118.40) double. AE, DC, MC, V. **Parking:** Public parking nearby.

Another tiny and tidy budget hotel, the Fita has rooms with some sort of private facilities. Recently renovated, the hotel is a family-run hostelry situated in the center of Amsterdam, near the Leidseplein and shopping areas, as well as theaters, museums, and diamond exhibitions.

Hotel Jan Luyken, Jan Luykenstraat 54–58, 1071 CS Amsterdam, Netherlands. ☎ **020/573-07-30.** Fax 020/676-38-41. 63 rms. MINIBAR TV TEL

Rates (including breakfast): Dfl 250–275 ($131.55–$144.75) single; Dfl 290–350 ($152.65–$184.20) double. Children 4–12 are charged half price; children under 4 stay free in parents room.
Additional person Dfl 70 ($36.85) extra. AE, DC, EU, V.

One block from the Vincent van Gogh Museum and from the elegant P. C. Hooftstraat shopping street, the Jan Luyken is best described as a small hotel with many of the amenities and facilities of a big hotel. The Jan Luyken maintains a balance between its sophisticated lineup of facilities (double sinks and bidets, elevator, lobby bar with fireplace, and meeting rooms for business) and an intimate and personalized approach that's appropriate to this residential neighborhood. The owners are proud of the atmosphere they've created, and they're constantly improving the look of the hotel.

Budget

$ **Hotel Casa Cara**, Emmastraat 24, 1075 HV Amsterdam, Netherlands. ☎ **020/662-31-35.** Fax 020/676-81-19. 9 rms (6 with bath). TEL **Transportation:** Tram 2 or 16 from Centraal Station to Emmastraat.

Rates (including breakfast): Dfl 55 ($28.95) single without bath, Dfl 75 ($39.45) single with bath; Dfl 75 ($39.45) double without bath, Dfl 100 ($52.65) double with bath; Dfl 130 ($68.40) triple with bath; Dfl 155 ($81.55) quad with bath. No credit cards.
Parking: Free on the street.

Gradually and faithfully trying to meet the demands of the 1990s traveler, the Casa Cara, near Vondelpark, is a simple but well-crafted conversion of a residential house in a neighborhood with deep front lawns. The hotel offers two large rooms with private shower/toilet on each floor, plus a trio of bathless rooms that, as a result, have the hall facilities almost to themselves.

Hotel P. C. Hooft, P. C. Hooftstraat 63, 1071 BN Amsterdam, Netherlands. ☎ **020/662-71-07.** Fax 020/675-89-61.
15 rms (3 with bath).
Rates: Dfl 65 ($34.20) single; Dfl 95 ($50) double without bath, Dfl 105 ($55.25) double with bath. Additional person Dfl 40 ($21.05) extra. V, MC.

One of the spiffiest little budget lodgings in town, the P. C. Hooft seems to have picked up a sense of style from the smart shops on the street without picking up the tendency to upscale pricing. Rooms are bright and tidy. Another plus: The building also houses a coffee shop, which is a handy spot to stop for a quick bite before you hit the sights or the shops.

Hotel Wynnobel, Vossiusstraat 9, 1071 AB Amsterdam, Netherlands. ☎ **020/662-22-98.** 12 rms (none with bath). **Transportation:** Tram 1, 2, or 5 to Leidseplein (six stops); cross the canal, turn left, and watch for the street on the far side of the Vondelpark entrance.
Rates (including breakfast): Dfl 70–75 ($36.50–$39.45) single; Dfl 95–110 ($50–$57.90) double; Dfl 150 ($78.95) triple; Dfl 200 ($105.25) quad. No credit cards.

The Wynnobel is just around the corner from the chic boutiques on P. C. Hoofstraat and only a few minutes' walk from the Rijksmuseum. It overlooks a corner of Vondelpark and is managed by Pierre Wynnobel and his wife, Joan, who always make sure the hotel is clean and their guests are happy. The large rooms are furnished with old-fashioned or antique pieces. A steep but striking central stairway winds around up to the hotel's four floors.

DORMS & HOSTELS

Arena Budget Hotel, s'Gravesandestraat 51, 1092 AA Amsterdam, Netherlands. ☎ **020/625-32-30.** Fax 020/663-26-49. 600 beds.
Transportation: Tram 6 or 10 from Centraal Station to Korte s'Gravesandestraat; 9 or 14 to Tropenmuseum; 3 to Oosterpark.
Rates: Dfl 80–90 ($42.10–$47.35) double with shower; Dfl 120–135 ($63.15–$71.05) triple with shower; Dfl 17.50–22.50 ($9.20–$11.85) in a dorm. No credit cards.

Here you'll find 8 dorms with up to 80 beds each, 8 smaller dorms with 8 bunk beds in each, 34 doubles, 4 triples, and one apartment with 6 beds. Located in a huge red-brick house built in 1890 as a hospital, it serves not only as a dorm but also as a cultural center. The Arena has an information counter, a concert hall, a TV video lounge, a restaurant, a garden, and bikes for rent. In summer all kinds of concerts, parties, movies, and other happenings enliven the atmosphere.

Bob's Youth Hostel, Nieuwe Zi Voorburgwal 92, 1012 SG Amsterdam, Netherlands. ☎ **020/623-0063.** 200 beds.
Transportation: Tram 1, 2, 5, 13, or 17 from Centraal Station (two stops).
Rates (including breakfast): Dfl 25 ($13.15).

At this very convenient location halfway between Centraal Station and Dam Square, guests are accommodated in dorms containing anywhere from 4 to 16 bunk beds. The atmosphere is very international. Although this place attracts primarily a young audience, drinking and drug taking are definitely banned, and there's a 3am curfew. During the summer a dinner for Dfl 8 ($4.20) is served.

In 1994, Bob's opened an annex around the corner at Spui 47, where there are six supermodern apartments with fully equipped kitchenettes accommodating two to four guests; they cost a low Dfl 125 ($65.80) per unit.

7 In Amsterdam South

Very Expensive

Amsterdam Hilton, Apollolaan 138, 1077 BG Amsterdam, Netherlands. ☎ **020/678-07-80.** Fax 020/662-66-88. 271 rms. MINIBAR TV TEL **Transportation:** KLM Hotel Shuttle service from Schiphol Airport.
Rates: Dfl 395–489 ($207.90–$252.65) single; Dfl 465–550 ($244.75–$289.45) double. Children stay free in parents' room. AE, DC, MC, V.

The Amsterdam Hilton was the first American chain hotel to open in Amsterdam and it's still among the most gracious—and spacious—well-appointed hotels in town. Located on one of Amsterdam's few boulevards, it's centered on its own city block with a vista of green lawn from the wide front porch and a view from both the lobby and the dining room over the Noorder Amstelkanaal (Northern Amstel Canal) to some of the large and expensive homes that give the neighborhood its local nickname of the "Gold Coast."

This place is where John Lennon and Yoko Ono staged their 1969 "bed-in for peace," and if you're willing to shell out more than $750 per night you can stay in the suite that's decorated with their memorabilia.

Dining/Entertainment: The hotel has a restaurant called Roberto's as well as a bar.

Services: Laundry/dry cleaning, water-taxi service.

Facilities: Couple of hotel shops.

Garden Hotel, Dijsselhofplantoen 7, 1077 BJ Amsterdam, Netherlands. ☎ **020/664-21-21.** Fax 020/679-93-56. 98 rms. A/C TEL **Transportation:** KLM Hotel Shuttle service stops nearby.

Rates: Dfl 375 ($197.35) single; Dfl 465 ($244.75) double. Additional person Dfl 75 ($39.45) extra. AE, DC, EU, MC, V.

The Garden Hotel, just off Apollolaan, has one of the most spectacular lobbies in town—all white and very bright, with white-leather armchairs, a wall-to-wall white fireplace with a copper-sheathed chimney, mirrored columns, and a sparkling contemporary chandelier. The guest rooms are decorated and arranged with contemporary good taste, in strong but subdued tones (cherry pink, caviar gray, salad green, and lilac of parfait d'amour). Bath are equipped with European-size tubs.

Dining/Entertainment: The hotel's De Kersentuin (Cherry Orchard) restaurant has been blessed with Michelin stars (see Chapter 5 for full details).

Services: Room service.

Hotel Okura Amsterdam, Ferdinand Bolstraat 333, 1072 LH Amsterdam, Netherlands. ☎ **020/678-71-11.** Fax 020/671-23-44. 370 rms and suites. A/C TV TEL

Rates: Dfl 350–450 ($184.70–$236.85) single twin, Dfl 610 ($321.05) executive single; Dfl 480–540 ($252.65–$284.20) double twin; Dfl 630 ($331.55) executive double; Dfl 1,250–2,350 ($657.90–$1,236.85) suite. AE, DC, EU, MC, V.

The largest, tallest, and most unusual hotel in Amsterdam is this 23-story establishment. Guest rooms are Western-style twin-bedded rooms with an easy-on-the-eyes decor and sweeping views over the city from their large windows.

Dining/Entertainment: Two Japanese restaurants, the Yamazato and the Teppan Yaki, are topnotch. The Yamazato has a sushi bar and seven private rooms, one of which is a tatami room. If you're not interested in Japanese food, the Camelia Brasserie may better suit your tastes. On the top floor of the Okura you'll find the Ciel Bleu Bar and the Ciel Bleu Restaurant, which specializes in French cuisine. La Serre Bar is a nice place for an informal drink.

Services: Room service, laundry, dry cleaning.

Facilities: Bank, sauna, massage, shopping arcade.

Moderate

Atlas Hotel, Van Eeghenstraat 64, 1071 GK Amsterdam, Netherlands. ☎ **020/676-63-36.** Fax 020/671-76-33. 23 rms. TV TEL

Rates (including breakfast): Dfl 150–195 ($78.95–$102.65) single; Dfl 180–225 ($94.75–$118.40) double; Dfl 255 ($134.20) triple. No charge for cribs. Additional person Dfl 40 ($21.05) extra. AE, MC, V. **Parking:** Free.

Near Vondelpark, off van Baerlestraat, the Atlas is a converted house with a convenient location for shoppers, concertgoers, and museum lovers. The guest rooms are small but tidy, decorated attractively in gray with blue comforters on the beds and a welcoming basket of oranges on the desk. Leather chairs fill the front lounge, which has a ticking grandfather clock in the corner; there is also a small bar/restaurant with 24-hour room service. One-day laundry and dry-cleaning service is available during the week.

Inexpensive

Hotel Terdam, Tesselschadestraat 23, 1054 Amsterdam, Netherlands. ☎ **020/612-68-76.** Fax 020/683-83-13. 95 rms. TV TEL **Transportation:** Tram 1, 2, 5, or 11 from Centraal Station to Leidseplein (six stops); walk over the bridge and you'll see the hotel.

Rates (including buffet breakfast): Dfl 170 ($189.45) single; Dfl 244 ($128.40) double. Additional person Dfl 60 ($31.55) extra. AE, DC, MC, V. **Parking:** Dfl 45 ($23.70) per day in nearby garage.

On a quiet street just off the Leidseplein, near all the famous museums, this huge hotel complex is ideal for single travelers, families, or longer-staying guests who appreciate fully equipped kitchenettes. The rooms are spacious, with large windows and modern furnishings. The Dutch breakfast offers an unusually large array of choices.

Hotel Toro, Koningslaan 64, 1075 AG Amsterdam, Netherlands. ☎ **020/673-72-23.** Fax 020/675-00-31. 22 rms. TV TEL **Transportation:** Tram 2 from Centraal Station to Emmaplein (about 15 minutes).

Rates (including buffet breakfast): Dfl 140 ($73.70) single with shower and toilet; Dfl 170 ($89.45) single with tub and toilet; Dfl 200 ($105.25) double with tub and toilet; Dfl 260 ($136.85) triple with tub and toilet. AE, DC, MC, V. **Parking:** Free.

On the fringes of Vondelpark in a quiet residential district, this beautiful hotel is one of my top budget choices. The house is furnished and decorated with taste, combining Louis XIV and Liberty styles and featuring stained-glass windows and Murano chandeliers. The guest rooms are worthy of being featured in *Better Homes & Gardens.* The house also affords guests a private garden and terrace. It's a 10-minute walk through Vondelpark to Leidseplein.

Hotel Zandbergen, Willemsparkweg 205, 1071 NB Amsterdam, Netherlands. ☎ **020/676-93-21.** Fax 020/676-18-60. 17 rms. TV TEL

Rates (including breakfast): Dfl 125 ($65.80) single; Dfl 185 ($97.35) double. Children 3 and under Dfl 25 ($13.15); additional person Dfl 55 ($28.95) extra. AE, DC, MC, V. **Parking:** Public parking nearby.

In the Vondelpark area, near Cornelius Schuystraat, this hotel nearly outdoes the Amstel in its use of shiny brass handrails and door pulls. Rebuilt in 1979, the Zandbergen has been efficiently divided into a variety of room types and sizes by the use of simple but attractive brick wall dividers between rooms. Wall-to-wall carpets and a color scheme based on bright tones of sand and gray make even the small single rooms more spacious and inviting. There's also a great family-size room here for two to four people, with a garden patio.

Owl Hotel, Roemer Visscherstraat 1, 1054 EV Amsterdam, Netherlands.
☎ **020/618-94-84.** Fax 020/618-94-41. 34 rms. TV TEL

Rates (including breakfast): Dfl 140 ($73.70) single; Dfl 165–190
($86.85–$100) double. Additional person Dfl 30 ($15.80) extra.
AE, MC, V.

If "small but chic, and reasonably priced" seems to describe the sort
of hotel you prefer, you'll be pleased to learn about the Owl, located
in the pleasant residential area around Vondelpark, behind the
Marriott. One of Amsterdam's best buys, the Owl Hotel is bright,
tidy, and well kept. Rooms are not very big but are not cramped,
and the baths are tiled floor to ceiling. There's a nice TV lounge/bar
overlooking a small garden.

A LOCAL HOTEL CHAIN

In the Amsterdam South neighborhood, the following three hotels
(along with the AMS Hotel Beethoven near the Museumplein) make
up a small local chain called the **AMS Hotel Group.** Together they
provide nearly 300 rooms within easy walking distance of museums,
concerts, shops, and the after-dark attractions of Leidseplein. Book-
ings for any of the hotels listed below can be made through the AMS
Museum Hotel address.

AMS Hotel Trianon, J. W. Brouwesstraat 3, 1071 LH Amsterdam,
Netherlands. ☎ **020/673-20-73.** Fax 020/673-88-68. 52 rms.
TV TEL

Rates (including breakfast): Dfl 120 ($63.15) single; Dfl 170 ($89.45)
double. Additional person Dfl 40 ($21.05). AE, DC, EU, MC, V.

The showplace of the AMS group is the Trianon, which a few years
ago underwent a top-to-bottom renovation, redecoration, and redi-
rection that took it from serviceable to sophisticated. Located directly
behind the Concertgebouw concert hall, it's also home to a gracious
little restaurant, with its own garden, called De Triangle.

AMS is a local chain that has several hotels, including the **AMS
Hotel Holland** at P. C. Hooftstraat 162 (☎ **020/676-42-53**) and
the **AMS Museum Hotel,** P. C. Hooftsraat 2 (☎ **020/662-14-02**).
All are priced as listed above.

5

Amsterdam Dining

Tʜᴇʀᴇ'ꜱ ɴᴏ ʀɪꜱᴋ ᴏꜰ ɢᴀꜱᴛʀᴏɴᴏᴍɪᴄ ʙᴏʀᴇᴅᴏᴍ ɪɴ Aᴍꜱᴛᴇʀᴅᴀᴍ. Yᴏᴜ ᴄᴀɴ ᴇᴀᴛ Italian one night and Indonesian the next; follow a typically Dutch lunch with an Argentine dinner; or, if it's your preference and passion, dine on fine French cuisine noon and night for a week and never eat at the same restaurant twice. Amsterdam's long history as a port and trading city and Holland's long tradition of welcoming immigrants from all over the world has resulted in a polyglot selection of restaurants that's a traveler's delight. Dutch cooking, of course, is part of this culinary smorgasbord, but you'll be far from stuck with **biefstuk** (Dutch beefsteak) and **kip** (chicken) every night—unless you want to be. Dutch practicality has also produced a wide selection of restaurants in all price ranges.

Restaurant Orientation

HOURS   As a general rule, and with the exception of a special group of late-night restaurants, kitchens in Amsterdam take their last dinner orders at 10 or 11pm.

TIPPING   Restaurants in Holland are required to include all taxes and the customary 15% service charge in the prices shown on their menus. You needn't concern yourself about leaving a tip beyond the amount shown on the tab, but if you want to do as the Dutch do, round up to the next guilder or, in the case of a large check, up to the next 5 or 10 guilders.

RESTAURANT CATEGORIES   The restaurants in this chapter have been grouped first by location and second by price. Based on an average cost of the main courses on the menus, the majority of the restaurants described here are in the moderate price range and are located in neighborhoods that are convenient to the hotels described in Chapter 4.

As you read through the following pages, please realize that although more than 70 restaurants are mentioned, this is only a personal selection—there are many other possibilities for you to discover on your own.

RESERVATIONS   Unless you eat early or late, reservations are generally required at top restaurants and at those on the high end of the moderate price range. A call ahead to check space is always a good idea in Amsterdam, where restaurants are often small and may be crowded with neighborhood devotees.

WINE WITH DINNER   Estate-bottled imported wines are expensive in Holland, and even a bottle of modest French wine can add at least Dfl 25 to 30 ($13.15 to $15.80) to a dinner tab. House wine, on the other hand—which may be a carefully selected French estate-bottled wine—will be a more economical choice in restaurants at any price level. Wine by the glass is generally anywhere from Dfl 5 to 8.50 ($2.65 to $4.50).

LUNCH & SNACK COSTS   Unless you want it to be, lunch doesn't have to be an elaborate affair (save that for the evening); and the most typically Dutch lunches are light, quick, and cheap (see the

"Food and Drink" section of Chapter 1). Whether you have two small sandwiches and a glass of milk; a pancake and coffee; or soup and French bread; or an omelet and glass of wine, a quick lunch in Amsterdam can be expected to cost Dfl 10 to 20 ($5.25 to $10.50). An afternoon stop for cake and coffee/cappuccino or pastry and tea will set you back approximately Dfl 6 to 10 ($3.15 to $5.30).

DINNER COSTS   As a guideline, here are relative costs for dinners in each category of restaurant, *without* wine, beer, cocktails, or coffee, ordered either à la carte or from a prix-fixe (fixed-price) menu:

At an **expensive** restaurant, you can expect to pay at least Dfl 70 ($36.80) per person for three courses, whether you choose soup or an appetizer, salad or a dessert, to accompany a main course; you could spend well over Dfl 100 ($52.60) for a lavish European-style five-course meal (soup or appetizer, fish, meat, vegetable or salad, cheese or dessert).

At the top end of the **moderate** price range, a three-course dinner can be expected to cost Dfl 50 to 80 ($26.30 to $42.15). For three courses at a low- to middle-priced restaurant, allow Dfl 40 to 55 ($21.05 to $28.90) for dinner.

Some **budget** restaurants offer three-course menus at prices in the Dfl 25 to 38 ($14.50 to $19.75) range; look, too, for traditional Dutch *dagschotels* (plates of the day, which are served with meat, vegetable, and salad all on one large plate) at inclusive prices ranging from Dfl 16.50 to 22 ($8.60 to $11.40) or more.

BUDGET DINING   Eating cheaply in Amsterdam is not an impossible dream. And, I'm happy to report, in some cases you can even eat cheaply with style (candles on the table, flowers in the window, and music in the air). The practical Dutch have as much trouble as you do parting with even one guilder more than necessary, so almost every neighborhood has its modestly priced restaurant, and new budget places pop up all over town with the regularity of spring tulips.

One way to combat escalating dinner tabs is to take advantage of the official **Dutch Tourist Menu.** This countrywide program sponsored by the Netherlands Board of Tourism promises you a three-course meal for the fixed price of Dfl 25 ($13.15), including taxes and service. You won't have your pick of the menu, but some 400 restaurants around the country, including more than a few in Amsterdam, take part in this program, and at least you know you can eat a square meal (soup or appetizer, main course, salad or dessert) for a no-surprise price. The VVV can give you a list of restaurants throughout Holland offering the Dutch Tourist Menu.

---

1   Overlooking the Amstel River

Expensive ─────────────────────────

Excelsior, in the Hôtel de l'Europe, Nieuwe Doelenstraat 2–8, at Muntplein. ☎ **623-48-36.**

Cuisine: CONTINENTAL. **Reservations:** Recommended.
Prices: Three-course meal Dfl 62.50–120 ($34.20–$63.15). AE,
DC, EU, V.
Open: Lunch Sun–Fri 12:30pm on dinner daily 6–11pm.

One of the most famous restaurants in Amsterdam is the Excelsior,
said to be a favorite of the queen's father, Prince Bernhard. Its fame
derives from its cuisine and service, recognized formally by a Michelin
star. Crystal chandeliers, elaborate moldings, crisp linens, fresh bouquets of flowers, and picture windows overlooking the Amstel River
help to give this lovely place a baronial atmosphere. If your budget
cannot compete with that of Prince Bernhard, the Excelsior offers
three-course menus that make fine gastronomy more affordable.

Conveniently situated en route to the new Musiektheater nearby,
the Excelsior offers a three-course *menu du théâtre*, which recently
included such choices as smoked eel with dill (a Dutch specialty) or
marinated sweetbreads of lamb with salad for starters, filet of halibut with caper sauce or filet of veal with leek sauce as main courses,
and desserts such as orange pie with frozen yogurt or raspberry
bavaroise with mango sauce. A lovely way to start an evening at the
ballet or the opera.

La Rive, in the Amstel Intercontinental Hotel, Professor Tulpplein 1.
☎ **622-60-60.**
Cuisine: FRENCH NOUVELLE. **Reservations:** Recommended.
Prices: Five-course fixed-price dinner Dfl 125 ($65.80). AE, DC,
EU, MC, V.
Open: Daily 7am–11pm.

La Rive overlooks the river, and in summer it opens onto a grassy
terrace along the embankment. The atmosphere here suggests a small
private library that has been called into service for a dinner party.
The walls are paneled in cherry and punctuated with tall cabinets
filled with books and brass objects. Along one wall is a row of private booths that are particularly romantic and overlook the other
tables for a view through tall french windows to the water. The service and wine cellar are in the finest modern French traditions. In
1994 La Rive was assigned a Michelin star.

Moderate

Le Relais, in the Hôtel de l'Europe, Nieuwe Doelenstraat 2–8,
at Muntplein. ☎ **623-48-36.**
Cuisine: FRENCH/CONTINENTAL. **Reservations:** Recommended
for dinner.
Prices: From Dfl 22.50 ($11.85) à la carte; fixed-price menu Dfl 49.50
($26.50). AE, DC, MC, V.
Open: Daily noon–2:30pm and 7–10:30pm

This second restaurant on the ground floor of the Hôtel de l'Europe
is moderately priced compared to the first-class Excelsior (see above).
Start with the beef carpaccio or a cold lobster and follow with leg
of lamb in honey and thyme. Cap it off with cassata ice cream or

coconut cake. Lighter luncheon dishes include a tuna sandwich with a salad as well as curried chicken soup. For open-air dining with a view of the canal and the Muntplein choose La Terrasse.

2 In the Center

Expensive

Le Bistro Suisse, in the Swissôtel Amsterdam Ascot Hotel, Damrak 95–98.
☎ **626-00-66.**
Cuisine: FRENCH. **Reservations:** Recommended.
Prices: Three-course meal Dfl 39.50–125 ($20.80–$65.80). AE, DC, MC, V.
Open: Daily noon–10pm.

Just off Dam Square, down a small alleyway that leads off the Damrak, you'll find Le Bistro Suisse. Even though it's the restaurant of the Swiss-owned Ascot, it looks like a bit of Paris dropped into the heart of Amsterdam. Dark woods and crisp white linens give a semiformal yet warm feeling to the place, and a newspaper rack with papers on wooden braces invites you to linger if you're dining alone. The menu is varied to suit a variety of appetites and budgets. To start you might try the famous Swiss Rösti (shredded baked potato) with different toppings, then choose an elaborate French dish to follow. Or try the chef's special wild boar steak.

Dorrius Restaurant, in the Holiday Inn Crowne Plaza, Nieuwe Zijds Voorburgwal 5. ☎ **620-05-00.**
Cuisine: SEAFOOD. **Reservations:** Recommended.
Prices: Three-course meal Dfl 80 ($42.10). AE, DC, EU, V.
Open: Daily noon–11pm.

Housed in adjoining canal houses, Dorrius is one of Amsterdam's most elegant dining rooms. The traditional feeling of the beamed ceilings and black-and-white marble floor is updated by coral-pink linens and a spacious arrangement of tables and fixtures. The bounty of the Dutch waters is the raison d'être of this fine restaurant: Zeeland oyster soup with spinach and champagne; poached rouget in lemon sauce; and Dover sole, grilled or à la meunière. Meat selections include tournedos with champagne-and-mustard sauce and filets of chicken breast with Parma ham, basil, and Noilly Prat sauce. Perhaps the most unique and sensible idea here, however, is the Trolley Specialties—each night beginning at 6pm a trolley is presented with various meat, game, and poultry choices to be carved at the table and served with vegetables, a potato, and sauce.

Edo Japanese Steak House, in the Golden Tulip Krasnapolsky, Dam 9. ☎ **554-60-96.**
Cuisine: JAPANESE. **Reservations:** Recommended.
Prices: Full meal Dfl 30–50 ($15.80–$26.30) at lunch, Dfl 60–110 ($31.55–$57.90) at dinner. AE, DC, MC, V.
Open: Lunch daily noon–2pm; dinner daily 6–10:45pm.

The Edo Japanese Steak House is a hibachi restaurant—chicken, steak, and delicate shrimp are quick fried on large table grills located right by the tables, so you can watch the cooking take place. Complete dinners include both appetizer and soup, salad and vegetables, and fried rice, plus ice cream with a choice of green tea or coffee.

Moderate

De Blauwe Parade, Nieuwe Zijds Voorburgwal 178. ☎ **624-00-47.**
   Cuisine: DUTCH. **Reservations:** Recommended.
   Prices: Fixed-price meal Dfl 45 ($23.70) for three courses, Dfl 60 ($31.60) for four courses, Dfl 75 ($39.45) for five courses. AE, MC, V.
   Open: Daily noon–9:30pm.

This restaurant, behind Dam Square, has been offering its steaks and typically Dutch dishes for more than 100 years in a beamed and tiled Dutch-tavern dining room. De Blauwe Parade still maintains a tradition that has become legendary among its patrons: Each of its steaks is numbered, and if the number on yours has "000" at the end, you're the winner of a free bottle of wine. It's also famous for its Dutch pea soup.

De Boemerang, Weteringschans 171. ☎ **623-42-51.**
   Cuisine: MUSSELS/STEAKS. **Reservations:** Recommended at dinner.
   Prices: Main courses Dfl 17.50–38 ($9.20–$20). AE, EU, V.
   Open: Mon–Fri noon–9pm, Sat–Sun 4–9pm.

This is the place to go for mussels. This restaurant, conveniently located for the Rijksmuseum, opened in 1915 and is still run by the same family. The original owner named it Boomerang because he hoped his customers would return like the Australian hunting weapon does—and return they have over the years. The decor is old and eclectic and includes hundreds of pieces of paper currency hanging from the ceiling, a jukebox with 40-year-old golden oldies, and old copper kettles and pans. But it's not the atmosphere that attracts customers, it's the most succulent mussels you've ever tasted, served in large pots in such huge quantities they're almost impossible to finish. Choose from any number of dipping sauces, all of which come with the mussels. The second reason people come here is for the juicy steaks served with fries.

Brasserie Noblesse, in the Amsterdam Renaissance Hotel, Kattengat 1.
   ☎ **551-20-44.**
   Cuisine: AMERICAN. **Reservations:** Recommended.
   Prices: Three-course meal Dfl 50 ($26.30); à la carte up to Dfl 120 ($63.15). AE, DC, EU, V.
   Open: Daily 6:30am–11pm.

One of the best restaurants in town for beef is the Brasserie Noblesse, which features aged prime rib flown in from the United States. Nearly as popular as American beef in Amsterdam is American regional cuisine, and the Brasserie Noblesse serves up a different distinctive American style of cooking—Cajun, Tex-Mex, or New England, for example—every three or four months. The prices are quite reasonable, and there's a nice wine list.

Dining in Central Amsterdam

Café von Puffelen, Prinsengracht 377. ☎ 624-62-70.

> **Cuisine:** DUTCH/CONTINENTAL. **Reservations:** Not required.
> **Prices:** Daily menu Dfl 27.50–32 ($14.50–$16.85); à la carte Dfl 12.50–
> 40 ($6.55–$21.05). AE, DC, MC, V.
> **Open:** Sun–Thurs noon–1am, Fri–Sat noon–2am.

At this large café/restaurant near the Westerkirk, the most popular
feature is the three menus that change daily. Among the dishes you

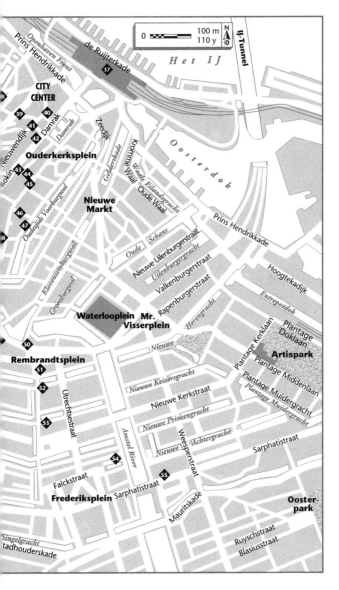

might find are suckling pig, veal steak, and grilled lamb chops. Other choices include vegetable platters and mozzarella with tomato. Save room for the house specialties—delicious handmade chocolates.

⭐ **Casa di David,** Singel 426. ☎ **624-50-93.**
Cuisine: ITALIAN. **Reservations:** Not required.
Prices: Full meal Dfl 20–50 ($13.15–$26.30). AE, DC, EU, MC, V.
Open: Dinner only, daily 5–11:30pm.

A friend recommended Casa di David as one of the best Italian restaurants he'd ever been to, and possibly the best in Amsterdam. The ambience is typically Italian—dark paneling, red-and-white-checked tablecloths, and wine casks. It's canal side and very romantic. Casa di David is most famous for its pizzas for one and its freshly made pasta. Each person at the table can choose his or her favorite toppings—there's even a vegetarian pizza.

China Treasure, Nieuwe Zijds Voorburgwal 115. ☎ **626-09-15.**

Cuisine: CHINESE. **Reservations:** Recommended.
Prices: Three-course meal Dfl 42 ($22.10). AE, DC, EU, V.
Open: Lunch daily noon–3pm; dinner daily 5–11pm.

In a city with a passion for Indonesian flavors, it can be difficult to find traditional Chinese cuisine, let alone good Chinese cuisine. But don't despair—make a beeline for China Treasure. Rated among the best restaurants in Amsterdam by Avante Garde, China Treasure offers classic Chinese culinary traditions and a wide array of choices, including complete menus.

Christophe, Leliegracht 46. ☎ **625-08-07.**

Cuisine: INTERNATIONAL. **Reservations:** Recommended.
Prices: Main courses Dfl 50–65 ($26.30–$34.20). AE, DC, MC, V.
Open: Dinner only, Mon–Sat 7–11pm.

The chef here uses traditional Mediterranean ingredients—figs, truffles, olives, and saffron—in exciting new ways. Try the pigeon roasted with spices, lobster with sweet garlic, quail risotto with truffle juice, or scallops with orange and saffron. Finish with baked figs accompanied by thyme ice cream. A traditional wooden decor prevails, with art deco touches.

Gauchos Grill, Damstraat 5. ☎ **623-96-32.**

Cuisine: ARGENTINIAN. **Reservations:** Not required.
Prices: Three-course meal Dfl 35–48 ($18.40–$25.25). No credit cards.
Open: Daily noon–1am.

Curiously enough, there are a number of Spanish and South American restaurants in Amsterdam. The decor at Gauchos transports you to the Argentine plains—rough paneling, appaloosa pony–skin bench covers, plank tables, and rancho-style seats with Indian tapestry covers. The specialty here is Argentine steaks served with chimichurri, a special sauce. Other top choices are the burgers and mixed grill.

You'll find three other Gauchos restaurants around town. Also open for both lunch and dinner is one at Geelvincksteeg 6, behind the Flower Market (☎ **626-59-77**); there are two Gauchos on Korte Leidsedwarsstraat at nos. 45 and 109 (☎ **623-80-87** or **627-03-18**) that are open for dinner only.

$ Haesje Claes, Spuistraat 273–275. ☎ **624-99-98.**

Cuisine: DUTCH. **Reservations:** Recommended.
Prices: Three-course meal Dfl 35–75 ($18.40–$39.45). AE, DC, EU, V.
Open: Daily noon–midnight.

If you're yearning for a cozy Old Dutch environment and hearty Dutch food at moderate prices, go to Haesje Claes. It's an inviting place with lots of nooks and crannies; brocaded benches and traditional Dutch hanging lamps with fringed covers give an intimate and comfortable feeling to the tables. The straightforward menu ranges from omelets to tournedos. You can get the official Dutch Tourist Menu or make à la carte choices.

Het Stuivertje, Hazenstraat 58. ☎ **623-13-49.**

Cuisine: DUTCH/FRENCH. **Reservations:** Essential.
Prices: Main courses Dfl 18–37.50 ($9.50–$19.70). AE, DC, MC, V.
Open: Lunch Tues–Sat noon–3pm; dinner Tues–Sun 5:30–11:30pm.

This traditional restaurant is always crowded with people enjoying the seasonal menu of the month or a selection from the regular menu. The latter features everything from vegetarian dishes like broccoli soufflé to goat stew with fennel and thyme, plus more traditional items like salmon with hollandaise and breast of veal stuffed with vegetables.

De Kleine Prins, Prinsengracht 604. ☎ **625-13-40.**

Cuisine: FRENCH/DUTCH. **Reservations:** Recommended.
Prices: Three-course meal Dfl 55 ($28.95). AE, DC, EU, V.
Open: Dinner only, Fri–Sun 5:30–11:30pm.

A good place in the neighborhood of antiques shops, De Kleine Prins ("The Small Prince") is located between Spiegelgracht and the Vijzelstraat. It's a quiet neighborhood restaurant—nothing fancy or trendy, but quite appealing. It's housed in a 17th-century canal house, and its walls are decorated with 18th-century engravings of Amsterdam. One of its regulars once described De Kleine Prins as having a "good price-to-quality ratio" for typically Dutch/French menu items at prices between the budget and moderate range.

Koh-I-Noor, Westermarkt 29. ☎ **623-31-33.**

Cuisine: INDIAN. **Reservations:** Recommended.
Prices: Three-course meal Dfl 26.50–49.50 ($13.95–$26.05). AE, DC, EU, V.
Open: Dinner only, daily from 5pm–midnight.

Facing the Westerkerk, Koh-I-Noor is a small and simple Indian restaurant that offers a choice of specials plus traditional favorites, including tandoori chicken and lamb vindaloo. There's another Koh-I-Noor at Rokin 18 (☎ **627-21-18**) that's also open at lunch.

Lucius Restaurant, Spuistraat 247. ☎ **624-18-31.**

Cuisine: SEAFOOD. **Reservations:** Recommended.
Prices: Three-course menu Dfl 47.50 ($25); main courses Dfl 10–95 ($5.25–$50). AE, DC, MC, V.
Open: Dinner only, Mon–Sat 5pm–midnight.

This restaurant, which opened in 1985, has established a reputation for fine seafood at fairly reasonable prices. Oysters and lobsters imported from Norway and Canada are the specialty. The three-course menu is also very popular. Among the half dozen or so choices featured on the chalkboard menu, you might find fish soup to start, followed by grilled plaice, Dover sole, bass, or John Dory. The spectacular seafood plate ($50) includes 6 oysters, 10 mussels, clams, shrimp, and half a lobster. The long, narrow dining room is cooled by ceiling fans and features an aquarium. In summer chairs are placed out on the sidewalk. (*Lucius,* by the way, means "pike" in Latin.)

De Nissen, Rokin 95. ☎ 624-28-25.

Cuisine: DUTCH. **Reservations:** Recommended.
Prices: Three- or four-course meal Dfl 28.50–65.50 ($15–$34.45). AE, DC, EU, V.
Open: Mon–Sat noon–9:30pm.

This Old Dutch–style spot, halfway between Dam Square and the Muntplein, has nooks and crannies that give it the atmosphere of an old wine cellar. The menu is typically Dutch and reasonably priced, and the mood is casual. Fresh fish here is a must, and you can order one of the set menus or à la carte. Try lobster bisque to start, fried flounder as a main dish, and fresh strawberries for dessert. At lunch De Nissen is popular with people who work nearby, so you may have to wait for a table.

Restaurant Manchurian, Leidseplein 10A. ☎ 623-13-30.

Cuisine: ASIAN. **Reservations:** Recommended for dinner.
Prices: Rijsttafel Dfl 39.50–79 ($20.80–$41.55); main courses Dfl 27.50–57.50 ($14.45–$30.25). AE, DC, MC, V.
Open: Daily noon–3pm and 5–11pm.

Apart from the lucky color red, the decor is minimal at this trilevel restaurant. The cuisine ranges from Cantonese, Szechuan, and Mongolian specialties to Thai dishes and rijsttafels with fantasy names like Tour of India and Imperial. Try the scallion lobster or Siam prawns, the Szechuan beef, or any of the sweet-and-sour dishes.

★ Rum Runners, Prinsengracht 277. ☎ 627-40-79.
$

Cuisine: CARIBBEAN. **Reservations:** Recommended.
Prices: Three-course meal Dfl 34–45 ($17.90–$23.70). AE, DC, EU, V.
Open: Mon–Thurs 4pm–1am, Fri 4pm–2am, Sat–Sun 2pm–2am.

Near the Anne Frankhuis, in the former storage room of the Westerkerk (yes, the church!), is Rum Runners, where atmosphere and cuisine are inspired by the Caribbean Islands. Two gigantic bamboo birdcages greet you as you enter, and you sit beneath gently circling ceiling fans; there are towering potted palms beneath the lofty rafters, and at night the music often has a reggae beat until the wee hours. Try *asopao,* a Caribbean rice dish, or shrimp-filled pineapples.

Sarang Mas, Damrak 44. ☎ 622-21-05.

Cuisine: INDONESIAN. **Reservations:** Recommended.
Prices: Full lunch Dfl 27.50 ($14.45); rijsttafels Dfl 45.50–57.50 ($23.95–$30.25). AE, DC, EU, V.
Open: Daily 11:30am–11pm.

This intimate Indonesian restaurant is located near the canal-boat piers—so you get a nice view while you dine on traditional Indonesian dishes, including a decent selection of rijsttafels. The pink, white, and green decor is a refreshing and contemporary alternative to the usual basic decor found in Indonesian restaurants.

Schiller, in the Schiller Crest Hotel, Rembrandtsplein 26–36.
☎ **623-16-60.**
Cuisine: CONTINENTAL. **Reservations:** Recommended.
Prices: Three-course meal Dfl 46 ($24.20). AE, DC, MC, V.
Open: Daily noon–10pm.

Beamed and paneled in well-aged oak and graced with etched-glass panels and stained-glass skylights, this 100-plus-year-old landmark is a splendid sight indeed. A particularly amusing little dining room is called the **sproekenzaal,** or "sayings rooms," because it's adorned with homey little mottos in five languages that are painted on the paneling in gold leaf; they include these contributions from the English language: "No two people are alike and both are glad of it" and "Candy is dandy but liquor is quicker."

Among the dishes on the traditional menu you'll find everything from stewed eel and potato-and-cabbage casserole to T-bone steak, roast leg of lamb with mint sauce, and spaghetti bolognese.

Tony's Pasta & Pizza Company, Reguliersdwarsstraat 55.
☎ **627-38-33.**
Cuisine: ITALIAN. **Reservations:** Recommended.
Prices: Three-course meal Dfl 25–88 ($13.15–$46.30). AE, DC, MC, V.
Open: Apr–Oct, daily from noon; Mar–Nov, dinner only, daily from 5pm.

When it's Italian you're after, go to Tony's. This trendy spot, located at the head of Amsterdam's restaurant row, is done up in black, gray, and white art deco with Campari ashtrays for color. The menu offers everything from individual pizzas to such enticing dishes as veal oregano with garlic sauce and sea bass with Mediterranean spices.

Budget

Café de Jaren, Nieuwe Doelenstraat 20–22. ☎ **625-57-71.**
Cuisine: DUTCH/CONTINENTAL. **Reservations:** Not required.
Prices: Set lunch Dfl 20 ($10.50); set dinner Dfl 28 ($14.75); main courses Dfl 7.50–25 ($3.95–$13.15). No credit cards.
Open: Daily 10am–1am.

One of the largest cafés in the city, Café de Jaren has 300 seats inside and 150 more out on the terrace. Many students who don't like the mensa food eat lunch here. The building originally served as a bank and so, besides being spacious, has unusually high ceilings. Here, you can enjoy everything from a cup of coffee or a glass of *jenever* to spaghetti bolognese and rib-eye steak.

Café Luxembourg, Spuistraat 24. ☎ **620-62-64.**
Cuisine: INTERNATIONAL. **Reservations:** Not required.
Prices: Dfl 3–13.50 ($1.60–$7.10). No credit cards.
Open: Sun–Thurs 10am–1am, Fri–Sat 10am–2am.

This large café opened eight years ago and soon became a favorite hangout for students, journalists, senior citizens, and other barflies. Unlike other coffeehouses in Amsterdam, which often draw a distinctive clientele, Café Luxembourg attracts all kinds of people because it offers amazingly large portions of food at reasonable prices. Soups, sandwiches, and such dishes as meat loaf are available. It's a relaxing place where people are encouraged to linger and read one of the many international newspapers that are available. In summer there's sidewalk dining.

Café-Restaurant Blincker, St. Barberenstraat 7. ☎ 627-19-38.

Cuisine: CONTINENTAL. **Reservations:** Recommended.
Prices: Main courses Dfl 8.50–26.50 ($4.45–$13.95). AE, DC, MC, V.
Open: Dinner only, Mon–Sat 4pm–1am.

This intimate restaurant in the Frascati Theater building, on a small side street off Rokin, attracts actors, journalists, artists, and other assorted bohemians. At night the place is jammed with people who cluster around the bar. To find Café Blincker, turn into Nesstreet from Dam Square (which runs parallel to Rokin), then turn left after the Frascati Theater.

Keuken van 1870, Spuistraat 4. ☎ 624-89-65.

Cuisine: DUTCH. **Reservations:** Not accepted.
Prices: Main courses Dfl 10–25 ($5.25–$13.15). AE, DC, EU, V.
Open: Mon–Fri 11:30am–8pm. Sat–Sun 4–9pm.

The Keuken van 1870, near the Amsterdam Sonesta Hotel, is said to be one of the cheapest places to eat in Amsterdam. It also must surely be the plainest place to eat: There's absolutely no attempt at decor here, meals are served cafeteria style, tables are bare, and dishes are plain—but the food is good. Pork chops, fish, and chicken—all accompanied by vegetables and potatoes—are some of the main courses available on the menu.

Restaurant Alfonso, Korte Leidsewasstraat 69. ☎ 627-05-80.

Cuisine: MEXICAN. **Reservations:** Recommended at dinner.
Prices: Two-course meal Dfl 35 ($18.40); à la carte main courses from Dfl 21.50 ($11.30). AE, DC, MC, V.
Open: Daily noon–midnight.

Of all the Latin American restaurants in Amsterdam, this is the best known and most popular. The large dining room is decorated in Mexican style, with sombreros, clay pottery, and cacti. Start with bean soup and follow with a combination plate of tacos, enchiladas, and burritos or chili con carne, chorizos, and quesadillas.

Restaurant Kopenhagen, Rokin 84. ☎ 624-93-76.

Cuisine: SEAFOOD/CONTINENTAL. **Reservations:** Recommended for dinner.
Prices: Three-course meal Dfl 30–38 ($15.80–$20); à la carte main courses Dfl 12.50–40 ($6.55–$21.05). AE, DC, MC, V.
Open: Mon–Sat noon–3pm and 5–11pm.

At lunchtime many Amsterdammers working in the area choose to eat here because the set menus are tasty and filling. The specialty is seafood, but the menu also features pasta, poultry, and meat dishes, too. For example, you might start with fish soup and follow with steamed catfish in white-wine sauce or mixed seafood platter—cod, salmon, plaice, and mussels. A variety of smørrebrød (open-face sandwiches) is offered, including the favorite treat—herring.

Restaurant Purnama, Korte Nieuwendijk 33. ☎ **620-53-25.**

Cuisine: INDONESIAN. **Reservations:** Recommended at dinner.
Prices: Rijsttafel Dfl 27.50–39.50 ($14.45–$20.80); main courses Dfl 6.50–19.50 ($43.40–$10.25). AE, DC, MC, V.
Open: Daily 1:30–10:30pm.

This small restaurant, only five minutes from the Centraal Station, is always crowded with locals enjoying the good-quality food. Among the favorite dishes are the minirijsttafel and the special rijsttafel. The first consists of 11 items, the second of 15 items that combine sweet and sour tastes and other contrasting spices and flavors. If this is too much for you, try the *nasi* or *bami goreng* or choose one of the 8 or 10 meat or fish dishes. For starters try the *sot ayam,* a spicy soup.

Restaurant Sukabumi, Geelvincksteeg 2. ☎ **625-14-46.**

Cuisine: INDONESIAN. **Reservations:** Suggested.
Prices: Daily platter Dfl 12.50 ($6.55); rijsttafel Dfl 35 ($18.40). No credit cards.
Open: Mon–Sat noon–10pm.

At lunch this tiny restaurant, located near the Flower Market and Muntplein, only five minutes' walk from the Leidseplein, is frequented by workers from the area. A typical one-plate dish is the so-called minirijsttafel—cooked rice garnished with different vegetables and spicy sauces. The best choice is the 17-item rijsttafel, or you can select such other dishes as *nasi* and *bami goreng* or *nasi kuming.* In summer you can enjoy sidewalk dining in this quiet pedestrian zone.

Ristorante Pizzeria Latina, Nieuwe Zijds Voorburgwal 61.
☎ **627-01-97.**

Cuisine: ITALIAN. **Reservations:** Not accepted.
Prices: Main courses Dfl 23.50–30 ($12.35–$15.80); pizza Dfl 8–14 ($4.20–$7.35). AE, DC, MC, V.
Open: Daily noon–midnight.

Stop here for a quick, unsophisticated Italian meal taken either in the large dining room or on the glassed-in veranda. The dishes are typical—minestrone, spaghetti bolognese, entrecote pizzaiola, and fried calamari, along with 22 different pizzas.

Rose's Cantina, Reguliersdwarsstraat 38–40. ☎ **625-97-97.**

Cuisine: MEXICAN. **Reservations:** Recommended.
Prices: Main courses Dfl 11.50–26.50 ($6.05–$13.95). AE, DC, MC, V.
Open: Dinner only, daily 5–11pm.

To attract English-speaking guests, Rose's Cantina advertises typical American favorites like hamburgers and meatballs, although the decor and most of the cuisine are Mexican inspired. A meal starting with tortilla chips and salsa, followed by a *prato mixto* or fried *galinhas* (roast chicken with fries and red peppers), and washed down with a Mexican beer will cost you less than Dfl 50 ($26.30). The tables are oak, the service is decent, and the atmosphere is Latin American. Rose's is near the Flower Market.

$ **The Station,** on Platform 1 of Centraal Station. ☎ **627-33-06.**
Cuisine: DUTCH. **Reservations:** Not accepted.
Prices: Full meal Dfl 18–30 ($9.45–$15.80). No credit cards.
Open: Mon–Sat 7am–10pm, Sun 8am–10pm.

For a little bit of elegance with your budget meal, try the Centraal
Station restaurant, a self-service spot in a lofty wood-paneled chamber with chandeliers. Each month there's a different special plate
offered here at a rock-bottom price, but if you're expecting a boring
choice, you should know that trout, jugged hare, and coq au vin have
found their way onto plates in the recent past, always with salad,
vegetable, and other appropriate accompaniments.

3 At Leidseplein

Expensive

'T Swarte Schaep, Korte Leidsedwarsstraat 24, at Leidseplein.
☎ **622-30-21.**
Cuisine: DUTCH. **Reservations:** Recommended.
Prices: Full meal Dfl 70–140 ($36.85–$73.70). AE, DC, EU, V.
Open: Daily noon–11pm.

'T Swarte Schaep is much better known by its English name, "The
Black Sheep." Located in a house that dates from 1687, this restaurant still seems like an old Dutch home. You climb a steep flight of
tiled steps to reach the second-floor dining room, where the beams
and ceiling panels are dark with age. It's a cozy, almost crowded place
made both fragrant and inviting by the fresh flowers on every table
and those that spill from the polished brass buckets hanging from
the ceiling beams. The Black Sheep is well known for its wine list
and its crêpes Suzette. Taking a peek at the menu choices, you might
find sole meunière with asparagus or grilled salmon with fresh thyme.

Moderate

Alphonso's, Korte Leidsedwarsstraat 69. ☎ **627-05-80.**
Cuisine: MEXICAN. **Reservations:** Recommended.
Prices: Full meal Dfl 30–55 ($15.80–$28.95). AE, DC, MC, V.
Open: Apr–Oct, daily noon–1am; Nov–Mar, daily 5pm–1am.

If you suddenly get a craving for Mexican food while you're in
Amsterdam, you won't have to go far to find Alphonso's, located just
off the Leidseplein. Alphonso's offers enchiladas con queso, burritos,
tacos, and other traditional favorites. You can even order margaritas
by the pitcher. There's another Alphonso's at Utrechtsestraat 32a
(☎ 625-94-26); it's open for dinner only, daily from 5pm to 1am.

Bistro La Forge, Korte Leidsedwarsstraat 26. ☎ **624-00-95.**
Cuisine: FRENCH/CONTINENTAL. **Reservations:** Recommended.
Prices: Three-course meal Dfl 62.50 ($32.90), including a glass of wine.
AE, DC, EU, V.
Open: Dinner only, daily 5pm–midnight.

Just off the Leidseplein and right next to the famous and pricey Black Sheep is Bistro La Forge, which serves a fairly traditional French/continental menu of meats and fish at moderate prices (like halibut and entrecote). The big attraction here is the open fireplace. You can order a fixed-price meal or à la carte dishes. Starters include escargots or frogs' legs. The à la carte menu has a variety of fish dishes, including salmon in puff pastry; there are such meat dishes as filet of rabbit or filet of beef with sweet-pepper sauce. The dessert menu includes a cheese plate, sorbet, crêpes, and cherries flambé served with vanilla ice cream. There is an extensive wine list.

De Blauwe Hollander, Leidsekrulestraat 28. ☎ **623-30-14.**

Cuisine: DUTCH. **Reservations:** Recommended.
Prices: Three-course meal Dfl 28–55 ($14.75–$28.95). No credit cards.
Open: Dinner only, daily from 5pm.

Depending on how you order, De Blauwe Hollander can be considered either a best buy as a moderate restaurant or a step-up alternative in the budget category. There's a small sidewalk gallery here that gives you a good view of the passing parade in this busy area of town, but be warned that the menu has very little that's more imaginative than roast beef, spareribs, or chicken. Everything is served with fries and a salad or vegetable, and there's usually a *budget schotel* (budget plate).

Café Americain, in the American Hotel, Leidsekade 97.
☎ **624-53-22.**

Cuisine: CONTINENTAL. **Reservations:** Recommended.
Prices: Three-course meal Dfl 55–85 ($28.95–$44.75). AE, DC, MC, V.
Open: Daily 10:30am–midnight.

You'll dine here in a lofty room that's a national monument of Dutch Jugendstijl and original art deco. Seductress/spy Mata Hari held her wedding reception here in her pre-espionage days, and since its 1897 opening the place has been a haven for Dutch and international artists, writers, dancers, and actors. Leaded windows, newspaper-littered reading tables, bargello-patterned velvet upholstery, frosted-glass chandeliers from the 1920s, and tall carved columns are all part of the dusky sit-and-chat atmosphere.

Castell, Lijnsbaangracht 252–254. ☎ **622-86-06.**

Cuisine: SOUTH AMERICAN. **Reservations:** Recommended.
Prices: Full meal Dfl 33.50–65 ($17.65–$34.20). No credit cards.
Open: Dinner only, Mon–Sun 5pm–12:30am.

Castell is nicely situated near the bustling Leidseplein. If you're going to be in the area, give Castell a call and make a reservation for the evening. The formula here is a simple one: beef, beef, and more beef. The menu includes a nice selection of tournedos, and expect to find Zeeland oysters on the menu when they're in season.

Kantjil and Tiger, Spuistraat 291. ☎ **620-09-94.**

Cuisine: JAVANESE/INDONESIAN. **Reservations:** Not required.
Prices: Main courses Dfl 25–90 ($13.15–$50). AE, DC, MC, V.
Open: Dinner only, daily 4:30–11pm.

The two best-sellers in this very popular large restaurant are *nasi goreng Kantjil* (fried rice with pork kebabs, stewed beef, pickled cucumbers, and mixed vegetables) and the 20-item rijsttafel for two. Other choices include stewed chicken in *soja* sauce, tofu omelet, shrimp with coconut dressing, Indonesian pumpkin, and mixed steamed vegetables with peanut-butter sauce. Finish off your meal with the multilayered cinnamon cake or (and try this once) the coffee with ginger liqueur and whipped cream. The restaurant attracts a young baby-boomer crowd with their children, as well as students from the nearby university who are tired of mensa meals. The name means "antelope and tiger."

De Oesterbar, Leidseplein 10. ☎ **623-29-88.**

Cuisine: SEAFOOD. **Reservations:** Recommended.
Prices: Three-course meal Dfl 45–125 ($23.70–$65.80). AE, DC, MC, V.
Open: Daily noon–1am.

More than 50 years old, De Oesterbar is the best-known and most popular fish restaurant in Amsterdam. The decor is a delight: all white tiles with fish tanks bubbling at your elbows on the street level, and Victorian brocades and etched glass in the more formal dining room upstairs. The menu is a directory of the variety of fish available in Holland and the variety of ways they can be prepared. The cuisine is traditional, however, and includes a few meat selections (tournedos or veal) for those who don't like fish or seafood. To whet your appetite, selections include sole Danoise with the tiny Dutch shrimp; sole Véronique with muscadet grapes; stewed eel in wine sauce; and the assorted fish plate of turbot, halibut, and fresh salmon.

Le Pêcheur, Reguliersdwarsstraat 32. ☎ **624-31-21.**

Cuisine: SEAFOOD. **Reservations:** Recommended.
Prices: Three-course lunch Dfl 47.50 ($25); five-course dinner Dfl 82.50 ($43.40). AE, EU, MC, V.
Open: Lunch Mon–Fri noon–midnight; dinner daily 5pm–midnight.

Appealing and popular, Le Pêcheur sports a marble floor, a muraled ceiling, and a garden for summer dining. If you know some French, you'll guess that fish is the principal preoccupation here. In season, come for the coquilles St-Jacques and the mussels and oysters from the southern province of Zeeland. You might try poached brill with onion sauce or fried wolffish with light mustard sauce. Of course, you can always have tournedos of beef cooked to your liking. There's a nice dessert menu, with such dishes as apple compote with cranberry sauce, sorbet, or crème caramel.

Budget

Tandoor, Leidseplein 19. ☎ **623-44-15.**

Cuisine: INDIAN. **Reservations:** Recommended.
Prices: Three-course meal Dfl 30–48 ($15.80–$25.25) AE, DC, MC, V.
Open: Dinner only, daily 5pm–1am.

When you have a hankering for Indian food and only a few rupees to spend, consider Tandoor, where you can have chicken or vegetable curry from the restaurant's Tourist Menu. The most popular items on the menu are the tandoori dishes, but like any good Indian restaurant, a variety of dishes from all over India is offered. There's a children's menu for kids who don't like spicy Indian food.

4   Along the Canals

Expensive

⭐ **Dynasty,** Reguliersdwarsstraat 30. ☎ **626-84-00.**
Cuisine: CHINESE/SOUTHEAST ASIAN. **Reservations:** Recommended.
Prices: Full meal Dfl 80–170 ($42.10–$89.45). AE, DC, EU, V.
Open: Dinner only, Wed–Mon 5:30–11pm.

For summer dining in a formal Louis XV–style canal-house garden or winter dining in a cozy cavern of exotic colors and upturned Chinese umbrellas, try Dynasty, located between the Singel and Herengracht Canals. It offers a selection of imaginative Chinese and Asian specialties, including Thai, Malay, and Philippine. Among the intriguing possibilities is the Promise of Spring, an appetizer of crisp pancakes filled with bamboo shoots and minced meat. Or perhaps it's more fun to get together a group of six like-minded diners to share Dynasty's magnificent 10-course Festive Meal, which is an extravaganza of flavors—among its delights are lobster, *coquillage,* duck, lamb, pigeon, and Szechuan beef.

De Goudsbloem, in the Hotel Pulitzer, Reestraat 8. ☎ **523-52-83.**
Cuisine: FRENCH. **Reservations:** Recommended.
Prices: Three-course meal Dfl 74.50 ($39.20). AE, DC, EU, MC, V.
Open: Dinner only, daily from 6pm.

Tucked into a small courtyard of the Hotel Pulitzer, the Goudsbloem is noted for its contemporary decor, its wildly colored service plates, its intimacy—so rare in hotel dining rooms—and a kitchen staff supervised by Pulitzer's executive chef. The wine card here lists hundreds of selections, all of them chosen with care by the Dutch sommelier.

Frommer's Cool for Kids: Restaurants

De Orient   (see p. 115) Kids will have fun at De Orient sampling the different Indonesian foods of the rijsttafels (comprised of 12, 19, or 25 dishes). There are a couple of dishes especially for children who don't like the spicy Indonesian food.

Pizzaland   (see p. 120) When your kids are longing for a piece of pizza, head to Pizzaland, Amsterdam's answer to Pizza Hut. You can order three different kinds of pizza—traditional, deep pan, or "whole meal."

Les Quatre Canetons, Prinsengracht 1111. ☎ **624-63-07.**
Cuisine: INTERNATIONAL. **Reservations:** Recommended.
Prices: Four-course meal Dfl 82.50 (43.40). AE, DC, EU, V.
Open: Lunch Mon–Fri from noon; dinner Mon–Sat from 6pm.

Located near the Amstel River, Les Quatre Canetons is the long-standing favorite restaurant of many Amsterdammers. The "Four Ducklings," located on the ground floor of an old canal-side warehouse, is described (as a result of its recent renovation) as one of Amsterdam's most "stylish" restaurants. However, the emphasis is still more on food than on fuss. Owners Ailko Faber and Jacques Roosenbred have worked in this restaurant since 1979 and are credited, along with others, for the new appreciation of Amsterdam as a European culinary capital by those who seek out and rate the restaurants of the world. Seasonal specialties and imaginative choices, such as duck breasts with prunes, make this a delightful place to dine, particularly if one has tickets for a performance at nearby Théâtre Carré.

Restaurant d'Vijff Vlieghen, Spuistraat 294–302. ☎ **624-83-69.**
Cuisine: DUTCH. **Reservations:** Recommended.
Prices: Four-course meal Dfl 55–300 ($28.95–$157.90). DC, EU, MC, V.
Open: Dinner only, daily 5:30pm–midnight.

Better known as "The Five Flies," Restaurant d'Vijff Vlieghen is one of the most famous restaurants in Amsterdam and occupies five canal houses (hence the name). The decor is decidedly Old Dutch, and there are interesting stories to be told about each of the six dining rooms, including the Glass Room, with its antique liqueur kegs, and the Rembrandt Room, with its original etchings. The blessing of this popular place is that, once seated in one of the dining rooms, you never realize how large this restaurant is.

Another blessing: a chef who is passionately chauvinistic about the exceptional quality and freshness of Dutch produce and determined to convey the culinary excellence inherent in many traditional Dutch recipes. For example, you can enjoy cutlets of wild boar from the Royal Estates with a stuffed apple, veal steak with prunes and apple, or smoked filet of turkey with mashed cranberry from the island of Terschilling. Another specialty here is the Flemish-Dutch traditional dish, waterzooi.

De Silveren Spiegel, Kattengat 4. ☎ **624-65-89.**
Cuisine: DUTCH/FRENCH. **Reservations:** Recommended.
Prices: Five-course meal Dfl 69.50–89.50 ($36.55–$47.10). AE, EU, MC, V.
Open: Lunch Mon–Sat from noon; dinner Mon–Sat from 6pm.

Directly across the street from the Amsterdam Sonesta Hotel, off Singel near the harbor, are two odd-looking little houses side by side that look as if they were transplanted from a children's fairy tale. In fact, they are survivors from the early 17th century that now house this well-known restaurant. It's typically Old Dutch inside, with the bar downstairs and more dining rooms where the bedrooms used to be. There's a pretty little garden in back, plus a traditionally Dutch tidiness that's very welcoming.

The menu is fun to read: For example, you're proudly told that your lamb from the Dutch island of Texel "is the best in the world" and that the filet of mullet is served with a sauce of mustard "made by a windmill near the Zaan."

Moderate

Espresso Corner Baton, Herengracht 82. ☎ **624-81-95.**

Cuisine: INTERNATIONAL. **Reservations:** Not required.
Prices: Main courses Dfl 5–12 ($2.65–$6.30). No credit cards.
Open: Mon–Sat 8am–6pm, Sun 9am–6pm.

This eatery deserves a special mention. Located on a canal at the corner of Herenstraat, it looks small from the outside but actually seats more than 100 people: 40 inside on two levels and 60 out on the sidewalk terrace. Salads, quiches, a choice of 30 hot or cold sandwiches—plus pastries and such desserts as tiramisù—make up the menu. A relaxing spot to while away a couple of hours watching the excursion boats slowly drifting past on the canal.

The Metz Restaurant, in The Metz department store, Keizersgracht 455. ☎ **624-88-10.**

Cuisine: DUTCH/INTERNATIONAL. **Reservations:** Recommended after 11:30am.
Prices: Main courses Dfl 14.50–30 ($7.65–$15.80). AE, DC, DISC, V.
Open: Mon 11:30am–5:30pm, Tues–Wed 9:30am–5:30pm, Thurs 9:30am–9pm, Fri–Sat 9:30am–5:30pm.

The Metz offers a spectacular panorama across the rooftops of Amsterdam from its sixth-floor restaurant at the corner of Leidsestraat, near Leidseplein. People drop in often for tea, which is served all day and consists of a pot of tea and a selection of cakes and/or sandwiches. Various one-plate meals, such as spaghetti with tomato sauce, grilled chicken, or vegetable stew, are also available.

Sluizer, Utrechtsestraat 43–45. ☎ **626-35-57.**

Cuisine: SEAFOOD. **Reservations:** Not required.
Prices: Main courses Dfl 30–40 ($15.90–$21.20) AE, DC, MC, V.
Open: Dinner only, daily 5pm–midnight.

This is a great place for seafood in an art deco atmosphere. There are at least 10 specials offered daily—from simple cod or eel to coquille St-Jacques, crab casserole, Dover sole, balibut, and octopus. A favorite specialty is the waterzooi, or fish stew.

Tempo Doeloe, Utrechtstraat 75. ☎ **625-67-18.**

Cuisine: INDONESIAN. **Reservations:** Recommended.
Prices: Five-course meal Dfl 75 ($39.50); à la carte dishes from Dfl 27.50 ($14.50).
Open: Dinner only, daily 6–11:30pm.

For authentic Indonesian cuisine this place is hard to beat. When a dish is described as *pedis,* or hot, that's indeed what it is. Try the rijsttafels, the *nasi koening*, or any of the vegetarian dishes. Finish with the *spekkoek*, a layered spice cake. The attractive decor and fine china are unexpected pluses.

5 In the Jordaan

Moderate

⭐ **Speciaal**, Nieuwe Leliestraat 140–142. ☎ **624-97-06.**
Cuisine: INDONESIAN. **Reservations:** Recommended.
Prices: Rijsttafel Dfl 50–70 ($26.30–$36.85) AE, EU, V.
Open: Dinner only, daily 5:30–11pm.

"Special" is the perfect word to describe Speciaal if you're a devoted fan and perpetual seeker of Amsterdam's finest rijsttafel restaurants. This cozy little place is owned and operated by a young Indonesian. Its walls are adorned with the mats that traditionally covered the spice crates that were sent to Speciaal from the East Indies. Equally true to the traditions of those islands is the cooking; for example, the satay, or kebabs, are of goat meat and are charcoal roasted. Here, too, you can sample the rich, multilayered Indonesian cake called *spekkoek*, which is served proudly as a specialty of the house.

6 Near the Museumplein

⭐ **Bodega Keyzer**, Van Baerkstraat 96. ☎ **671-14-41.**
Cuisine: CONTINENTAL. **Reservations:** Recommended.
Prices: Three-course meal Dfl 58 ($30.50); à la carte up to Dfl 120 ($63.15). AE, DC, EU, MC, V.
Open: Mon–Sat 9pm–midnight.

Whether or not you attend a concert at the Concertgebouw, you may want to plan a visit to its next-door neighbor, Bodega Keyzer. An Amsterdam landmark since 1903—it's said to have changed not a whit through the years—the Keyzer has enjoyed a colorful joint heritage with the world-famous concert hall. Among all the stories involving the great names of the music world is one about the night a customer mistook a concert soloist in search of a table for a waiter who might help with an order of whiskies. The musician, not missing a beat, lifted his violin case and said graciously, "Would a little Paganini do?" There's an elegance here that is a combination of traditional dark-and-dusky decor and highly starched pink linens. The menu leans heavily to fish from Dutch waters and, in season, to game specialties, such as hare and venison.

⭐ **Brasserie van Baerle**, Van Baerlestraat 158. ☎ **679-15-32.**
Cuisine: CONTINENTAL. **Reservations:** Recommended.
Prices: Three-course meal Dfl 44.50 ($20.45). AE, EU, MC, V.
Open: Mon–Fri from noon, Sun from 10am.

Filling the gap between sandwiches and haute cuisine was the goal of this restaurant's young owners. They've accomplished that aim and have created both culinary excitement and a gathering place for the writers, photographers, and advertising people who live in the area. It's nouvelle cuisine here—soups, salads, and other light dishes. In summer you can dine in the garden.

L'Entrecote, P. C. Hoofstraat 70. ☎ **020/673-77-76.**

Cuisine: FRENCH/AMERICAN. **Reservations:** Recommended.
Prices: Main courses Dfl 33–50 ($17.35-$26.30). AE, DC, DISC, V.
Open: Dinner only, Tues–Sat 5:30–11pm.

This small bilevel restaurant decorated in art deco style is famous for its rib steak dinners. Beef and veal steaks served with french fries and a salad are favorites, too. The upholstered chairs are comfortable, and some of the decor is quite dramatic, like the lamp standing next to the window. Service is swift, making this an ideal preconcert dining spot.

De Orient, Van Baerlestraat 21. ☎ **673-49-58.**

Cuisine: INDONESIAN. **Reservations:** Recommended.
Prices: Rijsttafel Dfl 30–65 ($15.80–$34.20). AE, DC, EU, MC, V.
Open: Dinner only, daily 5–10:30pm.

Owned since 1948 by a friendly Indonesian couple who lived in California for a while, De Orient offers three rijsttafels (12, 19, and 25 dishes), or you can come in on Wednesday night for the rijsttafel buffet. De Orient has a wide variety of vegetarian dishes available.

Ristorante Mirafiori, Hobbemastraat 2. ☎ **662-30-13.**

Cuisine: ITALIAN. **Reservations:** Recommended for dinner.
Prices: Three-course meal with wine Dfl 90 ($47.35). AE, DC, MC, V.
Open: Wed–Mon noon–3pm and 5pm–midnight.

Founded in 1941 by the same family who runs it today, this typical Italian restaurant has welcomed many famous guests to its three intimate dining rooms—the late Sammy Davis, Jr., Liza Minnelli, and Eddie Murphy, to name only a few. Soups and 13 pasta dishes introduce the menu, which also features cotoletta alla milanese, osso buco, fegato alla veneziana, and pollo alla diavola. For dessert, try the luscious zabaglione or the banana *al fuoco*. Service is included, but it's customary to leave a 10% tip if you're satisfied with the food and service. It's located between Leidseplein and the Rijksmuseum.

Sama Sebo, P. C. Hoofstraat 27. ☎ **662-81-46.**

Cuisine: INDONESIAN. **Reservations:** Recommended.
Prices: Rijsttafel Dfl 45 ($23.70). AE, DC, MC, V.
Open: Lunch Mon–Sat noon–2pm; dinner Mon–Sat 6pm–midnight.

Many Amsterdammers consider Sama Sebo, located at the corner of Hobbemastraat, to be the best Indonesian restaurant in town. Here a 20-dish rijsttafel is served in a small but very Indonesian environment of rush mats and batik.

Dining in the
Museumplein Area & Amsterdam South

 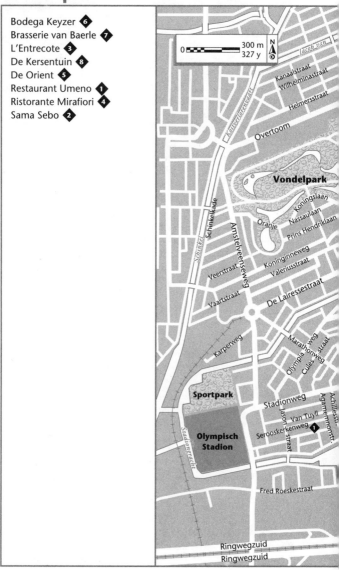

7 In Amsterdam South

Expensive

De Kersentuin, in the Garden Hotel, Dijsselhofplantsoen 7.
☎ 664-21-21.

Map labels:

Binnenkanaal

Helmersstraat
Overtoom
Vondelstraat

1e Constantijn Huygensstraat

Stad Houderskade

Singelgracht

P. C. Hooftstraat

Jan Luykenstraat

Paulus Potterstraat

Museumstraat

Horststraat

Hobbemakade

Halsstraat

Vondelpark

Museumplein

Vermeerstraat

Pieter de Hoochstraat

Quellijnstraat

Daniel Stalpertstraat

Frans

Van Eeghenstraat

Willems Parkweg

Van Breestraat

Valeriusstraat

Johannes Verhulststraat

Jacob Obrechtstraat

Van Baerlestraat

Nicolaas Maesstraat

Frans van Mierisstraat

straat

Govert Flinckstraat

1e Jan Steenstraat

Ruysdaelkade

Emmastraat

De Lairessestraat

Ruysdael straat

Ceintuurbaan

Van Ostadestraat

Rustenburgerstraat

Ferdinand Bolstr.

Reijner Vinkeleskade

Noorder Amstel Kanaal

Hobbemakade

Jan van Goyenkade

Apollolaan

Apollolaan

Jozef Israelskade

Amstel Kanaal

Amstelkade

Titiaanstraat

Jan van Eijckstraat

Gerrit v. d. Veenstraat

Michelangelostraat

Minervalaan

Ruebenstraat

Beethovenstraat

Schubert straat

Stadionweg

Richard Wagnerstraat

Diepenbrockstraat

Herman Heijermansweg

Haringvlietstraat

Churchilllaan

Deurloostraat

Scheldestraat

Olympiaplein

Sportpark
Olympiaplein

plein

Stadionweg

Parnassius

Watteaustr.

weg

Minervalaan

Stadionkade

Zuider Amstel Kanaal

Beatrixpark

Overtoom

Prinses Irenestraat

Ringwegzuid
Ringwegzuid

Railroad ┼┼┼┼

Cuisine: INTERNATIONAL. **Reservations:** Recommended.
Prices: Two-course menu Dfl 47.50 ($25); three-course menu Dfl 56 ($29.45); à la carte up to Dfl 125 ($65.80). AE, DC, EU, MC, V.
Open: Lunch Mon–Fri from noon; dinner Mon–Sat from 6pm.

All cherry red and gleaming brass, the spectacular "Cherry Orchard" has floor-to-ceiling windows looking onto the residential street outside and semiscreened interior windows looking into the glimmering kitchen inside. Attention to detail has made this restaurant a mecca for such superstars as Dionne Warwick and Grace Jones. It's consistently awarded a Michelin star. You eat with Christofle silver-plate flatware and drink wine or champagne that was personally sought out by the restaurateur and his chef. From nouvelle cuisine and a strictly French approach to cooking, they have progressed to their own unique culinary concept, based on regional recipes from around the world, using fresh ingredients from Dutch waters and farmlands. A sample is terrine of lightly smoked guinea fowl in aspic with Armagnac prunes.

Moderate

Restaurant Umeno, Agamemnonstraat 27. ☎ **676-60-89.**

> **Cuisine:** JAPANESE. **Reservations:** Recommended.
> **Prices:** Main courses Dfl 25–42.50 ($13.15–$22.35). AE, DC, MC, V.
> **Open:** Tues–Sun noon–2pm and 6–11pm.

This intimate Japanese eatery is off the beaten track, about 30 minutes from Centraal Station, near the Olympisch Stadion. The food and service are outstanding, and it's relatively easy to find a seat provided you call ahead—the restaurant can seat only 36. The sushi and sashimi are fresh. Other traditional dishes are offered, including shabu-shabu, sukiyaki, yakitori, and tonkatsu. Take tram 16 from Centraal Station to the Olympiaplein stop. The restaurant is at the corner of Tuyllweg.

8   Specialty Dining

Local Favorites

You'll have no trouble finding *broodjes* (small sandwiches) on menus all over Amsterdam, but to eat a broodje in a real *broodjeswinkel* (sandwich shop), you need to find the ever-crowded **Eetsalon Van Dobben,** at Korte Reguliersdwarsstraat 5–9, just off Rembrandtsplein, or one of two branches of **Broodje van Kootje,** conveniently located at Leidseplein and at Spui and easily identified by their bright-yellow broodje-shaped signs. A broodjeswinkel close to the Kalverstraat and Koningsplein shopping is the annex of **Tearoom Pott,** Voetboogstraat 22, near Heiligeweg.

Light, Casual & Fast Food

BAKERIES & CROISSANTERIES

Croissanteries are popping up along the shopping streets to offer the Dutch a crispy alternative to their traditional broodje. Three spots on the Damrak are **Outmeyer, Bakkerij de Waal,** and **Delifrance,** where you can have a quick breakfast of croissant, coffee or tea, and orange juice.

A lover of fresh-baked goodies will appreciate **Broodjevand Bakkar,** Wijde Heisteig 3–5, between Singel and the Herengracht, a bakery/coffee shop where your roll comes fresh from the oven; try one with a steaming cup of hot chocolate and you've got breakfast.

CAFÉS, COFFEE SHOPS & SWEET SHOPS

There are two sorts of cafés in Amsterdam: the museum or department-store lunchroom type and the Parisian people-watching type, many of which also have streetside terraces. In the first category, three of the best choices are **In de Oude Goliath,** Kalverstraat 92, at the entrance of the Amsterdam Historical Museum, a chic sort of place with high beamed ceiling and lofty painted-wood statues of *David and Goliath* salvaged from an amusement park that was a feature of Amsterdam's landscape for nearly 250 years (1625–1862); **La Ruche,** at De Bijenkorf department store, Dam Square, Rietveldkoepel, atop Metz & Co.; and the eating corners of **Maison de Bonneterie en Pander,** Kalverstraat 183, with windows on the Rokin.

Heading east from the Center, you'll also find half a dozen or so bright and trendy cafés in the streets and squares near Amsterdam's new Town Hall–Muziektheater complex. They have appropriate names like Mozart and Puccini, and there's also a café within the town hall theater building with the less appealing moniker of Waterloo, after the square the building now replaces.

Nearer the main canal areas, two trendy cafés that face each other across the square called Spui are **Café Luxembourg** and **Café Esprit** (located in the store of the same name); and at Rembrandtsplein, take your pick of several cafés, including **L'Opera** and **Café Schiller** (at the hotel of the same name).

For the Parisian sort of café in the same area, at the Leidseplein is an Amsterdam landmark, the **Café Americain** of the American Hotel (see earlier in this chapter), an art nouveau/art deco eyeful on the inside and a sun-worshiper's paradise when the outdoor terrace is set up in the summer months.

Other good stopping places in the Center, near the sights, are **Duke's,** Damrak 1–5, across from the canal-boat piers; **Berkhoff Coffee Shop,** Keizersgracht 504, off Leidsestraat; and **t'Singeltje,** Singel 494, at the Flower Market.

Perhaps Amsterdam's most crowded spot on Saturday morning is **Kweekboom,** on Damstraat or on Reguliersbreestraat between Muntplein and Rembrandtsplein. It's a coffee shop/candy store/pastry shop/ice-cream stand, where everything is freshly made and the management proudly displays awards won for everything from tarts, bonbons, and butter cookies to fantasy cakes (whatever they may be)! You may have to push your way to the back and wait for a table, but don't miss the spicy *croquetten* or the chocolate bonbons. Among the other cafés and tearooms that are conveniently located for shoppers are, near the Kalverstraat, the **Tearoom Pott,** Voetboogstraat 24, near Heiligeweg; and along the Leidsestraat, the **Berkhoff Tearoom** at no. 46 (sister of the coffeehouse mentioned above). Opposite Centraal Station and overlooking the inner harbor is **Noord-Zuid Holland Coffee House,** Stationsplein 10, which was built to duplicate a turn-of-the-century Amsterdam landmark. It's a restaurant and tearoom, and there's a waterside terrace in summer, a good place to watch the canal boats float by.

SMOKING COFFEE SHOPS

Tourists often get confused about "smoking" coffee shops and how they differ from "no-smoking" ones. Well, to begin with, "smoking" and "no-smoking" don't refer to cigarettes—they refer to hashish.

Not too long ago, before there was a crackdown on soft drugs in Amsterdam, these "smoking" coffee shops advertised that not only could patrons buy hashish within, but also they could sit and smoke it all day long if they so chose—their advertisement usually consisted of the shop sign with a marijuana leaf on it. Now, however, the marijuana leaves have been made illegal, although the same practice of smoking hashish often continues within. You won't be able to get any food here (except maybe a "space cake" or two), so don't expect to grab a quick breakfast, lunch, or dessert. Often, even the coffee in these places is horrible. Generally, these are the only places in Amsterdam called "coffee shops"—regular cafés are called *cafes* or *eet cafes,* so chances are, whether or not you want to smoke, you'll be able to find what you're looking for without too much difficulty.

FAST FOOD

I think you'll find that no matter how determined you may be to "eat well" or "eat native" whenever and wherever you travel, a glimpse of the Golden Arches is, occasionally, a welcome sight. For fast food in Amsterdam, you'll find **McDonald's** at the Muntplein, on Kalverstraat, on Leidsestraat, and at the Albert Cuypstraat market; and **Burger King** at Leidseplein.

Also on Damrak and Reguliersbreestraat is **Pizzaland.** Bright, clean, and decorated in the true splendor of Italy's colors (red, white, and bright green), this is Amsterdam's answer to Pizza Hut. Three kinds of pizza are served—traditional, deep pan, or "whole meal."

Another quick-bite alternative, especially for budget travelers, is **Febo Automatik** (there's one on Kalverstraat). Reminiscent of a bygone era for those who recall the old Horn & Hardart restaurants of New York, they open directly on the sidewalk and look like giant streetside vending machines. Drop your guilder coins in the appropriate slots and, as quickly and easily as you retrieve luggage in an airline terminal, you'll have a lunch of hamburger, fries, and a milk shake.

Breakfast

If you really can't start the day without your eggs and bacon, try the coffee shop called **De Roef** at the Stroomarkt, near the Sonesta Hotel. American breakfasts are served, just like at home.

And if you sleep late, keep in mind that the **Café Barbizon,** in the Golden Tulip Barbizon Palace Hotel, Prins Hendrikkade 59–72, serves late breakfast from 10:30am to noon at Dfl 28 ($14.75) for juice, two eggs, a broodje, and coffee or tea.

Two pancake houses you may want to visit are **Pancake Bakery,** Prinsengracht 191, near the Anne Frankhuis, which offers more than 30 kinds of pancakes; and **Bredero,** Oude Zijds Voorburgwal 244 (☎ **622-94-61**), in the canals east of Dam Square. Recommended by a reader is **De Leidse Inn,** Liedsestraat 23 (☎ **622-86-89**), which serves 28 kinds of pancakes, plus soups, salads, hamburgers, fish, and steak; this restaurant also has a marvelous Tourist Menu.

Late-Night Eateries

When hunger strikes late at night, head for the Leidseplein area for Indonesian snacks and minimeals at prices anyone can afford. **Bojo,** Lange Leidsedwarsstraat 51, is open Sunday through Thursday from 5pm to 2am and Friday and Saturday to 5am.

For French specialties in the same neighborhood, **Bistro La Forge,** Korte Leidsedwarsstraat 26, takes orders until midnight.

An Amsterdam Dinner Cruise

A delightful way to combine sightseeing and leisurely dining is the **Amsterdam Dinner Cruise** offered by Holland International (☎ **622-77-88**). It's a three-hour cruise on the canals (with a multilingual guide) while you enjoy a four-course dinner that includes a cocktail as well as wine with dinner, both pâté and consommé as starters, veal in mushroom-cream sauce served with four vegetables and a mixed salad; fruit salad with whipped cream, coffee with bonbons, and a glass of cognac or liqueur to finish. The cost is Dfl 145 ($76.30) per person and includes transportation from all major hotel areas. The cruise operates April to November, nightly at 8pm; November to April, on Tuesday and Friday at 7pm. Reservations are required.

6

What to See & Do in Amsterdam

Amsterdam is itself a museum. Nearly 7,000 of its historic 17th-century buildings and hundreds of its graceful bridges are listed with the Dutch government and permanently protected from alteration, destruction, and the ugliness of most modern urban development. Holland is proud of its history and wants the world to see and sense its greatest era, the 17th century. Amsterdam is also brimming with actual museums, with more than 40 collections of art and history, rarities and oddities: some as universally appreciated as the Rijksmuseum; others, such as a museum of the baking industry and a display of typewriters, possessed of a limited but nonetheless interesting appeal.

Suggested Itineraries

If You Have One Day

If you've got only one day in Amsterdam, the very first thing you should do is take a canal-boat tour. First of all, it will give you a better view of the architecture of the city than if you run around craning your neck to see straight up the canal-side facades. Second, it's faster and a lot easier on your feet than walking.

After the boat tour, you should grab a quick lunch since you don't have much time—maybe a broodje at a broodjeswinkel. Next, you might want to take the walking tour around the Old Jewish Quarter listed in Chapter 7. On that particular tour you'll walk right past the Jewish Historical Museum and also get to see the Waterlooplein Market. When you're finished with that, walk back across the Amstel River and head for the museum of your choice—probably one of the "big three": the Rijksmuseum, the Stedelijk Museum of Modern Art, or the Vincent van Gogh Museum (you should probably take a tram if you're running a little short on time).

After the museum(s), it will probably be late afternoon and you'll be pretty exhausted, so I'd suggest returning to the hotel for a drink at the bar before dinner (if your hotel has a bar) or a nap. Since you probably had a Dutch breakfast and a Dutch lunch, you might consider going for an Indonesian rijsttafel at dinner.

If you're still up for it, you really shouldn't miss having a drink in a brown café—your Amsterdam experience won't be complete without it.

If You Have Two Days

If you have two days, you should follow the first part of the itinerary above at a more relaxed pace. Take some notes while you're on the canal-boat tour about the things you'd like to see up close. Go for a short stroll along your favorite canal before lunch or between lunch and the walking tour of the Old Jewish Quarter. Spend more time in the Waterlooplein Market. Explore some of the shops and bookstores that you see along the way. Save the big museums for your second day. Spend the rest of the night as outlined above.

On the second day, sleep in a little (you'll probably need it) because the museums don't open until later in the morning, then plan to spend the day museum hopping. Before you leave the hotel you might want to try getting tickets to a concert, the ballet, or the opera, depending on your taste, so you can attend a show in the evening. If you have time, you might want to make a trip to the Anne Frankhuis—it's almost a requirement on a visit to Amsterdam—or the Amsterdam Historical Museum. Pick a place for dinner, maybe this time a Dutch meal. Finally, go see that show!

If You Have Three Days

Follow the itinerary above for the first two days of your stay in Amsterdam, excepting the visit to the Anne Frankhuis—save that for the third day since it's not in the same area as the other museums.

On the third day, I'd suggest spending the day shopping, sightseeing, and gallery hopping along the way. Walk along Kalverstraat (the more modern shopping street), then perhaps stroll along Nieuwe Spiegelstraat (antiques). After a leisurely lunch, the Anne Frankhuis is a good bet. While you're on that side of town, take a walk over to the Jordaan and explore some of the interesting little boutiques. It would also be a good time to go to the Looiersgracht Market on another antiques hunt.

Later, after you've had dinner, take a leisurely stroll along the canals—they're particularly beautiful at night when they're lit up.

Did You Know . . . ?

- More than 550,000 bicycles are in use in Amsterdam.
- There are close to 200 canals and more than 1,200 bridges in Amsterdam.
- In 1609 Henry Hudson set sail, like many navigators before and after, from the Schreierstoren (Tower of Tears) in Amsterdam aboard the *Halve Maen* (Half Moon). He discovered the Hudson River and established Nieuw Amsterdam.
- Rope and pulleys are still used to get furniture into homes where the staircases are too narrow and steep.
- There are about 2,400 legally occupied houseboats floating on Amsterdam's canals.
- Originally the Concertgebouw was built on 2,186 wooden piles; they were replaced by 400 metal tubes in 1983.
- Before Napoléon's occupation, engraved cartouches served as numbers for address identification purposes. Many of them can still be seen today.
- Rembrandt painted about 100 self-portraits—more than any other painter.

If You Have Five Days or More

Spend the first three days as outlined above, and the fourth day doing the rest of the things you've been meaning to get back to. On the fifth day, take a day trip to one or more of the places listed in Chapter 10.

1 The Top Attractions

⭐ **Rijksmuseum**, Stadhouderskade 42, at the Museumplein. ☎ **673-21-21.**

The most significant and permanent outgrowth of Holland's 17th-century golden age was the magnificent body of art it produced. These works are now housed in the Rijksmuseum, which ranks with the Louvre, the Uffizzi, and the Hermitage as a major museum of Western European painting and decorative arts.

The museum was founded in 1798 as the National Art Gallery located in The Hague. The steady growth of the collection of paintings and prints necessitated several moves: In 1808 King Louis Napoléon had it moved to his Royal Palace in Amsterdam and renamed the Royal Museum (the name Rijksmuseum—State Museum—dates from 1815). Then in 1816 it was moved to a large patrician residence called the Trippenhuis. However, this building soon proved too small and another was sought.

After years of negotiations, architect P. J. H. Cuypers designed the core of the present museum—located halfway between the Leidseplein and Weteringplantsoen—and this monumental Neo-Gothic building opened in 1885. Since then, many additions have been made to the collections and the building so that the museum now encompasses five collecting departments: Painting, Print Room, Sculpture and Decorative Arts, Dutch History, and Asiatic Art.

The Rijksmuseum contains the world's largest collection of paintings by the Dutch masters, including the most famous: Rembrandt's 1642 group portrait officially named *The Shooting Company of Captain Frans Banning Cocq and Lieutenant Willem van Ruytenbuch* yet better known as *The Night Watch*. Thankfully, this masterpiece was restored after being slashed in 1975.

Rembrandt, van Ruysdael, van Heemskerck, Frans Hals, Paulus Potter, Jan Steen, Vermeer, de Hooch, Terborch, and Gerard Dou are all represented, as are Fra Angelico, Tiepolo, Goya, Rubens, van Dyck, and later Dutch artists of the Hague school and the Amsterdam impressionist movement. There are individual portraits and guild paintings, landscapes and seascapes, domestic scenes and medieval religious subjects, allegories, and the incredible (and nearly photographic) Dutch still lifes; plus prints and sculptures, furniture, a collection of 17th-century dollhouses, Asian and Islamic art, china and porcelain, trinkets and glassware, armaments and ship models, costumes, screens, badges, and laces.

The Rijksmuseum

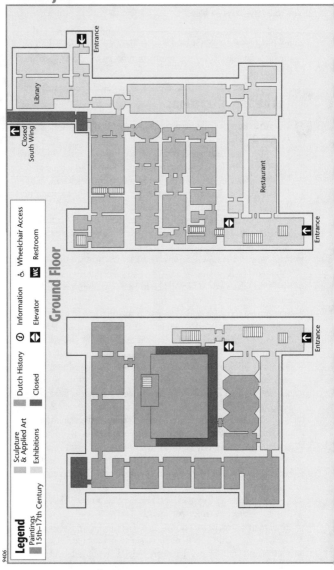

It will take you at least a day to do justice to this 200-plus-room museum, longer if you become fascinated by any one exhibit. Projected special exhibitions for 1995 include "The Art of Devotion, 1300–1500," the best examples of medieval objects of private devotion; "UKIYO-E," the finest Japanese prints; "Views of Windsor," watercolors from the collection of Britian's Elizabeth II; and "Saved for the Nation," the collection of the Royal Antiquarian Society.

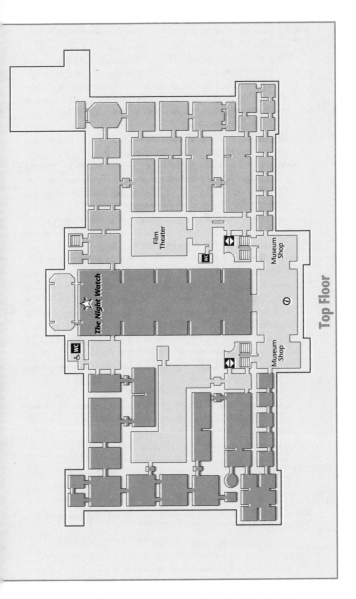

Top Floor

The Night Watch

Film Theater

Museum Shop

Museum Shop

Admission: Dfl 10 ($5.25) adults, Dfl 5 ($2.65) children 6–18, free for children under 6.

Open: Daily 10am–5pm. **Closed:** New Year's Day. **Tram:** 2 or 5 to Hobbemastraat or 6, 7, or 10 to Spiegelgracht. **Bus:** 26, 65, or 66 to Museumplein.

⭐ **Vincent van Gogh Museum**, Paulus Potterstraat 7–11, at the Museumplein. ☎ **570-52-00.**

Thanks to the chauvinism of his devoted family—in particular his brother's wife and a namesake nephew—nearly every painting, sketch, print, etching, and illustrated piece of correspondence that Vincent van Gogh ever produced has remained in his native country and since 1973 has been housed in its own three-story museum in Amsterdam. To the further consternation of van Gogh admirers and scholars elsewhere in the world, all but a few of the drawings and paintings that are not in the keeping of this museum are hanging in another of Holland's exceptional museums of art, the Kröller-Müller Museum in the Hoge Veluwe National Forest east of Amsterdam. In Amsterdam you can see more than 200 paintings displayed simply and in a straightforward chronological order according to the seven distinct periods and places of residence that defined van Gogh's short career (he painted for only 10 years and was on the threshold of success when he committed suicide in 1890 at the age of 37). One particularly splendid wall of art, on the second floor of the museum, is a progression of 18 paintings produced during the two-year period when Vincent lived in the south of France, generally considered to be the high point of his career (he, like Rembrandt, is referred to by his first name). It is a symphony of colors and color contrasts that includes *Gauguin's Chair; The Yellow House; Self-portrait with Pipe and Straw Hat; Vincent's Bedroom at Arles; Wheatfield with Reaper; Bugler of the Zouave Regiment;* and one of the most famous paintings of modern times, *Still Life Vase with Fourteen Sunflowers,* best known simply as *Sunflowers.*

A new wing that houses temporary exhibitions of van Gogh's work has recently been added to the museum. Surrounded by water gardens, it's a wonderful place to relax and enjoy the genius of the artist.

Admission: Dfl 10 ($5.25) adults, Dfl 5 ($2.65) children 18 and under.

Open: Tues–Sat 10am–5pm, Sun and holidays 1–5pm. **Tram:** 2 or 5 to Paulus Potterstraat or no. 16 to Museumplein-Concertgebouw. **Bus:** 26, 65, or 66 to Museumplein.

⭐ **Anne Frankhuis,** Prinsengracht 263, just below Westermarkt. ☎ **556-71-00.**

No one should miss seeing and experiencing this house, where eight people from three separate families lived together in nearly total silence for more than two years during World War II. The hiding place Otto Frank found for his family and some friends kept them all safe until, tragically close to the end of the war, it was discovered and raided by Nazi occupation forces. It was here that the famous diary was written, day by day, as a way to deal with the boredom and the jumble of thoughts its young author was sorting out at the time, which had as much to do with male-female relationships as with the war and the horrifying things happening beyond her attic hiding place.

The rooms of this building, which was an office and warehouse at that time, are still as bare as they were when Anne's father returned, the only survivor of the eight *onderduikers* (divers or hiders); and nothing has been changed, except that protective Plexiglas panels have been placed over the wall where Anne pinned up photos of her favorite actress, Deanna Durbin, and of the little English princesses Elizabeth and Margaret.

Admission: Dfl 6 ($3.35) adults, Dfl 3 ($1.70) children 10–17.

Open: Mon–Sat 9am–5pm, Sun and holidays 10am–5pm (June–Sept 1, open till 7pm). **Tram:** 13, 14, or 17 to Westermarkt, then walk past the Westerkerk along the canal.

The Canals & Canal Houses

A boat ride around the canals is the first thing you should do in Amsterdam. Why? Because no matter how many times you walk past the gabled houses or sight your camera's viewfinder along the length of a canal, you'll never see or appreciate the gables and the waterways the way they were built to be seen unless you see them from canal level aboard a glass-roofed motor launch. Besides, this is the best and only way to see Amsterdam's surprisingly large and busy harbor, one of the biggest in Europe.

A typical canal-boat itinerary (and they are all essentially the same) will include Centraal Station, the Harlemmersluis floodgates (used in the nightly flushing of the canals), the Cat Boat (a houseboat with a permanent population of as many as 150 wayward felines), and both the narrowest building in the city and one of the largest houses still in private hands and in use as a single-family residence. Plus, you will see the official residence of the burgomaster (mayor) of Amsterdam, the "Golden Bend" of the Herengracht (traditionally the best address in the city), many picturesque bridges (including the famous Skinny Bridge over the Amstel), and the Amsterdam Drydocks (capable of lifting ships of up to 40,000 tons). To explain what you're seeing as you cruise along there will be either a guide fluent in several languages or a prerecorded commentary that repeats each description in four languages (Dutch, German, French, and English).

Trips last approximately one hour and leave at regular intervals from *rondvaart* (canal circuit) piers in key locations around town. The majority of launches, however, are docked along Damrak or Prins Hendrikkade near Centraal Station and on the Rokin near the Muntplein and near the Leidseplein; they leave every 45 minutes in winter (10am to 4pm), every 15 to 30 minutes during the summer season (9am to 9:30pm).

Major operators of canal-boat cruises are **Rederij Amstel** (☎ **626-56-36**); **Holland International** (☎ **622-77-88**), **Lovers** (☎ **622-21-81**), **Rederij Plas** (☎ **624-54-06**), **Meyers** (☎ **623-42-08**), **Rederij P. Kooy** (☎ **623-38-10**), **Rederij Noord-Zuid** (☎ **679-13-70**), and **Rederij Wisman** (☎ **638-03-38**). The average fare is Dfl 10 to 15 ($5.25 to $7.90) for adults, Dfl 8 to 10 ($4.20 to $5.25) for children 4 to 13.

The Red Light District (Walletjes)

This warren of streets around Oudezijds Achterburgwal and Oudezijds Voorburgwal by the Oude Kerk is on most people's sightseeing agenda—however, a visit to this area is not for everyone, and if you do choose to go you need to exercise some caution because the area is a center of crime, vice, and drugs. Stick to the crowded streets, and be wary of pickpockets. Do not take photographs unless you want to lose your camera or have it broken.

Still, it's extraordinary to view the prostitutes in leather and lace sitting in their storefronts with their radios and TVs blaring as they do their knitting or adjust their makeup, waiting patiently for customers. It seems to reflect the Dutch pragmatism: If you can't stop the oldest trade in the world, you can at least confine it to a particular area and impose health and other regulations on it.

Open: Mon–Sun 10am–12:30pm and 1–4pm. **Tram:** 9 or 14 to Mr. Visserplein. **Metro:** Waterlooplein.

2 More Attractions

Churches & Synagogues

The history of the city can be traced through its many churches and synagogues. The most important are the **Nieuwe Kerk,** at Dam Square, where Queen Beatrix was crowned on April 30, 1980; the 17th-century **Westerkerk,** on the Prinsengracht at Westermarkt, which has the tallest and most beautiful tower in Amsterdam (topped by the crown of the Holy Roman Empire) and is the burial place of Rembrandt; the **Oude Kerk,** at Oudekerksplein on Oude Zijds Voorburgwal, which dates from the 14th century and is surrounded by small almshouses; and the 17th-century **Portuguese Synagogue** (see below).

The churches of Amsterdam can be seen by attending services or, in some cases, during limited visiting hours that can be supplied by the VVV Tourist Office.

The Portuguese Synagogue, Mr. Visserplein 3. ☎ **624-53-51.**

One of the startling facts of the history of Amsterdam is the tremendous growth the city experienced during the 16th and early 17th

---

Frommer's Favorite Amsterdam Experiences

A Canal-Boat Ride   At any time of the day, it's the best way to see the city.

A Trip to the Waterlooplein Market   Visit on a warm weekend afternoon, in hopes of finding a real Amsterdam bargain.

A Leisurely Evening in a Brown Café   Here you can spend an evening drinking jenever or tasting different types of beer with the locals.

centuries—from a population of 10,000 in the year 1500 to approximately 200,000 by 1650. A factor in that expansion was an influx of Sephardic Jews fleeing Spain and Portugal, and it was they who established the neighborhood east of the Center known as the Jewish Quarter. In 1665 they built an elegant Ionic-style synagogue within an existing courtyard facing what is now a busy traffic circle called Mr. Visserplein. They spent 186,000 guilders—a tremendous sum even now, but a veritable king's ransom in those days—because for the first time in 200 years they could at last build a place to worship together openly. The building was restored in the 1950s, but essentially it is unchanged from what it was 320 years ago, with its women's gallery supported by 12 stone columns to represent the Twelve Tribes of Israel and the large, low-hanging brass chandeliers that together hold 1,000 candles, all of which are lighted for the private weekly services. Attendance at the services is by advance appointment, so call ahead.

Admission: Dfl 5 ($2.65) adults, Dfl 2.50 ($1.30) children.

Open: Mon–Sun 10am–12:30pm and 1–4pm. **Tram:** 9 or 14 to Mr. Visserplein. **Metro:** Waterlooplein.

Diamond-Cutting Demonstrations

Visitors to Amsterdam during the 1950s and 1960s—when the diamond business was booming—were able to go to the diamond-cutting factories of Amsterdam and take tours through their workrooms. Now you'll be lucky to see one lone polisher working at a small wheel set up in the back of a jewelry store or in the lobby of a factory building. But never mind, you still can get an idea of how a diamond is cut and polished. You need no special directions or instructions to find this sightseeing activity; you'll see signs all over town for diamond-cutting demonstrations. You're also on your own if you decide to buy.

The major diamond factories and showrooms in Amsterdam are the **Amsterdam Diamond Center,** Rokin 1, just off Dam Square (☎ **624-57-87**); **Coster Diamonds,** Paulus Potterstraat 2–4, near the Rijksmuseum (☎ **676-22-22**); **Gassan Diamonds,** Nieuwe Uilenbuergerstraat 173–175 (☎ **622-53-33**); **Holshuijsen Stoeltie,** Wagenstraat 13–17 (☎ **623-76-01**); **Van Moppes Diamonds,** Albert Cuypstraat 2–6, at the daily street market (☎ **676-12-42**); and **Reuter Diamonds,** Kalverstraat 165 or Singel 526 (☎ **623-35-00**).

A Brewery Tour

The **Heineken Brewery Museum,** Stadhouderskade 78 (☎ **523-92-39**), located a short walk along the Singelgracht from the Rijksmuseum, operates tours of the brewing facilities Monday through Friday at 9:30 and 11am and 1 and 2:30pm in summer. Heineken opened its first Amsterdam brewery in 1864 and is now one of the world's best-known beers. The guides explain the brewing process and show a film about the company's history. Then you can enjoy a beer in the large drinking hall overlooking the city. The

Attractions in Central Amsterdam

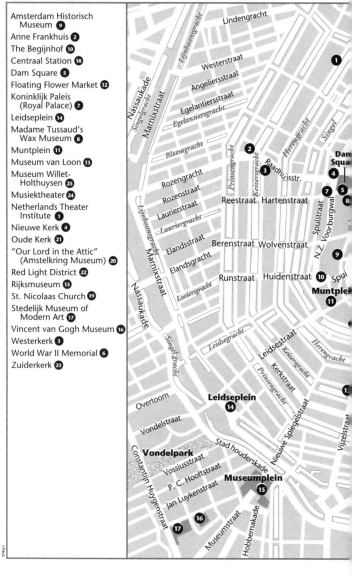

tours are free, but you are expected to donate Dfl 2 ($1.05) to a charity like UNICEF.

Historic Buildings & Monuments

Koninklijk Paleis (Royal Palace), Nieuwe Zijds Voorburgwal 147, at Dam Square. ☎ **624-86-98.**

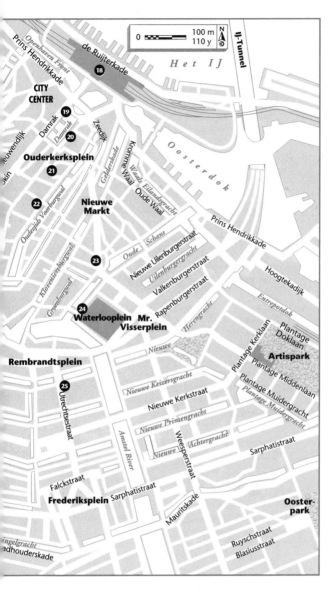

One of the year-round pleasures of strolling on Dam Square is looking at the 17th-century facade of the Royal Palace, which was designed by Jacob van Campen, the Thomas Jefferson of the Dutch
Republic. If your visit to Amsterdam is in summer, you can have the
added pleasure of seeing the inside of this impressive building. If it
seems unpalatial—perhaps more like an office building than a royal

residence—the reason is that for the first 153 years of its existence this was the town hall of Amsterdam, where the city council met and the town clerk signed and sealed everything from orders of execution to marriage licenses. Its first use as a palace was during the five-year French rule of the city by Napoléon in the early 19th century, when the French emperor's brother, Louis Bonaparte, was king of Holland. Since the return to the throne of the Dutch House of Orange, this has been the official palace of the reigning king or queen of the Netherlands; few, however, have used it for more than an occasional reception or official ceremony (such as the inauguration of Queen Beatrix) or as their pied-à-terre in the capital.

Admission: Dfl 5 ($2.65) adults, Dfl 1.50 (80¢) children 12 and under.

Open: Two weeks at Easter, mid-June to first week in Sept, and second week in Oct, daily 12:30–5pm. **Tram:** 1, 2, 4, 5, 9, 13, 14, 16, 17, 24, 25 to Dam Square or the Dam Square stop on the Nieuwe Zijds Voorburgwal.

The Begijnhof, Spui. No phone.

When you leave the Amsterdam Historisch Museum (see "Museums and Galleries," below), cut through the Civic Guard Gallery, a narrow, skylighted chamber that rises to a full height of two stories and on the walls of which hang perhaps a dozen large and impressive 17th-century group portraits. This gallery is the back entrance to the Begijnhof, a 14th-century cloister of small homes around a garden courtyard that too few tourists take the time to see.

There's nothing in particular to do here, unless you attend one of the two churches on Sunday, and there are no placards to read. But it's here that you can best appreciate the earliest history of the city, when Amsterdam was a mecca for religious pilgrims and an important location on the European map of Roman Catholic nunneries. The Begijnhof was not a convent (that was located next door, where the Historisch Museum now stands); it was an almshouse for pious lay women—the *begijnes*—who were involved in religious and charitable work for the nunnery. All but one of the old wooden houses from the early period are gone now, but even the drastic, about-face changeover of the city from Catholicism to Protestantism in the late 16th century had little effect on the Begijnhof—its tiny 17th- and 18th-century houses surrounding the small medieval courtyard still house the city's elderly poor.

Admission: Free.

Open: Daily until sunset. **Tram:** 1, 2, or 5 to Spui, walk east one block, and turn left on the Gedempte Begijnensloot; the main gate of the Begijnhof is on the left, halfway along the block.

Museums & Galleries

 Amsterdam Historisch Museum, Kalverstraat 359. ☎ 523-18-22.

The Amsterdam Historisch (Historical) Museum is housed in the huge, beautifully restored 17th-century buildings of the former city orphanage. It has three courtyards and a civic-guard gallery and is located next to the Begijnhof.

Few cities in the world have gone to as much trouble and expense as Amsterdam to display and explain the history of the city, and few museums in the world have found as many ways to make such dry material as population growth and urban development as interesting as the latest electronic board game. And don't say you have little interest in the history of Amsterdam—just come to this museum. It's a beautiful and fascinating place to visit that will give you a better understanding of everything you see when you go out to explore the city on your own. Gallery by gallery, century by century, you see how a small fishing village became a major world power; you also see many of the famous paintings by the "Dutch masters" in the context of their time and place in history.

Display descriptions are in Dutch, but there are English-language introductions posted in every gallery (look for the symbol of a small British flag); plus, the museum provides free loose-leaf notebooks in English, German, or French to carry with you, which explain in detail the history that relates to the various display areas.

Admission: Dfl 7.50 ($3.95) adults, Dfl 3.75 ($1.95) children 6–16.

Open: Mon–Fri 10am–5pm, Sat–Sun 11am–5pm. **Tram:** 1, 2, 4, 5, 9, 14, 16, 24, or 25 to Spui. At Dam Square, walk along Kalverstraat; the museum is on the right, just past St. Luciensteeg.

Madame Tussaud's Wax Museum, Dam 20. ☎ **622-99-49.**

If you like your celebrities with a waxen stare, don't miss Madame Tussaud's. Located in the midst of the Kalverstraat shopping mall, this is a uniquely Amsterdam version of the London attraction, with its own cast of Dutch characters (Rembrandt, Wilhelmina, Erasmus, and Mata Hari) among the international favorites (Churchill, Kennedy, Gandhi, and Pope John XXIII).

Admission: Dfl 18 ($9.45) adults, Dfl 13 ($6.85) seniors and children 14 and under.

Open: Daily 10am–5:30pm. **Tram:** 1, 2, 4, 5, 9, 14, 16, 24, or 25 to Dam Square.

⭐ **Scheepvaartmuseum (Netherlands Maritime Museum),** Kattenburgerplein 1. ☎ **523-22-22.**

The newest museum in Amsterdam is the Netherlands Maritime Museum, now appropriately housed in a former rigging house of the Amsterdam Admiralty, overlooking the busy Amsterdam harbor. Here you'll see room after room of ships and ship models, seascapes, and old maps, including a 15th-century Ptolemaic atlas and a sumptuously bound edition of the *Great Atlas, or Description of the World,* produced over a lifetime by Jan Blaeu, who was the stay-at-home master cartographer of Holland's golden age. Among the important papers on display are several pertaining to the Dutch colonies of Nieuwe Amsterdam (New York City) and Nieuwe Nederland (New York State), including a receipt for the land that now surrounds the New York State capital at Albany.

Attractions in the
Museumplein Area & Amsterdam South

 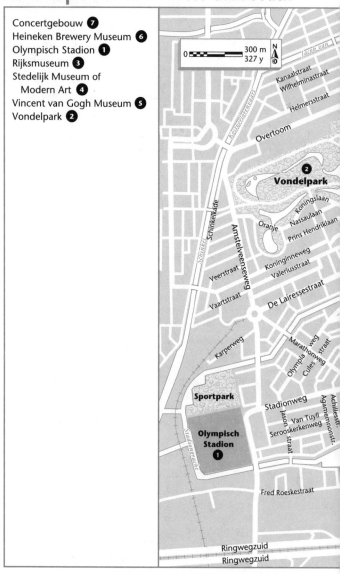

Admission: Dfl 12.50 ($6.55) adults, Dfl 8 ($4.20) children 16 and under.

Open: Tues–Sat 10am–5pm, Sun and holidays noon–5pm. **Bus:** 22 or 28 from Centraal Station to Kattenburgerplein; the museum is on the left.

Museum van Loon, Keizersgracht 672, above Vijzelstraat.
☎ **624-52-55.**

The history of this magnificent house—one of a matched pair built in 1671—is a long saga of ne'er-do-well spouses and ailing orphans, of misguided inheritances and successive bankruptcies; yet the achievements of the people whose portraits now hang in the house are as illustrious as any you can imagine. On the walls of this elegant patrician home hang more than 80 van Loon family portraits, including those of Willem van Loon, one of the founding fathers of the Dutch East India Company; Nicolaes Ruychaver, who liberated Amsterdam from the Spanish in 1578; and another, later, Willem van Loon, who became mayor of Amsterdam in 1686. Also unique among the treasures this house contains are a family album in which you can see tempera portraits of all living van Loons painted at two successive dates (1650 and 1675), and a series of commemorative coins struck to honor seven different golden wedding anniversaries celebrated between the years 1621 and 1722.

Admission: Dfl 5 ($2.65) adults, Dfl 4 ($2.10) children 16 and under.

Open: Sun 1–5pm, Mon 10am–5pm. **Tram:** 16, 24, or 25 to the Keizersgracht stop on Vijzelstraat, then walk toward the river; the museum is on the right-hand side of the canal.

Museum Willet-Holthuysen, Herengracht 605, near Amstel. ☎ **523-18-70.**

This museum is housed in an elegant 17th-century canal house built in 1687 and renovated several times before its last inhabitant gave both the house and its contents to the city of Amsterdam in 1889. Among the rooms that are particularly interesting to see are the Victorian-era bedroom on the second floor, a large reception room with tapestry wall panels, and the 18th-century basement kitchen that's still so completely furnished and functional you could swear the cook had merely stepped out to buy provisions.

Admission: Dfl 5 ($2.65) adults, Dfl 2.50 ($1.30) children 16 and under.

Open: Mon–Fri 10am–5pm, Sat–Sun 11am–5pm. **Tram:** 4 to the Herengracht stop on Utrechtsestraat and walk toward the river; the museum is on the left-hand side of the canal.

Museum Het Rembrandthuis, Jodenbreestraat 4–6, near Waterlooplein. ☎ **624-94-86.**

This is not much of an art museum compared to Amsterdam's big three, but it's a museum of art and a shrine to one of the greatest painters the world has ever known. The house now tilts sadly, just as Rembrandt must have "tilted" sadly from the shame of bankruptcy when he left the house in 1658 (the company of Capt. Banning Cocq *hated* the artistic freedom Rembrandt had exercised on their group portrait and this ruined his previously brilliant career). Now, thanks to an inventory made for the sake of his creditors, his house has been faithfully restored to the way it looked when he lived and worked here. His printing press is back in place, and more than 260 of his etchings now hang on the walls, including self-portraits, landscapes, and several that relate to the traditionally Jewish character of the neighborhood, such as the portrait of Rabbi Menassah ben Israel, who lived across the street and was an early teacher of another illustrious Amsterdammer, Baruch Spinoza.

Admission: Dfl 5 ($2.65) adults, Dfl 3.50 ($1.85) children.

Open: Mon–Sat 10am–5pm, Sun and holidays 1–5pm. **Tram:** 9 or 14 to Mr. Visserplein. **Metro:** Waterlooplein; walk west one block and the museum is on the left just before the canal.

★ **Stedelijk Museum of Modern Art**, Paulus Potterstraat 13, at Museumplein. ☎ **573-29-11.**

This is the contemporary art museum of Amsterdam and the place to see the works of such modern Dutch painters as Karel Appel, Willem de Kooning, and Piet Mondrian; there are also works by French artists Chagall, Cézanne, Picasso, Renoir, Monet, and Manet as well as those by Americans Calder, Oldenburg, Rosenquist, and Warhol. Recently restored as closely as possible to its original 1895 Neo-Renaissance facade, the Stedelijk centers its collection around the following schools of modern art: De Stijl Cobra, and post-Cobra painting, nouveau réalisme, pop art, color-field painting, zero and minimal art, and conceptual art. The Stedelijk Museum also houses the largest collection outside Russia of the abstract paintings of Kasimir Malevich.

Admission: Dfl 7.50 ($3.95) adults, Dfl 3.75 ($1.95) children 7–16, free for children under 7.

Open: Daily 11am–5pm. **Tram:** 2 or 5 to Paulus Potterstraat or 16 to Museumplein-Concertgebouw. **Bus:** 26, 65, or 66 to Museumplein.

★ **Tropenmuseum**, Linnaeusstraat 2, at Mauritskade. ☎ **568-84-22.**

One of the more intriguing museums of Amsterdam is the curious (and curiously named) Tropenmuseum, or "Tropical Museum," of the Royal Tropical Institute, a foundation devoted to the study of the cultures and cultural problems of tropical areas around the world (the interest reflects Holland's centuries as a landlord in such areas of the globe as Indonesia; Surinam on the northern coast of South America; and the islands of St. Maarten, Saba, St. Eustatius, Aruba, Bonaire, and Curaçao in the West Indies). The Tropical Institute building complex alone is worth the trip to Amsterdam East and the Oosterpark, or East Park; its heavily ornamented facade is an amalgam of Dutch architectural styles—turrets, stepped gables, arched windows, delicate spires—and the monumental galleried interior court (a popular spot for concerts) is one of the most impressive spots in town.

Of the exhibits, the most interesting are the walk-through model villages that seem to capture a moment in the daily life of such places as India and Indonesia (except for the lack of inhabitants); the displays of tools and techniques used to produce batik, the distinctively dyed Indonesian fabrics; and also displays of the tools, instruments, and ornaments that clutter a tropical residence.

Admission: Dfl 10 ($5.25) adults, Dfl 4 ($2.65) children 18 and under.

Open: Mon–Fri 10am–5pm, Sat–Sun and holidays noon–5pm. **Tram:** 9 to Mauritskade.

Religious Heritage Sights

 Joods Historisch Museum (Jewish Historical Museum), Jonas Daniel Meijerplein 2–4, near Waterlooplein. ☎ **626-99-45.**

For more than 350 years Amsterdam has been a center of Jewish life, and its Jewish population has been a major contributor to the vitality and prosperity of the city. The area around the Waterlooplein (site of the new Town Hall–Muziektheater complex) was their neighborhood, where they held their market and built their synagogues. Of the five synagogues that were built in the 17th and 18th centuries, however, only the Portuguese Synagogue continued to serve as a house of worship after the devastating depletion of Amsterdam's Jewish population in World War II. The other buildings, sold to the city in 1955, stood unused and in great need of repairs for many years. During those same years, the city authorities and the curators of the Jewish Historical Collection of the Amsterdam Historisch Museum were patiently reestablishing the collection of paintings, decorations, and ceremonial objects that had been confiscated during World War II.

Finally, in 1987, the new Jewish Historical Museum opened in the restored Ashkenazi Synagogue Complex. Allow plenty of time for your visit here; the collection is large. The museum was designed to tell three complex, intertwining stories through its objects, photographs, artworks, and interactive displays; these are the stories of Jewish identity, Jewish religion and culture, and Jewish history in the Netherlands. Leave time, too, to appreciate the beauty and size of the buildings themselves, which include the oldest public synagogue in Europe. It's important to note that this is a museum for everyone—Jewish or otherwise—that presents the community through both good times and bad times and provides insights into the Jewish way of life over the centuries. A thought-provoking display of photographs taken on the occasion of the community's 350th anniversary celebrations in 1985 closes the chronological exhibit.

Admission: Dfl 7 ($3.70) adults, Dfl 3.50 ($1.85) children 10–16.

Open: Daily 11am–5pm. **Tram:** 9 or 14 to Waterlooplein and walk past the Portuguese Synagogue.

Hollandse Schouwburg, on the Plantage Middenlaan. No phone.

Not far from the Jewish Historical Museum and Portuguese Synagogue is "the place where we commemorate our compatriots who were deported between 1940 and 1945 and did not return." All that remains of the former Yiddish Theatre is its facade, behind which is only a simple memorial plaza of grass and walkways.

Admission: Free.

Open: Mon–Fri 10am–4pm, Sat–Sun 11am–4pm. **Tram:** 9 or 14 to Plantage Middenlaan.

Museum Amstelkring ("Our Lord in the Attic"), Oude Zijds Voorburgwal 40, at Heintje Hoecksteeg. ☎ **624-66-04.**

Attractions in Amsterdam East

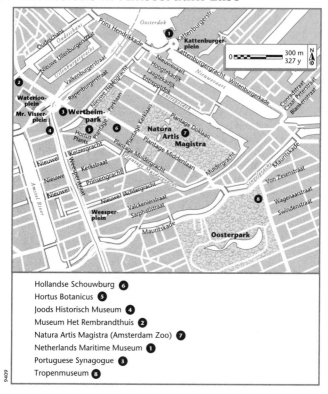

One of the quirks in the history of Amsterdam is that this traditionally tolerant city had a law on its books for more than 200 years that prohibited any religious services other than those of the officially favored Dutch Reformed church. As a result, the city's Catholics, Mennonites, Lutherans, and Jews were forced to hold services in private homes and other secret locations. The museum known as "Our Lord in the Attic" incorporates the best preserved of these clandestine churches in Holland; it's also one of the oldest canal-house museums you can visit in Amsterdam. The church is located in the common attic of three houses built during the years 1661–63. Worshipers entered by a door on a side street and climbed a narrow flight of stairs to the third floor (notice the well-worn stair treads). An 18th-century redecoration created the chapel-size church you see today, with its baroque altar, spinet-size pipe organ, and two narrow upper balconies. The church is used today for services and concerts. Take time to look through the sparsely furnished rooms of this interesting little house-museum; notice particularly the symmetry in the proportions of floors, ceilings, and walls, a characteristic feature of classic Dutch architecture of the 17th century.

Admission: Dfl 5 ($2.65) adults, Dfl 3.50 ($1.85) students and seniors.

Open: Mon–Sat 10am–5pm, Sun and holidays 1–5pm. **Tram:** Take any tram to Dam Square and walk; the best route is via Damstraat to the Oude Zijds Voorburgwal canal, where you turn left and continue two blocks past the Oude Kerk.

3 Cool for Kids

Though kids may get a little bored with the Amsterdam art museums listed above, they might be interested in seeing the **Anne Frankhuis** (see "The Top Attractions," above, for details). There's a section of the Tropenmuseum (see "More Attractions," above) reserved just for them called **Kindermuseum TM Junior** (☎ 568-83-00 for information). It's open only to children age 6 to 12 (one adult per child is allowed). **Madame Tussaud's Wax Museum** (see "More Attractions," above, for details) is always fun for kids, though if they're too small they might be a little frightened by the wax statues.

★ **Artis Zoo,** Plantage Kerklaan 40. ☎ 523-34-00.

I haven't met one kid who didn't like a zoo. If you're at a loss for what to do with the kids, the Artis Zoo is a safe bet. Established in 1838, it is the oldest zoo in the Netherlands, housing over 6,000 animals. Also on the property are a planetarium, an aquarium, and a geological and zoological museum. In addition to the rest of the zoo, there's also a children's farm.

Admission (including zoo, children's farm, planetarium, and zoological museum): Dfl 19 ($10) adults, Dfl 12.50 ($6.55) children 10 and under.

Open: Daily 9am–5pm.

4 Organized Tours

BY BUS

For many travelers, a quick bus tour is the best way to launch a sightseeing program in a strange city, and although Amsterdam offers its own unique alternative—a canal-boat ride—you may want to get your bearings on land as well. A three-hour tour costs Dfl 28 to 40 ($14.75 to $21.05); children are charged half price. Major companies offering these and other motor-coach sightseeing trips are **Holland International Excursions,** Dam 6 (☎ 551-28-00); **Keytours,** Dam Square 19 (☎ 624-73-04); and **Lindbergh Excursions,** Damrak 26 (☎ 622-27-66).

BY BOAT

Ever resourceful and ever aware of the transportation resource their canals represent, the Dutch have introduced **Museum Boot** (Boat), Stationsplein 8 (☎ 622-21-81), to carry weary tourists on their pilgrimages from museum to museum. It's an easy way to travel and, for those with limited time in Amsterdam, also provides some of the advantages of a canal-boat cruise. Stops are made every 45 minutes at seven key spots around the city, providing access to a total of 16 museums, including, at Stop 1, the Anne Frankhuis; at Stop 2, the Rijksmuseum, Vincent van Gogh Museum, and Stedelijk Museum of Modern Art; at Stop 3, Madame Tussaud's and the Amsterdam Historisch Museum; at Stop 4, Museum Het Rembrandthuis and the Jewish Historical Museum; and at Stop 5, the Netherlands Maritime Museum and the Tropenmuseum. Fare for the Museum Boot, which is for the whole day and includes a 50% discount on museum admissions, is Dfl 19 ($10) for adults and Dfl 13 ($6.85) for children ages 13 and under; or there is a "combi-ticket" at Dfl 35 ($18.40) that offers travel for the whole day and free admission to any three museums you choose.

5   Sports & Recreation

SPORTS

GOLF   There are two public golf courses in Amsterdam: one at the **Golf en Conference Center Amstelborgh,** Borchlandweg 6 (☎ **697-50-00**), and **Sloten,** at Sloterweg 1045 (☎ **614-24-02**). The Amstelborgh complex includes a nine-hole course, a restaurant, conference facilities, locker rooms, and Europe's largest driving range (lit at night). It is open Monday through Friday from 8am to 10:30pm and Saturday and Sunday from 8am to 9pm. Call ahead for greens fees and tee times at both courses.

SOCCER   Called football in Europe, soccer is absolutely the biggest game in Holland. Ajax is the world-famous Amsterdam team; matches are held in **Olympisch Stadion** (Olympic Stadium), Stadionplein 20 (☎ **671-11-15**; tram 16 or 24).

TENNIS & SQUASH   You'll find indoor courts at **Frans Otten Stadion,** Stadionstraat 10 (☎ **662-87-67**). For both indoor and outdoor courts, try **Gold Star,** Karel Lotsylaan 20 (☎ **644-54-83**).
Squash courts can be found at **Squash City,** Ketelmarkerstraat, near Centraal Station (☎ **626-78-83**).

RECREATION

BOATING & CANOEING   From March 15 to October 15 you can go to Loosdrecht, outside Amsterdam, to rent sailing equipment at **Ottenhome** (☎ **2158-233-31**). **Yacht Haven Robinson,** Dorpstraat 3, Landsmeer (☎ **2908-213-46**), rents rowing equipment.
Sadly, the outfit that used to rent canoes for canal use no longer does so, but canoes can be rented in Amsterdamse Bos (woodland), south of the city, for use in the park only.

BOWLING   If you're an avid bowler and can't go for long without knocking down some pins, try **Knijn Bowling,** Scheldeplein 3 (☎ **664-22-11**).

CYCLING   South of the city is Amsterdamse Bos, where you can rent bicycles (☎ **644-54-73**) for touring the woodland's special paths. Of course, you can always do as Amsterdammers do and explore all those bridges and canals by bike (see "By Bicycle" under "Getting Around" in Chapter 3 for rental information).

FISHING   Anglers should try the Bosbaan artificial pond in Amsterdamse Bos, south of the city. You can obtain a license there at Nikolaswetsantraat 10 (☎ **626-49-88**), open Monday through Friday; or at any fishing supply store in the area.

FITNESS CENTERS   If you're worried about missing a day or two of your exercise routine, there are several centers you can try: **Fitness Aerobic Center Jansen,** Rokin 109–111 (☎ **626-93-66**); **Gym '86,** Tweede vd Helstraat 2 (☎ **675-05-03**); and **Sporting Club Leidseplein,** Korte Leidsedwarsstraat 18 (☎ **620-66-31**). For aerobics classes conducted in English, go to **H '88,** Herengracht 88 (☎ **638-06-50**).

HORSEBACK RIDING   Indoor and ring riding only are offered at **Amsterdamse Manege,** Nieuwe Kalfjeslaan 25 (☎ **643-13-42**). Horses rented at **De Ruif Manege,** Sloterweg 675 (☎ **615-66-67**), can be ridden in Amsterdamse Bos.

ICE SKATING   All those Dutch paintings of people skating and sledding (and the story of Hans Brinker and his silver skates) will surely get you thinking about skating on Amsterdam's ponds and canals. However, doing this won't be easy unless you're willing to shell out for a new pair of skates—there are very few places that rent skates, and most locals have their own.

You can rent skates from November through February at **Jaap Eden Baan,** Radioweg 64 (☎ **694-98-94**), and they'll even allow you to take them out of the rink. It is possible to skate on the canals (in winter, of course), though they rarely freeze over. Don't attempt to skate on a canal or pond unless locals are doing so—they know when the ice is thick enough for safe skating.

JOGGING   The two main jogging areas are Vondelpark in the city center and Amsterdamse Bos on the southern edge of the city. You can also run along the Amstel River.

SWIMMING   Amsterdam's state-of-the-art swimming facility is **De Mirandabad,** De Mirandalaan 9 (☎ **642-80-80**). This ultramodern complex features indoor and outdoor pools with wave machines, slides, and other amusements. The **Marnixbad,** Marnixplein 5 (☎ **625-48-43**), is a glass-enclosed public pool.

Also, try calling **Floralparkbad,** Sneeuwbalweg 5 (☎ **636-81-21**), or **Sloterparkbad,** Slotermeerlaan 2 (☎ **611-45-65**), to see if they're open.

7

Strolling Around Amsterdam

Tʜᴇ ʙᴇsᴛ ᴡᴀʏ ᴛᴏ ᴅɪsᴄᴏᴠᴇʀ ᴀɴʏ ᴄɪᴛʏ ɪs ᴏɴ ꜰᴏᴏᴛ. Tʜɪs ɪs ᴇsᴘᴇᴄɪᴀʟʟʏ ᴛʀᴜᴇ of Amsterdam. You'll find that the Amsterdam VVV Tourist Office has several walking tour folders available. You can follow the two listed below, which are adaptations of the tourist office's "Voyage of Discovery Through the Centre" and "Jewish Amsterdam," or stop by and pick up their walking tours.

Walking Tour 1

The Center

Start The VVV office at Stationsplein, in front of Centraal Station.
Finish Oude Brugsteeg.
Time 2¹/₂ to 4 hours, depending on how long you spend in museums or shops.
Best Times Anytime.

Across from the VVV office, the starting point of our walking tour is:

1. **Centraal Station,** designed by P. J. H Cuypers and built between 1884 and 1889. Walk straight ahead along the Damrak, a street bordered by a series of shops, cafés, and department stores. When you reach:
2. **Damrak 28–30,** look up at the office building and you'll see 4 baboons and 22 owls peering down at you. Across the street is the:
3. **Stock Exchange,** built by Berlage between 1896 and 1903. Also here is:
4. **'y Beursmannetje,** a statue of a man with a newspaper under his arm, given to the city by *Financieel Dagblad,* the financial newspaper of Holland. Beyond is the:
5. **Zoutsteeg,** a narrow street of restaurants and shops; centuries ago, when the Damrak was part of the Amstel River, ships unloaded salt here (*zout* means "salt" in Dutch).
   Turn right onto Gravenstraat and cross the Nieuwendijk, passing:
6. **De Drie Fleschjes,** a tasting house dating from the 17th century. From here you can see the:
7. **Nieuwe Kerk** and its late Gothic choir. The Nieuwe Kerk is where all kings and queens of Holland have had their coronations since 1815. Continue around the church and you'll see, across the Nieuwe Zijds Voorburgwal, the:
8. **"Perenburg,"** the former post office, so nicknamed because of the pear-shaped tower decorations. Walk from there into Dam Square, which is bordered on one side by the:

Walking Tour—The Center

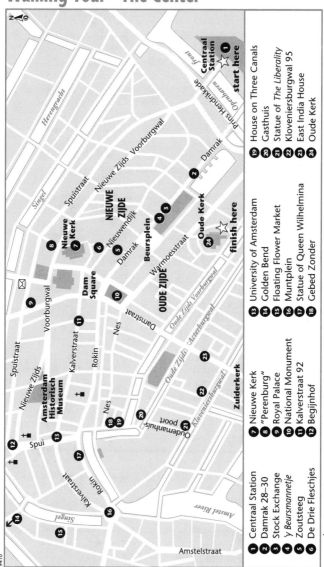

N

start here

finish here

① Centraal Station
② Damrak 28–30
③ Stock Exchange
④ 't Beursmannetje
⑤ Zoutsteeg
⑥ De Drie Fleschjes

⑦ Nieuwe Kerk
⑧ "Perenburg"
⑨ Royal Palace
⑩ National Monument
⑪ Kalverstraat 92
⑫ Begijnhof

⑬ University of Amsterdam
⑭ Golden Bend
⑮ Floating Flower Market
⑯ Muntplein
⑰ Statue of Queen Wilhelmina
⑱ Gebed Zonder

⑲ House on Three Canals
⑳ Gasthuis
㉑ Statue of The Liberality
㉒ Kloveniersburgwal 95
㉓ East India House
㉔ Oude Kerk

Church ✝ Post Office ⊠

9. **Royal Palace,** built as a town hall between 1648 and 1655 and later chosen as an official residence of the royal family. Directly across the square from the Royal Palace is the:

10. **National Monument,** built in 1956 to honor the dead of World War II. To the left, if you're facing the palace, is Kalverstraat, the busiest pedestrian shopping street in Holland.

Stroll onto Kalverstraat and look for:

11. **Kalverstraat 92.** You'll see a porch dating from 1592 that used to be the entrance to the city orphanage and is now the entrance to the Amsterdam Historisch Museum. Pass under and look around. The first courtyard was for the boys; to the left are the cupboards where they stored their tools. The inner courtyard was for the girls; it's now the museum entrance. The museum itself is fascinating (see "More Attractions" in Chapter 6 for a full description).

   After visiting the museum, pass through a small alleyway with a magnificent gallery of regimental paintings to the:

12. **Begijnhof,** where devout women have lived since the 14th century—no. 34, the oldest house in Amsterdam, was built in 1475.

   Pass between nos. 37 and 38 into Spui. Opposite is the main building of the:

13. **University of Amsterdam.** You probably wouldn't even notice the presence of a university if no one pointed it out to you. Here you'll also see a statue of a small boy, typical of Amsterdam.

   Take the small street next to Café Hoppe and cross the bridges—first, over Singel, and then, via Wijde Heisteeg, over the Herengracht to one of the most-photographed parts of Amsterdam. The views are of gables and canals. Continue along the Herengracht, crossing over Leidsestraat to the:

14. **Golden Bend,** so named because of the magnificent homes there, which were built on double lots with double steps and central entrances. The entrance to Nieuwe Spiegelstraat, a street lined with antiques shops, is also here. At the end of the street you can see the Rijksmuseum, built by P. J. H. Cuypers in 1885.

   Continue along the Herengracht, turn left at Vijzelstraat, and walk to the:

15. **Floating Flower Market,** which is worth a quick detour. If you keep going, past the flower market, you'll see the:

16. **Muntplein,** with its 17th-century tower. This square is, in fact, a bridge across the Amstel River. Turn left at Rokin, pass the:

17. **Statue of Queen Wilhelmina** and walk into Lange Brugsteeg. Past Nes is:

18. **Gebed Zonder** (Prayer Without Ending), an alley, the name of which comes from the convents that used to be here and in which one could always hear the murmur of prayers from behind the walls. Follow Grimburgwal across Oude Zijds Voorburgwall and Oude Zijds Acterburgwal. Between these canals is the:

19. **House on Three Canals.** From here, cross the bridge to the far side of Oude Zijds Achterburgwal, where you'll pass the:

20. **Gasthuis.** Turn into the Oudemanhuispoort. At the end of the arcade, turn left onto Kloveniersburgwal and look for the:

21. **Statue of** *The Liberality* above the doorway. She has a cornucopia at her feet and is flanked by two elderly Amsterdammers.

    As you continue on Kloveniersburgwal, notice:

22. **Kloveniersburgwal 95.** This lovely canal house was built in 1642. Turn left onto Oude Hoogstraat, passing the:

23. **East India House,** and its courtyard, which dates from 1606. Via Oude Doelenstraat (straight ahead) you come to Oude Zijds Voorburgwal, where you turn right after the bridge and continue to the:

24. **Oude Kerk,** a late Gothic church begun in the year 1300; in its southern porch, to the right of the sexton's house, you will see a coat of arms belonging to Maximilian of Austria, who, with his son Philip, contributed to the building of this porch.

    Finally, turn right through the Enge Kersteeg, right again onto Warmoesstraat, and left onto Oude Brugsteeg. At the end of this small street, on your left you will see a gable decorated with a coat of arms protected by two lions. The building was the custom-house of early Amsterdam and you're looking at the crest of the city—a fitting end to your walk through the heart of Amsterdam.

Walking Tour 2
The Old Jewish Quarter

Start   Rembrandtsplein.
Finish   *The Dockworker,* on Jonas Daniel Meijerplein.
Time   Allow between 1¹/₂ and 3 hours, not including museum and rest stops.
Best Times   Anytime.

From Rembrandtsplein—named in tribute to the city's most famous artist—follow Utrechtsestraat to Kerkstraat. Continue along Kerkstraat over the Magere Brug, a white drawbridge spanning the Amstel River. Kerkstraat will become Nieuwe Kerkstraat on the opposite side. Go left immediately after crossing the bridge and head for Nieuwe Amstelstraat. Here, you'll find the:

1. **Jewish Historical Museum** (see "More Attractions" in Chapter 6 for a full description). Note that across the

street from the museum is the Arsenal, which served as a storage space for munitions in the 19th century and has now been incorporated as part of the museum.

Go right from the museum to the end of the street. Turn left, cross Mr. Visserplein, and you'll pass the:

2. **Moses and Aaron Church,** which actually has nothing to do with Jewish history—in fact, it started out as a secret church for Catholics who were forbidden to worship by the Calvinists when they rose to power in the late 16th century.

Turn left onto:

3. **Jodenbreestraat,** which used to be the center of Jewish Amsterdam. Now it's mostly modern buildings, and unfortunately the right side of the street was knocked down in 1965, destroying any character that was left of the street.

Cross the road and turn right onto Uilenburgersteeg. Keep going straight onto Nieuwe Uilenburgerstraat. On the right is:

4. **Gassan Diamonds,** where you can watch a diamond-cutting demonstration (see "More Attractions" in Chapter 6 for a full description). A great number of Jews in Amsterdam were diamond polishers.

Walk back to Jodenbreestraat where you'll find:

5. **Het Rembrandthuis.** Rembrandt was not Jewish, but because he lived in this once primarily Jewish neighborhood, he often painted portraits of Jews who were his friends or neighbors.

Cross the bridge leading to St. Antoniebreestraat to the left, just after Rembrandt Museum onto Waterlooplein, where you'll find the:

6. **Waterlooplein Flea Market,** one of Amsterdam's best-known markets. If you don't like flea-market shopping, you might just enjoy people-watching here—there's as wide a diversity of people as there is a diversity of items. If you enjoy flea-market shopping, beware: You might have to continue this walking tour tomorrow.

On your way around, when you come to the bridge at Staalstraat that leads to Zwanenburgwal, cross the bridge to find:

A Refueling Stop

A delightful place called **Puccini.** Its a wonderful place to stop for coffee and some homemade desserts—you can actually see them preparing the desserts next door.

Go back over the bridge and turn right; you'll be able to see the:

7. **Jewish Resistance Fighters Memorial,** a black-marble monument to the Jews who tried to resist or escape Nazi

oppression, and the Dutch people who tried to help them.

Turn left at the monument (the Grand Café Danzig will be on your left, the River Amstel will be on your right), and walk about 200 yards toward the bridge. Just before the bridge, look for the outline of:

8. **Megadlei Yethomin,** which, starting in 1836, was an orphanage for German and Eastern European Jewish boys. During World War II the boys were taken to a Nazi concentration camp (Sobibor concentration camp). After the war, it was reopened, this time as a home for boys who wanted to go to Israel.

Keep going straight to the:

9. **Blauwbrug.** This bridge used to be the main road connecting the Jewish Quarter and the center of Amsterdam.

Don't cross the bridge; instead, continue along with the river to your right. Turn left into Nieuwe Herengracht just before the drawbridge and continue along to:

10. **Nieuwe Herengracht 33,** which used to be the Portuguese Jewish home for the elderly. There was apparently room for 10 people, and they had their own synagogue within. Note the stonework on the house diagonally to the left across the street from where you're standing.

Walk to the end of Nieuwe Herengracht and turn right across Vaz Diasbrug. Take a look back down the canal as you cross the bridge—there's a wonderful view of canal houses and houseboats that's very typically Amsterdam.

Continue along this road, which is now Weesperstraat, until you reach:

11. **A small garden.** There is a monument to the Dutch people who protected the Jews during World War II. This is a wonderful place to sit and rest for a few minutes—an oasis in the midst of the modern buildings and construction sites around the area. Take a look at the monument up close, then have a seat on one of the benches.

After you're sufficiently rested, continue on Weesperstraat until you get to Nieuwe Keizersgracht, where you'll go right to:

12. **Nieuwe Keizersgracht 58,** where the offices of the Jewish Council were once located. During World War II, the Jewish Council followed the Germans' orders hoping that they would be seen as cooperative and would therefore be treated leniently. Tragically, their cooperation only served to make it easier for the

Germans to find and deport most of the Jews in Holland.

Return to Weesperstraat, turn right, cross at the traffic light, and continue along Weesperstraat to the entrance to Nieuwe Kerkstraat, which is under the Metropool Building. Go left under the Metropool to:

13. **Nieuwe Kerkstraat 127**, formerly the Metaarhuis, where corpses from the Nieuwe Keizersgracht hospital were cleansed according to the strict Jewish ritual.

Walk farther along and cross the bridge at the end of Nieuwe Kerkstraat (veer to the left a bit) and you'll be on Plantage Kerklaan. Walk down Plantage Kerklaan to the traffic lights and take a left onto Plantage Middenlaan. On your left you'll see:

14. **Hollandse Shouwburg**. Many Jews who were to be deported during the war were ordered to report to this once Dutch playhouse. It is said that the children of these Jews were sent across the street to the kindergarten, and many of them were saved by being taken "underground" through the attached houses. There is a plaque on the school building that celebrates the escape of some of the children.

Go back to the traffic lights, turn left, and, continuing along Plantage Kerklaan, you'll soon see:

15. **Plantage Kerklaan 36**, where a plaque commemorates the Jewish resistance fighters who tried to destroy the city registers so the Germans wouldn't know how many Jews were living in Amsterdam, or where they were living. This would have prevented them from being able to identify most of the Jews, and it could have prevented thousands from dying in concentration camps. Unfortunately, the attack failed and 12 people were executed.

Staying on Plantage Kerklaan, you'll soon arrive at Henri Polaklaan, which is opposite the entrance to:

16. **Artis**, Amsterdam's zoo (see "Cool for Kids" in Chapter 6 for a full description). Now, if you've been dragging the kids along with you the whole way and you're tired of keeping them away from canal edges and hearing them complain about being tired, the zoo is the perfect spot—they'll forget their aching feet, and you won't have to worry about their falling headlong into the canal. Even if you don't have kids, you might want to stop and have a look—the zoo is beautiful, especially in the spring.

After your romp at the zoo, go back out the way you came in, and follow Henri Polaklaan to:

17. **Henri Polaklaan 6–12**, the former Portuguese Jewish Hospital built in 1916. The pelican on the facade is a symbol of the Portuguese Jewish community.

Walking Tour—The Old Jewish Quarter

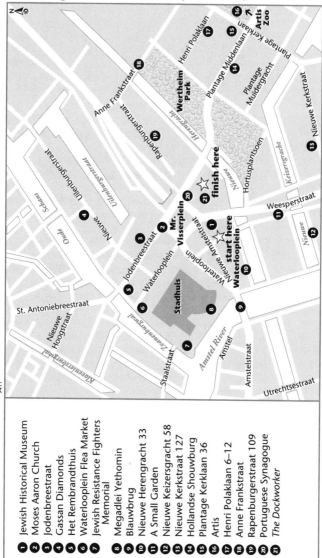

Legend:

1. Jewish Historical Museum
2. Moses Aaron Church
3. Jodenbreestraat
4. Gassan Diamonds
5. Het Rembrandthuis
6. Waterlooplein Flea Market
7. Jewish Resistance Fighters Memorial
8. Megadlei Yethomin
9. Blauwbrug
10. Nieuwe Herengracht 33
11. A Small Garden
12. Nieuwe Keizersgracht 58
13. Nieuwe Kerkstraat 127
14. Hollandse Shouwburg
15. Plantage Kerklaan 36
16. Artis
17. Henri Polaklaan 6–12
18. Anne Frankstraat
19. Rapenburgerstraat 109
20. Portuguese Synagogue
21. The Dockworker

Right at the end of Henri Polaklaan, cross Plantage Parklaan. Note the tile entrances and wooden doors at nos. 24 and 25; they're quite typical of the entryways to the canal houses. Follow the road left as it leads into:

18. **Anne Frankstraat,** obviously named for Anne Frank, of diary fame (for more about Anne Frank and the Anne Frankhuis, see "The Top Attractions," in Chapter 6).

Cross the bridge and go straight until you get to Rapenburgerstraat. Turn left until you see:

19. **Rapenburgerstraat 109**, Beth Hamidrash Ets Chaim (now the home of *NIW*, Holland's Jewish weekly newspaper), once the place where Jews of Amsterdam could study the Jewish law and commentaries. Though the building dates from 1883, the study hall was founded in 1740.

At the end of Rapenburgerstraat, cross back to Mr. Visserplein. When you cross the road, the:

20. **Portuguese Synagogue** will be on your left (see "More Attractions" in Chapter 6 for a full description).

Make a left onto Jonas Daniel Meijerplein, and in the square between the synagogue and the Jewish Historical Museum, you'll see:

21. *The Dockworker.* The street, Jonas Daniel Meijerplein, is where many Jews were forced to wait for their deportation to concentration camps, and this statue was erected in commemoration of the 1941 February Strike by the workers of Amsterdam in protest of the deportation of the Jews. The strike was one of the biggest collective protests in all of occupied Europe regarding the treatment of the Jews by the Germans during the war.

This concludes your tour.

8

Amsterdam Shopping

Fʀᴏᴍ ɪᴛs ᴇᴀʀʟɪᴇsᴛ ᴅᴀʏs Aᴍsᴛᴇʀᴅᴀᴍ ʜᴀs ʙᴇᴇɴ ᴀ ᴛʀᴀᴅɪɴɢ ᴄɪᴛʏ. Fɪʀsᴛ, ᴛʀᴀᴅᴇ centered on the fish that the original dammers of the Amstel caught in the rivers and the North Sea; later, during the 17th century, on the spices, furs, flower bulbs, and artifacts carried back to Europe by the ships of the Dutch East and West India Companies.

The fish were sold on the same spot where a major department store now stands, and the early townspeople brought calves to market on the same street you will walk along to begin a shopper's walking tour through Amsterdam. The luxury items you buy to take home today are the same sort of goods Dutch merchants sold to one another in the golden age of the 17th century, and the junk you find to buy in the flea market at Waterlooplein is much the same as it has been for hundreds of years.

Adding a modern dimension to this tradition-laden scene are the funky boutiques you find scattered around Amsterdam, and adding sparkle are the diamond cutters.

1 The Shopping Scene

Shopping Orientation

HOURS Regular shopping hours in Amsterdam are Monday from 11am to 6pm; Tuesday, Wednesday, and Friday from 9am to 6pm; Thursday from 9am to 9pm; and Saturday from 9am to 5pm.

PRICES Prices in Holland are fixed, with all applicable taxes included in the amounts shown on tags and counter display cards. Although end-of-season and other special sales occur from time to time throughout the year, the practice of discounting as we know it is not yet part of the Dutch pricing system, so there's little use running from shop to shop trying to find a better price on ordinary consumer goods. If you want a bargain, go to the Waterlooplein flea market, although even there you'll find that the Dutch have much less interest in the sport of haggling—or margin in their prices—than their counterparts in countries farther south. They're too practical, with your time and money as well as their own, to quote a ridiculous price in the expectation that it will be cut in half or that you'll be fool enough to pay it.

VAT & THE VAT REFUND As a visitor, you're entitled to a refund of the VAT—value-added tax—you pay on your purchases in Holland. It's not worth the trouble for small purchases, and many stores require a minimum purchase before they will bother with the paperwork involved (for example, De Bijenkorf department store will process the VAT refund only for items priced Dfl 300 [$157.90] or more). But on high-ticket items, the savings can be significant. To obtain your VAT refund, get a special refund form from the shop at the time you make your purchase. When you leave Holland, present the form and show your purchases to the Dutch Customs officers. They stamp the form and return it to the store; the store then mails your tax refund to you in a few months or issues credit to a charge card.

DUTY-FREE ITEMS   If nothing else has convinced you that the Dutch are the world's most sophisticated and dedicated buyers and sellers of luxury goods, wait until you leave Holland and see the array of shops at Amsterdam's **Schiphol Airport.** You can buy anything, even a fully equipped Mercedes, with less fuss and bother than it takes to buy a newspaper at most airports. There are shopping areas scattered all over the terminal building for duty-free liquor, smokes, perfume, cameras, appliances, designer accessories, cheese, chocolates, tulip bulbs, leather goods, clothing, crystal, pewter, earthenware, even diamonds. Plus, there's a duty-free car and motorcycle showroom called **ShipSide,** across from the main terminal (☎ **02503-14500** for information). To give you an idea of the buys you may find at the Amsterdam Airport Shopping Centre, the Sony Walkman (rechargeable) is Dfl 83 ($43.70), the Sharp pocket computer IQ 8300 is Dfl 599 ($315.25), and an 18-karat gold men's Rolex quartz watch, with date display and President's wrist band, is Dfl 22,725 ($11,960); 15 grams of Estée Lauder Private Collection perfume is Dfl 125 ($65.80); and a Hermès scarf is Dfl 325 ($171.05). Simpler choices are Godiva Chocolates (1 kg/2.2 lb., for Dfl 65 ($34.20) or farmer's Gouda cheese (3 kg, or 6.6 lb., for Dfl 25/$13.15).

Best Buys

If an item in an Amsterdam shop window takes your fancy or fills a specific need, buy it, of course. But often both prices and selections in Holland are too close to what you can find at home to justify the extra weight in your suitcase or the expense and trouble of shipping. Exceptions are the special items that the Dutch produce to perfection (delftware, pewter, crystal, and old-fashioned clocks), or commodities in which they have significantly cornered a market, like diamonds. None of these is a cheap commodity, unfortunately, and you'll want to do some homework in order to make canny shopping decisions (see below), but if you know enough and care enough, you can find excellent values and take home beautiful, and in some cases valuable, treasures from Holland that will please you much more and much longer than the usual souvenirs. And if money is a consideration, remember that the Dutch also have inexpensive specialties, such as cheese, flower bulbs, and chocolate.

DELFTWARE/DELFT BLUE

There are three types of delftware available in Amsterdam—Delftware, Makkumware, and junk—and since none of it is cheap, you need to know what the differences are between the three types and what to look for to determine quality. But first, a few words of historical background and explanation: delftware (with a small "d") has actually become an umbrella name for all Dutch hand-painted earthenware pottery resembling ancient Chinese porcelain, whether it is blue and white, red and white, or multicolored, and regardless of the city in which it was produced. Delftware, or Delft Blue (with a capital "D"), on the other hand, refers to the predominantly blue-and-white products of one firm, **De Porceleyne Fles** of Delft, which is the only survivor of the original 30 potteries in Delft that during the 17th century worked overtime in that tiny city to meet the clamoring demand of the newly affluent Dutch for Chinese-style vases, urns, wall tiles, and knickknacks—real or reproduced, porcelain or pottery.

Similarly, the term makkumware is becoming synonymous with multicolored—or polychrome—pottery, whereas Makkumware is, in fact, the hand-painted earthenware produced only in the town of Makkum in the northern province of Friesland and only by the 300-plus-year-old firm of **Tichelaars,** which was founded in 1660 and now is in its 10th generation of family management. Copies of the products of these two firms are numerous, with some copies nearly equal in quality and others missing by miles the delicacy of the brush stroke, the richness of color, or the sheen of the secret glazes that make the items produced by De Porceleyne Fles and Tichelaars so highly prized, and so expensive.

Your eye should tell you which pieces of pottery are worth their prices, but to be sure that yours is a *real* Delft vase, for instance, look on the bottom for the distinctive three-part hallmark of De Porceleyne Fles: an outline of a small pot, above an initial *J* crossed with a short stroke (actually it's a combined initial, *J* and *T*), above the scripted word "Delft," with the *D* distinctively written like a backward *C*.

To distinguish the products of Tichelaars, look for a mark that incorporates a crown above a shield showing the word "Makkum" and two scripted *T*s, overlapped like crossed swords (or look simply for the crossed *T*s, since the crown is a rather recent addition to their mark, the result of a royal honor bestowed on the company for its 300th anniversary in 1960).

CRYSTAL & PEWTER

Holland is not the only country that produces fine pewter ware and crystal, but the Dutch contribute both a refined sense of design and a respect for craftsmanship that combine to produce items of exceptional beauty and quality. Also, if you remember the classic Dutch still-life paintings and happy scenes of 17th-century family life, pewter objects are part of Holland's heritage. As with hand-painted earthenware, there are Dutch towns associated with each of these crafts and long-established firms whose names are well known as quality producers. Crystal, for example, has long been associated with the cities of Leerdam, south of Utrecht, and Maastricht, in South Limburg, whose manufacturers have recently joined together to market under the names of Royal Netherlands in the United States and Kristalunie in Holland. Look for the four triangles of the Royal Leerdam label.

Traditionally, pewter was the specialty of the little town of Tiel, near Arnhem in the eastern part of Holland. Gradually, though, the old firms are disappearing, making it more difficult to find fine spun pewter produced in the old way and in the old molds. An important shopping note on pewter is that although the Dutch government now bans the use of lead as a hardening agent, this assurance protects you from toxicity only with *new* pewter. Don't buy any antiques for use with food or drink. If you're not sure, look inside the pitcher or goblet; if it's light in color, it's fine; if it's dark and has a blue shine, buy it for decorative purposes only.

OLD-FASHIONED CLOCKS

It's true that the Swiss make the finest clocks in the world, but what they do well for the inner workings the Dutch do well for the outside, particularly if you like a clock to be old-fashioned, handcrafted, and highly decorated with figures and mottos or small peekaboo panels to show you the innards.

There are two types of clocks that have survived the centuries and the shift in Dutch taste to more contemporary timepieces. One is the Zaandam clock, or Zaanseklok, from the small city across the harbor from Amsterdam, which is identified by its ornately carved oak or walnut case and brass panels, its tiny windows on the dial face, and the motto NU EICK SYN SIN, which basically translates from Old Dutch as "To Each His Own." The other popular clock style is the Friese Stoelklok, or Frisian clock, which is even more heavily decorated, customarily with hand-painted scenes of the Dutch countryside or ships at sea (that may even bob back and forth in time with the ticks) or possibly with both motifs and also with a smiling moon face.

DIAMONDS

Amsterdam has been a major center of the diamond-cutting industry since the 15th century and is one of the best places in the world to shop for diamond jewelry and unmounted stones in all gradations of color and quality.

Dutch jewelers generally adhere to the standards of both the Gemological Institute of America and the U.S. Federal Trade Commission, and most will issue a certificate with a diamond they sell that spells out the carat weight, cut, color, and other pertinent identifying details, including any imperfections.

Should you decide to buy a diamond, there are four factors influencing its quality that should be considered. The first is its weight, which will be stated either as points or carats (100 points equals 1 carat equals 200 milligrams, or 3.47 grains troy). Next is the cut, which may be a classic round (brilliant) cut, a pear shape, a rectangular emerald cut, an oval, or a long and narrow, double-pointed marquise. This is initially a matter of design preference rather than a factor of a stone's value; it is also, however, the test of the diamond cutter's ability to polish each of 58 facets at an angle that varies no more than half a degree from every other angle. To evaluate a diamond's cut, hold it to the light and look into the table (which is the name of the flattened top and the diamond's largest facet); if you see a dark circle, you know the stone is well cut and is reflecting light to its full capacity; if you don't, expect to pay less and to get less sparkle. Also expect to pay more or less according to the clarity and color of a diamond. The clarity can be reliably evaluated only by a jeweler, who uses a loupe, or small eyeglass, to magnify the stone 10 times; the fewer the imperfections, the better the diamond and the higher the price (and, by the way, only a stone with *no* visible imperfections at that magnification can be described as "perfect" according to the guidelines of the Gemological Institute). Likewise, the whiter the diamond, the better the quality and the greater its value. To see for yourself whether a stone you are considering is closer to white than yellow or even brown, hold it with tweezers and look at it from the side, against a pure background (do this preferably in daylight through a north window, and never in direct sunlight). But don't expect to see blue unless you're looking at what a diamond dealer calls a "fancy" (a colored diamond), similar to the yellow Tiffany diamond or the deep-blue Hope.

ANTIQUES

Antiques lovers love Holland! And why not, when you think of all those tankards, pipes, cabinets, clocks, kettles, vases, and other bric-a-brac you see in the old Dutch paintings that still show up among the treasures of shops on Amsterdam's Nieuwe Spiegelstraat. It's the 20th century's good fortune that since the 17th century the Dutch have collected everything—from Chinese urns to silver boxes, from cookie molds to towering armoires—and should you find that while you're in Amsterdam there is a *kijkdag* (looking day) for an upcoming auction, you will realize that antiques still pour forth from the attics of the old canal houses.

CHEESE

Holland is the Wisconsin of Europe, well known around the world for its butter and cheese. Gouda (correctly pronounced, in Dutch, "*how*-duh") and Edam are the two cheeses most familiar to us because they have been exported from Holland so long—since the 1700s—but once inside a Dutch cheese shop, you'll quickly realize that there are many other interesting Dutch choices, including a nettle cheese that's a specialty of Friesland. Before you simply point to any cheese and say "I'll take that one," you need to know that in Holland you have the choice of factory cheese, made of pasteurized milk, or *boerenkaas,* which is farm cheese that is produced in the old careful way with fresh, unpasteurized milk straight from the cow. Boerenkaas is more expensive, of course, but it also can be expected to be more delicious. Look for the boerenkaas stamp. Another choice that you will make is between young and old cheese; it's a difference of sweetness, moistness, and a melting quality in the mouth (*jonge,* or young, cheese) and a sharper, drier taste, and a crumbly texture (oude, or old, cheese).

FLOWER BULBS

Nothing is more Dutch than a tulip, and no gift to yourself will bring more pleasure than to take home some bulbs to remind you of Holland all over again when they pop up every spring. You may have a problem making your choices, however, since there are more than 800 different varieties of tulip bulbs available in Holland, not to mention more than 500 kinds of daffodils and narcissi, and 60 different varieties of hyacinth and crocus. Many growers and distributors put together combination packages in various amounts of bulbs that are coordinated according to the colors of the flowers they will produce, but it's great fun—since so many bulbs are named for famous people—to put together your own garden party with Sophia Loren, President Kennedy, Queen Juliana, and Cyrano de Bergerac!

If you worry about the failure rates or bug-ridden bulbs, don't! The Dutch have been perfecting their growing methods and strengthening their stock for more than 400 years, and as in everything they do, perfection is not simply a standard to strive for, it's an obligation. Do check before buying, however, since not all bulbs are certified for entry into the United States. Packages are marked; look for the numbered phyto-sanitary certificate attached to the label.

CHOCOLATE

There's little to tell about Dutch chocolate except that it deserves its excellent reputation. **Droste, Verkade,** and **Van Houten** are three of the best Dutch brand names to look for, or you can seek out the small specialty chocolate shops that still home-make and hand-fill the boxes of bonbons.

Great Shopping Areas ─────────────────────────

The easiest way to approach shopping in Amsterdam is to devote a day to the project, put on your most comfortable shoes, and walk. You can window-shop all the way from Dam Square to the Concertgebouw if you have the stamina, and as long as you remember a few key jogs in the path you won't even need to consult a map. A few are pedestrians-only shopping streets, some are busy thoroughfares, others are peaceful canal-side esplanades or fashionable promenades; but each segment in this ever-growing network of commercial enterprises has developed its own identity or predominant selection of goods as a specialty. To get you on your way, here are three suggested shopping walks:

If you're looking for jewelry, trendy clothing, or athletic gear, begin at the department stores at Dam Square and follow Kalverstraat to Heiligeweg; turn right there and continue shopping until you reach the Leidseplein. (Heiligeweg becomes Leidsestraat after it crosses the Koningsplein, but it's really one long street, so you can't possibly get lost.)

If you're feeling rich or simply want to feast your eyes on lovely things (fashion, antiques, and art), begin at the Concertgebouw and walk along Van Baerlestraat toward Vondelpark; turn right at the elegant P. C. Hoofstraat. At the end of the street, by the canal, turn right again and walk to the Rijksmuseum, then turn left across the canal. Straight ahead is the Spiegelgracht, a small and quiet bit of canal that's the gateway to the best antiques-shopping street in Amsterdam, if not in all of Europe.

Finally, if your idea of a good day of shopping includes fashion boutiques, funky little specialty shops, and a good browse through a flea market or secondhand store, cut a path from west to east through the old city by beginning at the Westermarkt and crisscrossing among the canals. Reestraat, Hartenstraat, Wolvenstraat, and Runstraat are particularly good choices with lots of fun shops, including one that boasts of selling Europe's largest selection of ribbons and braid, and another with elaborately painted toilet bowls. At Dam Square you can take Damstraat and its continuations (Oude Doelenstraat, Hoogstraat, and Nieuwe Hoogstraat) to St. Antoniesbreestraat (and its continuation, Jodenbreestraat) to Nieuwe Uilenburgerstraat to Waterlooplein and the market. Or at Dam Square, follow Rokin to the Muntplein and walk from there, or take tram no. 9 or 14 to the stop for the Muziektheater/Waterlooplein.

For more ideas on shopping routes and to combine your buying with a historical walking tour, look at the three small booklets with titles beginning "On the Lookout for . . . ," which are excellent pictorial guides, with maps. The types of shopping covered by their guides, published by the VVV Amsterdam Tourist Office, are art and antiques, "the chic and the beautiful," and simply "between the canals," which covers the wide range of shopping available in that area.

To plan your own shopping route through Amsterdam, here are brief descriptions of the major shopping streets and what you can expect to find along each of them:

KALVERSTRAAT

This is the busiest stretch of pedestrian shopping in the city. At one end is Dam Square with its department stores; at the other end, the Muntplein traffic hub. In between, Kalverstraat is a hodgepodge of shopping possibilities. Punk-tinged boutiques for the young and athletic-shoe emporiums are side by side with shops selling dowdy raincoats and conservative business suits, bookstores, fur salons, maternity and baby stores, and record shops.

The big and busy **Vroom & Dreesman** department store has its main entrance on Kalverstraat, as does the elegant **Maison de Bonneterie en Pander;** also along the way are **Benetton** and **Fiorucci,** plus everything in the way of fast food from frites to poffertjes.

The more conservative and well-established fashion shops for men and women on Kalverstraat are **Maison de Vries, Claudia Sträter,** and **Austin Reed;** for leather goods, **Zumpolle** offers elegant and high-quality handbags and leather suitcases.

ROKIN

Parallel to Kalverstraat and also running from Dam Square to the Muntplein is Rokin, one of the busiest tram routes in the city. Along here you will find art galleries and antiques shops, and elegant fashion boutiques such as **Claudia Sträter** for lingerie, **Le Papillon** for fitness/dance wear, **Jan Jensen** for shoes, **Emmy Landkroon** and **Sheila** for haute couture, or the straightforward chic of **agnès b.**

HEILIGEWEG, KONINGSPLEIN & LEIDSESTRAAT

The fashion parade that begins on Kalverstraat continues around the corner on Heiligeweg, across the Koningsplein and along Leidsestraat, all the way to the Leidseplein. But the mood changes: The shops are more elegant, and instead of a sprinkling of fast-food outlets and souvenir shops, you find congenial cafés and airline ticket offices. Along the way, look for **Espirit, Pauw Boutique, Rodier Paris, Smit-Bally,** and **van der Heijden;** the Amsterdam branches of **Studio Haus** for modern china and crystal and **Cartier** for gold and silver; **Metz & Co.,** a dry-goods store at the corner of the Keizersgracht; and for men's and women's fashions, **Meddens** on Heiligeweg. **Morris** has suedes and leather on Leidsestraat; **Crabtree & Evelyn** has its usual array of fragrant soaps, sachets, and cosmetics; and **Shoe-Ba-Loo** has, you guessed it, a choice selection of shoes.

P. C. HOOFTSTRAAT & VAN BAERLESTRAAT

P. C. Hoofstraat (known locally as "P.C.," or "pay-say") is the Madison Avenue of Amsterdam, where well-dressed and well-coiffed Amsterdammers buy everything from lingerie to light bulbs. Along its three short blocks you'll find shops selling furniture, antiques, toys, shoes, chocolates, Persian rugs, designer clothes, fresh-baked bread and fresh-caught fish, china, books, furs, perfume, leather goods, office supplies, flowers, and jewelry. And around the corner on Van Baerlestraat are more boutiques, shoe shops, and enough branches of the major banks to guarantee that you can continue to buy as long as your traveler's checks hold out. Worth special mention are the Amsterdam branches of **Godiva Chocolatier, Pauw Boutique** (in five locations), **Daniel Hechter,** and **Kenzo;** two spots for children's clothes, **Pauw Junior** on van Baerlestraat, and three branches of **Hobbit, Rodier Paris, MacGregor,** and **Society Shop;** and for women's fashions, look for the shops of Holland's current crop of name designers, including **Edgar Vos, Frans Molenaar,** and **Tim Bonig,** plus **Rob Kroner, Jacques d'Ariege,** and, at the corner of Van Baerlestraat, **Azurro,** all of which catch a fashion mood and find an elegant compromise between haute couture and everyday living.

SPIEGELSTRAAT (NIEUWE SPIEGELSTRAAT TO SPIEGELGRACHT)

This is the antiques esplanade of Amsterdam, and although it covers only a short, four-block stretch of street-plus-canal, it's one of the finest antiques-hunting grounds in Europe. No wonder! At one end of this shopping street is the Rijksmuseum; at the other, the Golden Bend of the Herengracht canal, where Amsterdam's wealthiest burghers traditionally kept house. It seems that, now that their beautiful gabled homes have been turned over to banks and embassies, all the treasures they contained have simply found their way around the corner to the antiques shops. Among the items you might expect to see are dolls with china heads, rare editions of early children's books, Indonesian puppets, Persian tapestries and rugs, landscape paintings, prints, reproductions and modern art, brass Bible stands and candlesticks, copper kettles, music boxes, old Dutch clocks, and, of course, the little spiegels, or mirrors that give this street its name, and which the Dutch use beside upper-story windows to see who's knocking at their door.

OTHER SHOPPING STREETS/AREAS

For more antiques shops, look along the Prinsengracht between Leidsestraat and Westermarkt, or visit the **Kunst- & Antiekcentrum de Looier** (see "Shopping A to Z" below). For the up-and-coming funky boutiques of Amsterdam, look among the canals east and west of Dam Square, or in the nest of streets beyond the Westermarkt known as **the Jordaan.**

2 Shopping A to Z

Here, as a tip sheet from one shopper to another, is a selection of stores in Amsterdam you might not find otherwise. It can save you time and trouble with your shopping list or simply provide interesting shops to visit.

Antiques

A van der Meer, P. C. Hooftstraat 112. ☎ **673-41-15.**

For more than 30 years, A van der Meer has been a landmark amid the fashionable shops of P. C. Hooftstraat and a quiet place to enjoy a beautiful collection of antique maps, prints, and engravings. And 17th- and 18th-century Dutch world maps by the early cartographers Bleau, Hondius, and Mercator are a specialty. Also, there is a small collection of Jewish prints by Picart as well as 18th-century botanicals by Baptista Morandi and 19th-century works by Jacob Jung, mostly of roses, as well as 19th-century lithographs of hunting scenes by Harris. Open Monday through Saturday from 10am to 6pm.

⭐ **Kunst- & Antiekcentrum de Looier,** Elandsgracht 109. ☎ **624-90-38.**

This big indoor antiques market spreads through several old warehouses along the canals in the Jordaan. As in New York, London, and other cities, individual dealers rent small stalls and corners to show their best wares. The old armoires and other pieces of heavy Dutch traditional furniture are too large to consider buying, but many dealers also offer antique jewelry, prints and engravings, and the omnipresent Dutch knickknacks. Open Saturday through Wednesday from 11am to 5pm, Thursday to 9pm.

Premsela & Hamburger, Rokin 120. ☎ **624-96-88 or 627-54-54.**

On the Rokin, opposite the Allard-Pierson Museum is Premsela & Hamburger, fine jewelers and antique silver dealers in Amsterdam since 1823 and purveyors to the Dutch court. Inside their brocaded display cases and richly carved cabinets is a variety of exquisite and distinctive items. Here it's possible to find decorative modern and antique silver objects as well as Old Dutch silver fashioned by 17th-century craftsmen. Here you can feast your eye on an 18th-century perpetual calendar, a silver plaque depicting the entrance to an Amsterdam hospital, and a variety of sterling silverware. Their workshop can design, make, and repair jewelry. Recently a limited quantity of rings with symbols of love were cast and chased after an original dating back to around 1620. Purchase and delivery of these 18-karat gold love rings can be arranged at the Rokin shop. Open Monday through Friday from 9am to 5:30pm; on Sunday, by appointment only.

Art

Galleries abound in Amsterdam, particularly in the canal area near the Rijksmuseum; and a quick look at the listings of their exhibitions proves that Dutch painters are as prolific in the 20th century as they were in the golden age. The VVV Tourist Information Office publication *This Week* is your best guide to who is showing, where; your own eye and sense of value will be the best guide to artistic merit and investment value.

On the other hand, posters and poster reproductions of famous artworks are an excellent item to buy in Amsterdam. The Dutch are well known for their high-quality printing and color-reproduction work, and one of their favorite subjects is Holland's rich artistic treasure trove, foreign as well as domestic. Choose any of the three major art museums as a starting point for a search for an artistic souvenir, but if you like modern art—say, from the impressionists onward—you will be particularly delighted by the wide selection at the **Stedelijk Museum of Modern Art,** and if you particularly like van Gogh, the **Vincent van Gogh Museum** is another good source of reproductions. Or at **Het Rembrandthuis** you can buy a Rembrandt etching for Dfl 30 ($15.80) or Dfl 40 ($21.05) mounted; it's not an original, of course, but it is a high-quality modern printing produced individually, by hand, in the traditional manner from a plate that was directly and photographically produced from an original print in the collection of Rembrandthuis. Or for something simpler and cheaper to remind you of the great master, Het Rembrandthuis also sells mass-printed reproductions of the etchings, or small packets of postcard-size reproductions in sepia or black and white on a thick, fine-quality paper stock (including a packet of self-portraits).

Perhaps your interest is to have an artistic, rather than photographic, view of Amsterdam or the Dutch countryside. **Mattieu Hart,** which has been in its location on the Rokin since 1878, sells color etchings of Dutch cities.

Other galleries that hold contemporary as well as modern art, photography, sculpture, and African art are listed below.

★ **ABK Gallery for Sculpture,** Zeilmakersstraat 15.
☎ **625-63-32.**

This place is a cooperative gallery for Amsterdam sculptors. If you're particularly interested in the latest sculpture in Amsterdam, this is definitely the place to go. Call before you head out, since it's open only by appointment on Wednesday through Sunday from 1 to 6pm.

★ **Animation Art,** Borenstraat 39. ☎ **627-76-00.**

Got a favorite cartoon character? Well, Animation Art has original drawings and cell-paintings of all different kinds of cartoons. A fun place for the kid in everyone. Open Tuesday through Friday from 11am to 6pm and Saturday from 11am to 5pm.

Art Rages, Spiegelgracht 2a. ☎ **627-36-45.**

Here you'll find some interesting contemporary ceramics, glass, jewelry, and mixed-media pieces from all over Europe, as well as the United States and Canada. Open Monday through Saturday from 11am to 6pm.

Italiaander Galleries, Prinsengracht 526. ☎ **625-09-42.**

Here there's a permanent exhibition of African and Asian art, as well as all sorts of ethnic jewelry. Open Monday through Saturday from noon to 5:30pm.

Books

American Book Center, Kalverstraat 185. ☎ **625-55-37.**

You'll swear you never left the States when you see the array of best-sellers and paperbacks in the American Book Center on Kalverstraat near Munt Square. Plus, there are magazines (risqué and otherwise) and hardcover editions, hot off the presses. Prices are higher than you'd pay at home, but the selection beats any airport or hotel gift shop, with categories ranging from ancient civilizations, astrology, and baby care to science, science fiction, and war. If you think you'll buy a lot of books, you can buy a one-year discount card for Dfl 15 ($7.90) that allows 10% off; also, students and teachers can get 10% off simply by showing a school ID. Open Monday through Wednesday and Friday and Saturday from 10am to 8pm, Thursday from 10am to 10pm, and Sunday from 11am to 6pm.

★ **Athenaeum Booksellers,** Spuistraat 14–16. ☎ **622-62-48.**

You can't really miss this place if you're on the Spui. It's always crowded with book lovers, students, and scholars, and there are magazine stands on the sidewalk. Better known for its nonfiction collection, it has books in a number of different languages.

De Slegte, Kalverstraat 48–52. ☎ **622-59-33.**

You won't find too many books in English here—most are in Dutch or other languages—but you'll find some, and if you collect books as a hobby, you might run across a real gem. It's probably one of the biggest, most-often-visited bookstores in Amsterdam. Open Monday from 11am to 6pm, Tuesday through Friday from 9:30am to 6pm, and Saturday from 8am to 6pm.

The English Bookshop, Lauriergracht 71. ☎ **626-42-30.**

Located just on the edge of the Jordaan, this bookstore is small, but it has a wonderful selection of books in English (mainly fiction and biography). Occasionally you'll be able to find a great book at a discount. There's also a small selection of British magazines, including *Time Out,* a magazine that reports monthly on happenings in Amsterdam. Open Monday through Friday from 11am to 6pm and Saturday from 11am to 5pm.

⭐ **W. H. Smith,** Kalverstraat 152. ☎ **638-38-21.**

W. H. Smith is a chain in England that has a large stock of fiction and nonfiction titles. You'll probably be able to find almost anything you're looking for on one of the three floors here. Open Monday from 11am to 6pm, Tuesday and Saturday from 10am to 6pm, Wednesday and Friday from 9am to 6pm, Thursday from 9am to 9pm, and Sunday from 11am to 5pm.

Cigars, Pipes & Smoking Articles

Smokers know that Holland is one of the cigar-producing centers of the world; they also know that Dutch cigars are different, and drier, than Cuban or American smokes. It's partly because of the Indonesian tobacco and partly because of the way the cigar is made.

P. G. C. Hajenius, Rokin 92–96. ☎ **623-74-94.**

P. G. C. Hajenius has been the leading purveyor of cigars and smoking articles in Amsterdam since 1826, first with a store on Dam Square and then since 1915 in its present elegant headquarters. Their cigars are the specialty of the house, and there's a room full of Havanas, too. Hajenius also sells the long, uniquely Dutch, handmade clay pipes you see in the old paintings (a good gift idea), as well as ceramic pipes, some painted in the blue-and-white Chinese-inspired patterns of Delftware; plus you'll find lighters, cigarette holders, clippers, and flasks. Open Monday through Wednesday and Friday and Saturday from 9:30am to 6pm, Thursday until 9pm.

Delftware

Folke & Meltzer, P. C. Hooftstraat 65–67. ☎ **664-23-11.**

The best one-stop shop you'll find for authentic Delft Blue and Makkumware, as well as Hummel figurines, Leerdam crystal, and a world of other fine china, porcelain, silver, glass, or crystal products, is the main branch of Folke & Meltzer. Open Monday through Friday from 9:30am to 5:30pm and Saturday from 9:30am to 5pm.

Heinen, Prinsengracht 440, just off Leideestraat. ☎ **627-82-99.**

Unless you simply *have* to have the brand-name articles, you can save considerably on your hand-painted pottery and also have the fun of seeing the product made by visiting *Heinen.* Run by a father-son team who sit inside their canal-house window, quietly painting the days away in the age-old European tradition of master and apprentice, Heinen offers good quality and a good selection of useful, well-priced items. Best of all, Jaap (father) and Jorrit (son) both paint in five techniques: blue and white (Delft), polychrome (Makkum/multicolor), Japanese Imari, Kwartjes, (a modern-looking Delft with blue, red, and gold), and Sepia (brown and red). For an idea of prices: a delftware vase is Dfl 149 ($78.40), an Imari egg cup, Dfl 32.50 ($17.50); and a polychrome powder jar, Dfl 97.50 ($51.30). Open Monday from 11am to 6pm and Tuesday through Saturday from 9:30am to 6pm.

Department Stores —————————————————————————

De Bijenkorf, Dam 1. ☎ **621-80-80.**

Amsterdam's best-known department store, and the one with the best variety of goods, is De Bijenkorf. Ongoing expansion and renovation is gradually changing this once-frumpy little dry-goods emporium into Amsterdam's answer to New York's Bloomingdale's. You find the usual ranks of cosmetic counters holding down the center section of the ground floor, plus a men's department, and odds and ends such as socks and stockings, handbags and belts, costume jewelry, and stationery. And umbrellas—plenty of umbrellas! On upper floors you find everything from ladies' fashions to *dekbedden* (down comforters), plus a bookstore, several eating spots, and even a luggage section where you can pick up an extra suitcase or tote bag to take home purchases you make. Records, color TV sets, shoes, clothing, personal effects, appliances . . . it's all here. Open Monday from 11am to 6pm; Tuesday, Wednesday, and Friday from 9:30am to 6pm; Thursday from 9:30am to 9pm; and Saturday from 9am to 6pm.

Hema, Reguliersbreestraat 10. ☎ **624-65-06.**

Hema has all the merchandise you'd expect to find in a Woolworth store in the United States. You can get things like socks, toothbrushes, chocolate, cookies, and cheeses. If you can't figure out where to find it, your best bet is to look here. Open Monday from 11am to 6pm, Tuesday through Friday from 9:30am to 6pm, and Saturday from 9am to 6pm.

Metz & Co, Keizersgracht 455. ☎ **624-88-10.**

This dramatic store founded in 1740 is now owned by Liberty of London and sells furniture, fabrics, kitchenware, and other traditional department-store items. The cupola and café are worth stopping for. Open Monday from 11am to 6pm and Tuesday through Saturday from 9:30am to 6pm.

Vroom & Dreesman, Kalverstraat 201–221 and 212–224. ☎ **622-01-71.**

Less polished and pretentious, and highly successful as a result, is the Amsterdam branch of Vroom & Dreesman, a Dutch chain of department stores that pop up in key shopping locations wherever you go in Holland. Here you find V&D near the Muntplein. It's a no-nonsense sort of store with a wide range of middle-of-the-road goods and prices and services to match. Open Monday through Saturday from 9am to 6pm.

Fashions —————————————————————————————————

WOMEN'S

Paris may set the styles, but young Dutch women—and some of their mothers—often know better than the French how to make them work. Whatever the current European fashion rage is, you can expect to see it in shop windows all over Amsterdam, and in all price ranges. Some boutique faithfuls claim that they buy Paris designer fashions in Amsterdam at lower-than-Paris prices, but one quick check says that designer wear is still expensive, whether you pay in guilders, francs, or hard-earned dollars.

It's more fun to ferret out the new, young crop of Dutch designers who regularly open shops in unpredictable locations all over town. Although boutiques and their designers have a way of fading with the sunset as the tides of fashion change from dazzling to demure and back again, the current top names and locations along the Rokin are: **Carla V., Sheila de Vries, Jan Jensen** (shoes), and **Puck & Hans,** whose pseudo-Japanese look catches the eye as you walk along.

Maison de Bonneterie, Beethovenstraat 32. ☎ **676-11-91.**

Here you find exclusive women's fashions, as well as Gucci bags and Fieldcrest towels and a star-studded cast of brand names on household goods, and personal items.Open Monday from 1 to 5:30pm and Tuesday through Saturday from 10am to 5:30pm.

Peek and Cloppenburg, Dam 20. ☎ **623-26-37.**

Peek and Cloppenburg is a different sort of department store, or perhaps a better description is that P&C is an overgrown clothing store. Open Monday from noon to 6pm and Tuesday through Saturday from 9:30am to 6pm.

MEN'S

In addition to the department stores listed above, it's possible to find men's fashions at **Tie Rack,** Heiligeweg 7 (☎ **627-29-78**), and **Guus de Winter,** Linnaeusstraat 197 (☎ **694-02-52**).

CHILDREN'S

Children's stores are everywhere. Among them are **'t Hummeltje,** De Clercqustraat 122 (☎ **683-82-25**); **'t Schooltje,** Overtoom 87 (☎ **683-04-44**), with expensive but cute clothes for babies and children (well into the teen years); and the more affordable **Spetter Children's Fashion,** Van de Helstraat 58 le (☎ **671-62-49**).

Food & Wine

Jacob Hooy & Co., Kloveniersburgwal 12. ☎ **624-30-41.**

You'll feel you've stepped back into history if you visit Jacob Hooy & Co. This shop, opened in 1743 and operated for the past 130 years by the same family, is a wonderland of fragrant smells that offers more than 500 different herbs and spices, and 30 different teas, sold loose, by weight. Everything is stored in wooden drawers and wooden barrels with the names of the contents hand scripted in gold, and across the counter are fishbowl jars in racks containing 30 or more different types of *dropjes* (drops or lozenges) that range in taste from sweet to sour to salty. Open Monday from 1 to 6pm and Tuesday through Friday from 8:30am to 6pm.

★ **H. Keijzer,** Prinsengracht 180. ☎ **622-84-28.**

Specializing in coffee as well as tea, H. Keijzer was founded in 1839. Keijzer offers 90 different kinds of tea and 22 coffees at prices that change with the market and generally range from Dfl 4 ($2.10) to Dfl 16.50 ($8.70) per 100 grams. To try teas that are popular with the Dutch, consider taking home several 100-gram packets of teas from different parts of the tea-growing world: Ceylon Melange (or Delmar Melange), an English-style blend, from Sri Lanka; Darjeeling First Flush, from India; Yunnan, from China; and Java O.P. (Orange Pekoe), from Indonesia. Select from an assortment of tea boxes to make a nice gift; the small box that shows the store and other buildings and discreetly displays the company name and the words "sinds 1839" (since 1839) is Dfl 4.50 ($2.35). Open Monday through Friday from 8:30am to 5:30pm and Sautrday from 8:30am to 5pm.

Patisserie Pompadour, Huidenstraat 12. ☎ **623-95-54.**

The counter display here is amazing—close to 50 luscious pastries that can be enjoyed in this exquisite Louis XVI tearoom. Open Tuesday through Friday from 9am to 6pm and Saturday from 9am to 5pm.

H. P. de Vreng en Zonen, Nieuwendijk 75. ☎ **624-45-81.**

This distillery creates Dutch liqueurs and gins according to the old-fashioned methods, sans additives. Try the traditional Old Amsterdam jenever or some of the more flamboyantly colored liquids, like the brilliant green *Pruimpje prik in.* Some supposedly have aphrodisiac power. Open Monday through Friday from 9am to 6pm and Saturday from 9am to 5pm.

Markets

Amsterdammers are traders to the tips of their money-counting fingers, and nothing proves it more quickly than a visit to a street market. It's not that the Dutch will bargain for hours like a Moroccan in his souk, or follow you around a square pulling bigger and brighter samples from beneath a poncho like a bowler-hatted Ecuadorian. No, the Dutch street merchants prove they are incurable traders in a more stolid way—by their permanence. Many of Amsterdam's open-air salesmen are at their stalls, vans, tents, and barges 6 days a week, 52 weeks a year. They're as permanent as any rent payer. In all, there are more than 50 outdoor markets every week in Amsterdam and its outlying neighborhoods, and on any given day—except Sunday—you have a choice of several.

Besides the markets listed below, you may also enjoy visiting the **Textile Market** (at Noordermarkt, on Prinsengracht), held on Monday mornings; the **Garden Market** (at Amstelveld, on Prinsengracht near Vijzelstraat), also on Monday; and the **Stamp Market** (at the post office), held on Wednesday and Saturday afternoons. Finally, the **Bird Market** (at Noordermarkt, on Prinsengracht) is held on Saturday mornings.

★ **Albert Cuyp Markt,** Albert Cuypstraat.

You'll find just about anything and everything your imagination can conjure up at this market. All different types of foods, clothing, flowers, and plants, as well as textiles. The market houses 350 different stalls and is held six days a week.

Bookmarket, Spui.

Every Friday there's a book market held on the Spui. Usually, there are about 25 different booths that offer secondhand books. Often you can find some great books (in English)—perhaps even a rare book or two. Just about any subject is available, including many fiction and nonfiction titles.

Kunst- & Antiekcentrum de Looier, Elandsgracht 109.
☎ **624-90-38.**

This market is located in an old milk factory, and it's a lot of fun. You'll find some true antiques here, but, like any good "antiques" market, you'll also find an enormous number of curios, old paintings, glass, flatware, and toys that don't necessarily deserve the label "antique."

★ **Floating Flower Market,** on the Singel at the Muntplein.

A row of barges has permanently parked here to sell a selection of fresh-cut flowers, bright- and healthy-looking plants, ready-to-travel packets of tulip bulbs, and all the necessary accessories of home gardening. You'll find tulips that cost a few pennies less than at flower stands all over town—10 tulips for Dfl 6 to 7 ($3.15 to $5.25). But buying at the Singel flower market is as much a ritual as a bargain, and prices definitely beat the cost of fresh flowers at home.

Thorbecke Sunday Art Market, Thorbeckeplein.

This market runs from March through December. Local artists come and show their wares, putting them on display for sale. You'll find sculptures, paintings, jewelry, and mixed-media pieces. It's kind of nice on a Sunday afternoon (if it's not raining) to go and pick your way through and around the artists' tables here.

★ **Waterlooplein Flea Market,** Waterlooplein.

Waterlooplein is the classic market of Amsterdam, and perhaps of all Europe. It's often said that, before the war robbed the neighborhood of its most colorful citizens, you could find real antiques among the junk and possibly even a proverbial dusty Rembrandt. Today your luck is more apt to run in the opposite direction, but Dfl 10 ($5.25) isn't a bad price for an old record album, and Dfl 100 ($52.65) will buy a leather jacket to keep you warm if there's a change in the weather. Most of the merchants now work out of tents and sell *patates frites met mayonnaise* (french fries, eaten Dutch style, with mayonnaise) from vans that are a long way from the pushcarts of yesteryear, but you still find baseball jackets, cooking pots, mariner's telescopes, coal scuttles, bargain watches, nuts and bolts, and not-too-bad prints of Dutch cities. On Sunday in the summer (late May to the end of September), the junk goes away for a day and the antiques and books come in.

Ribbons, Laces, Tassels & Beautiful Buttons

Knopen Winkel, Wolvenstraat 14. ☎ **624-04-79.**

"The Button Shop," an amusing store in the canal area, stocks over 8,000 different buttons for a total stock of 50,000, plus or minus.

Prices range from Dfl 0.15 (10¢) to Dfl 20 ($10.50) per button, and buttons are sorted by color and displayed in specially designed cases around this tiny shop. There's also a special section of children's buttons, as well as sections for buttons of wood, leather, glass and metal, and pearl. Open Monday from 1 to 6pm, Tuesday through Friday from 11am to 6pm, and Saturday from 11am to 5pm.

H. J. van de Kerkhof Passementen, Wolvenstraat 9–11.
☎ **623-46-66.**

The walls of this store are filled with spools of ribbon and cord, and notebooks are filled with examples of patches and appliqués. There also are key tassels and tiebacks in all sizes (including very large/ "canal house" size) at prices ranging from Dfl 18 ($9.45) to Dfl 365 ($192.10) for the tassels, Dfl 7 ($3.70) to Dfl 3,000 ($1,578.95) for the tiebacks. Open Monday through Friday from 9am to 6pm and Saturday from 11am to 5pm.

9

Amsterdam Nights

NIGHTLIFE IN AMSTERDAM, LIKE AN INDONESIAN RIJSTTAFEL, IS A BIT OF THIS and a bit of that. The cultural calendar is full, but not jammed: There's a strong jazz scene, and the club and dance bar front proved to be amusing if not outrageous. I did hear a Leidseplein bartender lament that "the good nightlife is finished in Amsterdam," but I think your fun will depend on the scale and bent of your expectations. Yes, the grand nightclub shows are gone (it's rumored they will soon make a comeback). The dance clubs may indeed seem quiet and small to those used to the flash of clubs in New York or Los Angeles. However, the brown cafés—the typical Amsterdam pubs—have never been better, the ballet and opera seasons never more fully subscribed. The music clubs can be good fun, and the little cabarets and dusty theaters along the canals also can be counted on for English-language shows on a regular basis. Or there's always the movies, since Amsterdam is one of the few cities on the European continent where you can see first-run blockbuster hits from home with their English-language soundtracks intact. There's also another diversion in town—gambling.

A simpler evening pleasure in Amsterdam, one totally free of charge, is walking along the canals and looking into the houses as you pass. You may think I'm making the shocking suggestion that you spy on people, but in Amsterdam it's not spying, or even peeking. The Dutch live their lives as open books and take great pride in their homes; they keep their curtains open in the evening because they want you to see how tidy and *gezellig* (cozy, homey, warm, and inviting) their living quarters are. This doesn't mean that you're meant to linger on the sidewalk watching them, but a leisurely stroll past an Amsterdam canal house and a quick peek at the decor is quite all right. If you're reticent to engage in this Dutch national sport, look up to admire the elegant gables (illuminated in the summer months, April to October, from 30 minutes after sundown to 11:30pm), or look down to watch the flickering reflections of the street lamps on the canals. The evening hours are the magic time in Amsterdam; if nothing else has brought you around, a sparkling ripple on the water can make you fall hopelessly in love with the city.

Entertainment Orientation

AN INFORMATION SOURCE   Your best source of information on all the nightlife and cultural possibilities of Amsterdam is a publication called *What's On in Amsterdam.* It's the VVV Amsterdam Tourist Office's official bi-weekly program for visitors to the city. Many hotels have copies available for guests, or you can easily get one at the VVV Information Office (see Chapter 3 for addresses and hours). Also, look around town for *Time Out,* a newspaper, and *Uitgaan,* a magazine; they're in Dutch, but together constitute a complete cultural guide to Amsterdam; day by day, with listings for concerts and recitals, theater, cabaret, opera, dance performances, rock concerts, art films, and film festivals. They also provide a complete review of who is showing, when, in all of Amsterdam's art galleries. Perhaps the best reason for picking up *Time Out* is that it also lists which buses or trams to take to get to the various theaters.

TICKETS   If you want to attend any of Amsterdam's theatrical or musical events (including rock concerts), make it your first task on arrival to get tickets; box office information is given below, or you can also arrange tickets through the VVV Tourist Information Offices (see Chapter 3 for addresses and hours); they charge Dfl 5 ($2.65) for the service.

HOURS & PERFORMANCE TIMES   Concert, theater, opera, and dance performances generally begin at 8:15pm; jazz concerts begin at 11 or 11:30pm. Jazz clubs and music spots are usually open from 10pm to 2am, and as late as 4am on weekends. Dance clubs open at 9pm and close at 4am, 5am on weekends.

DRINK PRICES   With the exception of the dance clubs, nightclubs, and other high-ticket nightspots in Amsterdam, you can expect to pay Dfl 2.50 to 5 ($1.30 to $2.65) for a beer or a Coke and Dfl 3 to 5 ($1.55 to $2.65) for *jenever* (Dutch gin, the national drink; try it at least once, *without* ice). To order your favorite whisky and water will probably cost you at least Dfl 6 ($3.15), and a mixed cocktail can be as much as Dfl 11 ($5.80). But, remember, these are average prices around town; the cost at a brown café (pub) could be less, a hotel bar could charge more.

SAFETY   Whenever and wherever you wander in Amsterdam—and particularly after dark—it's wise to be mindful of your surroundings. Amsterdam is a big city with big city problems, and its population is as mixed in demeanor and proclivity as the cast of a Fellini movie. Fortunately, Amsterdam's less desirable citizens tend to congregate in the less desirable neighborhoods, and none of the nightspots described here is in a "problem area" (although taxis are advised in a few cases). You're on your own if you venture off the main thoroughfares, and remember that there are no cruising taxis in Amsterdam. Your best bet if you begin to feel uneasy is to find a restaurant or brown café and ask to use the phone; the numbers you need are **677-77-77** to call a taxicab or **622-22-22** to call the police.

---

1 The Performing Arts

Orchestras & Opera Companies

In addition to perusing the well-filled schedule of the Concertgebouw (see below), check the listings in *What's On in Amsterdam*. There you may find information on concerts in special Amsterdam buildings, including Beurs van Berlage, the former home of the Amsterdam Beurs (Stock Exchange). What was once the trading floor is now a concert hall where you can see performers such as the Netherlands Chamber Orchestra or the Netherlands Philharmonic Orchestra, fondly known as NedPho, which has made its home here for several years.

Koninklijk Concertgebouworkest (Royal Concertgebouw Orchestra), in the Concertgebouw, Concertgebouwplein 2–6. ☎ **671-83-45.**

Music in Amsterdam is focused around one world-famous orchestra—the Royal Concertgebouw Orchestra—based in the Concertgebouw, an elegant, colonnaded, and newly refurbished building with a sculpted lyre on its rooftop.

Admission: Tickets, Dfl 10–150 ($5.25–$78.95).

De Nederlandse Opera (Netherlands Opera Society), Het Muziektheater, Waterlooplein 22. ☎ **625-54-55.**

Another enjoyable way to spend an evening in Amsterdam during the musical season (September through March) is to hear an opera performed by the Netherlands Opera Society, whose productions of classics dominate the schedule of the Muziektheater. Although less illustrious internationally than the Royal Concertgebouw Orchestra or either of Holland's major dance companies, the Netherlands Opera has its own well-known performers and devoted following of opera lovers.

Admission: Tickets, Dfl 10–180 ($5.25–$94.75).

Dance Companies

Besides the Muziektheater (which hosts the dance companies listed below), dance performances are also occasionally held in other theaters in Amsterdam, including **Felix Meritis**, Keizersgracht 324, below Leidsestraat (☎ **626-23-21**), and **Studio Danslab**, Overamstelstraat 39 (☎ **694-94-66**). Check *What's On . . .* for listings.

Het Nationale Ballet (Dutch National Ballet), Het Muziektheater, Waterlooplein 22. ☎ **625-54-55.**

As every dance lover knows, a mania for ballet and dance in all forms is sweeping the world. One of the surprises to some people is to see so many Dutch names among those of the dance world's rising stars. But the Dutch aren't surprised, and take pride in the increasing popularity and prestige of this major dance company. To find out if it will be possible to see this company perform while you're in Amsterdam, check the listings in *What's On, Time Out,* or *Uitgaan;* ask at the VVV Tourist Information Office; or go directly to the theater, open Monday through Saturday from 10am to 8pm and Sunday from 11:30am to 8pm.

Admission: Tickets, Dfl 17.50–50 ($9.20–$26.30).

Nederlands Dans Theater (Netherlands Dance Theater), Het Musiektheater, Amstel 3 at Waterlooplein. ☎ **625-54-55.**

This dance company is one of the best in Holland. The Czechoslovakian artistic director/choreographer, Jiří Kylián, has enjoyed great success during his 18-year tenure with the Dance Theater, helping to give the company a solid reputation throughout Europe. In fact, the Dance Theater now consists of three companies: NDT 1, the main company; NDT 2, for dancers under 21; and NDT 3, a ground-breaking, elite corps of older dancers. The theater's box office is open Monday through Saturday from 10am to 8pm and Sunday from 11:30am to 8pm.

Admission: Tickets, Dfl 17.50–50 ($9.20–$26.30)

Major Concert Halls & All-Purpose Auditoriums

Concertgebouw, Concertgebouwplein 2–6. ☎ **671-83-45.**

The Concertgebouw, which means "concert building," is one of the most acoustically perfect concert halls in the world. Throughout both the musical season (September through March) and the annual Holland Festival, the world's greatest orchestras, ensembles, conductors, and soloists regularly travel to Amsterdam to perform. The richness of tone possible in this building surely is as much a pleasure for the performer as for the audience. Concerts and recitals are scheduled every day of the week during the season and often there's a choice of two programs at the same time on the same evening, one performed in the famous Grote Zaal, or Great Hall, and the other in a smaller recital hall, the Kleine Zaal, or Little Hall. Given a choice, treat yourself to the rich and unparalleled experience of great music in a nearly perfect acoustical setting, and don't worry about the location of your seat. The Concertgebouw Grote Zaal is an almost-unobstructed space in which every seat has a clear view. It's even possible to sit on the stage, behind the performers; tonal perfection is slightly altered there, however, so seats are cheaper as a result. In addition to the Concertgebouw Orchestra, you might be able to hear international orchestras and such artists as Jessye Norman, Kathleen Battle, or Yo-Yo Ma.

The box office is open daily from 9:30am to 7pm for advance tickets, to 8pm for same-day tickets; phone orders from 10am to 3pm only. Ticket prices vary according to seat location and program.

Admission: Tickets, Dfl 20–200 ($10.50–$105.25).

Muziektheater, Waterlooplein 22. ☎ **625-54-55.**

When it's not hosting the Netherlands National Ballet or the Netherlands Dance Theater, the Muziektheater offers a special treat during the concert season—musical lunches. These are free 30-minute concerts offered on Wednesday at 12:30pm (doors open at 12:15pm).

Admission: Tickets to most events, Dfl 15–50 ($7.90–$26.30), free to musical lunches.

The Major Concert & Performance Halls

Concertgebouw, Concertgebouwplein 2–6 (☎ **671-83-45**).

Felix Meritis, Keizersgracht 324 (☎ **623-13-11**).

De Melkweg, Lijnbaansgracht 234 (☎ **624-17-77**).

Muziektheater, Waterlooplein 22 (☎ **625-54-55**).

Théâter Carré, Amstel 115–125 (☎ **622-52-25**).

Theaters

Amsterdammers speak English so well that Broadway road shows and English-language touring companies (such as the Young Vic company) often make Amsterdam a stop on their European itineraries (check *What's On . . .*, *Time Out*, or *Uitgaan* for listings. Broadway and London musicals also come to Amsterdam from time to time.

It's not out of the question that you'll find a production of Shakespeare's *As You Like It* or Agatha Christie's *The Mouse Trap* here, but don't count on it: Many of the theatergoing opportunities in Amsterdam are experimental and avant-garde.

Royal Théâtre Carré, Amstel 115–125. ☎ **622-52-25.**

Look for touring shows on the schedule at the Royal Théâtre Carré. Recently, *Les Misérables* had a run there. *The Phantom of the Opera, Miss Saigon,* and *Cats* were also on the 1994 schedule. But get your tickets as far in advance as possible—the hot shows sell out quickly. Box office is open Monday through Saturday from 10am to 7pm and Sunday from 1 to 7pm.

Admission: Tickets, Dfl 30–80 ($15.80–$42.10)

Melkweg, Lijnbaansgracht 234a. ☎ **624-17-77.**

De Melkweg means "milky way" in Dutch, and so the people who in 1970 brought theater to this building named it in tribute to its past—it had been a dairy factory. Its organizers have always embraced liberalism and experimentalism, and so the theater showcases new groups—international, as well as local. You might find comedy, multicultural, or gay and lesbian theater here; Melkweg also has a dance club and movie theater, both of which are a smart bet for a good time.

Admission: Tickets, Dfl 12–35 ($6.30–$18.40).

Dinner Theater

Lido, Max Euweplein 64.

Located near the Leidseplein, Lido offers a dinner show every Thursday, Friday, and Saturday night (and in summer, also on Wednesday). Before the show, you'll choose from among three different dinner menus: Menu Spectacle, a four-course dinner; Menu Lido, a four-course dinner with four glasses of wine, coffee, and assorted chocolates; and Menu Jacquart, a four-course dinner with half a bottle of champagne, coffee, and assorted chocolates. The restaurant is open at 7pm, and dinner begins at about 8pm.

Admission: Prices vary according to dinner, Dfl 150–260 ($78.95–$136.85).

2 The Club & Music Scene

Rock & Pop

Nothing changes faster in Holland—or exhibits more variety—than the pop music scene, whether rock, reggae, new wave, or whatever comes along to be the next craze. Performers en route to (or from) world-class stardom always seem to turn up in Amsterdam (or Rotterdam, or Leiden, or Utrecht), and few of them have difficulty selling out. Big stars and large-scale productions—Diana Ross or Charles Aznavour—occasionally perform at **Théâter Carré,** Amstel 115–125 (☎ **622-52-25**), or, in the case of rock stars, at Fijenoord Stadium or the Ahoy Congress Hall, both of which are in Rotterdam.

The two best sources of information about who might be appearing in Amsterdam while you're there is *Time Out* or *What's On. . . .*

Jazz & Blues

Jazz, Dixieland, and rhythm and blues may be American musical forms, but Europeans—and certainly the Dutch—have adopted them with gusto. July is the best month of the year for a jazz lover to travel to Europe. That's when three major festivals are scheduled almost back-to-back in France, Switzerland, and Holland, including the three-day **North Sea Jazz Festival,** P.O. Box 87840, 2508 DE, The Hague (☎ **070/350-16-04**), held each year at the Congresgebouw in The Hague. It's a convention of the biggest names in the international jazz world, with more than 100 concerts—involving more than 600 artists—scheduled in 10 halls in three days.

Described below are a few of the jazz hangouts that dot Amsterdam's cityscape.

Alto Jazz Café, Korte Leidsedwarsstraat 115. ☎ **626-32-49.**

There's a regular crowd and a regular quartet that plays jazz nightly in this small, comfortable café. It's open Sunday through Thursday from 9pm to 3am and on Friday and Saturday from 9pm to 4am.
Admission: Free.

Bimhuis, Oudeschans 73–77. ☎ **623-13-61.**

Near the harbor, this theater regularly features European and American artists. The atmosphere is relaxed and serious about jazz. You'll neither feel that you can't have a conversation nor struggle to hear the music. It offers a regular schedule of concerts. This is one spot where it pays to take a cab—it's far away and hard to find.
Admission: Free Mon and Wed, Dfl 10–20 ($5.25–$10.50) Tues and Thurs–Sun.

Bourbon Street, Leidsekruisstraat 6–8. ☎ **623-34-40.**

Bourbon Street is a wonderful little jazz place. It hosts local talent as well as guests from the States and elsewhere. Sometimes there's a cover charge for better-known jazz groups or musicians. The music plays well into the night; the place is open Sunday through Thursday from 10pm to 4am and on Friday and Saturday from 10pm to 5am.
Admission: Free most nights, but call ahead to be sure.

Rum Runners, Prinsengracht 277. ☎ **627-40-79.**

Rum Runners (see Chapter 5 for details) features live jazz on Sunday. It's located between the Westerkerk and the Anne Frankhuis. You can't really miss it. It's open Monday through Thursday from 4pm to 1am, on Friday from 4pm to 2am, on Saturday from noon to 2am, and on Sunday from noon to 1am.
Admission: Free.

Dance Clubs

For local residents, the club scene in Amsterdam is generally a "members only" situation. But as a tourist, you can simply show up and, as long as your attire and your behavior suit the sensibilities of the management, and you're willing to pay the price of admission—typically Dfl 12 ($6.30)—you shouldn't have any problems getting past the bouncer. Drinks can be expensive, to be sure—a beer or Coke averages Dfl 7 ($3.70), and a whisky or cocktail, Dfl 14 ($7.35)— but you can nurse one drink along while you dance your feet off, or down a quick beer if the crowd or the music mix is not your style.

The places listed below are those that are most popular at press time. Don't hesitate to ask around for new places once you get to Amsterdam. Of course, you can always consult the trusty *What's On* . . . for listings.

Melkweg, Lijnbaansgracht 234. ☎ **624-17-77.**

Melkweg, the old dairy factory described above, is a multipurpose venue that also houses a club. One of my favorites, and the most interesting club around, it houses a dance floor, theater, and movie theater, all on three different floors. Admission to clubs is often extremely difficult—here you must pay for a temporary membership before they'll let you in, but believe me, it's worth it!

Admission: Dfl 7.50–25 ($3.95–$13.15) plus Dfl 5 ($2.65) monthly club membership.

Paradiso, Weteringschans 6–8. ☎ **623-73-48.**

Paradiso is located in an old church, and presents an eclectic variety of music, mostly Latin and African. You might not want to go in initially, but the inside is bright, and you might catch some great acts before they become really famous. It isn't open every day, but hours are usually between 8pm and 2am. Call for exact days and times while you're in town.

Admission: Dfl 8.50–19.50 ($4.45–$10.25).

Roxy, Singel 465–467. ☎ **620-03-54.**

The Roxy is one of the hippest, trendiest places in Amsterdam. The membership policy is extremely strict, so it might be difficult for you to get in. Some nights, however, the rules for admittance are dropped and anyone can enter. It has been said that the Roxy was the first club in Amsterdam to play house music, so it's understandable that it has gained a reputation for being "the place to be." The decor changes every month. Open on Wednesday, Thursday, and Sunday from 11pm to 4am, and on Friday and Saturday from 11pm to 5am.

Admission: Dfl 8–15 ($4.20–$7.90).

World Music

World music is the name that has been given to a kind of dance-oriented music that blends elements of musical traditions from all over the globe, and it's extremely popular with Amsterdammers. Some of the places at which you can go to hear music with roots in India, Turkey, Portugal, Brazil, a host of African nations, and more are **Akhnaton,** Nieuwezijds Kolk 25 (☎ **624-33-96**); **Paradiso,** Weteringschans 6–8 (☎ **623-73-48**); and **Soeterijn,** Linnaeusstraat 2 (☎ **568-82-00**). If you're not too interested in the rock dance-club scene, world music might be a fun and educational alternative. You'll find more information about what's going on where in *What's On.* . . .

3 The Bar Scene

Brown Cafés

Whoever has sipped a frothy beer has heard of the Dutch talent for brewing the stuff. But you haven't really tasted Dutch beer until you've tasted it in Holland, served Dutch style in a real *bruine kroeg,* or brown café. Although it's unfair to all three institutions to say that a brown café is the Amsterdam equivalent of a London pub or your neighborhood bar at home, at least this comparison helps you to anticipate the camaraderie you'll encounter and appreciate the unpolished environment of a place where pouring another beer is much more important than dusting off the back bottles on the bar. And it's the Dutch beer-pouring process you go to a brown café to see: It's a remarkable ritual of drawing a beer to get as much foam as possible and then using a wet knife to shave the head between a series of final fill-ups.

Even if you're not a beer lover, venturing into a brown café in Amsterdam will give you a peek into the everyday life of the city. You'll find brown cafés on almost every corner in the old neighborhoods of the city, and you can't miss them. Most have lacy curtains on the bottom half of the window, and perhaps a cat will be sleeping in the sun on the ledge (even if it has a name, it surely will be called simply *pussje,* little kitty). In winter the front door will be hung with a thick drape to keep out drafts, and you may find it still there long into spring. There will be no mistaking you've found the right place once you're inside; the smoky, mustard brownness of the interior is unique to an Amsterdam brown café, the result of years—no, centuries—of thick smoke and heated conversation. There may be booths or little tables sprinkled around the place, but the only spots of color and light are sure to be the shining metal of the beer tap and, perhaps, a touch of red still showing in the Persian rugs thrown across the tables (that's typically Dutch, if you recall the old paintings) to catch *tosti* crumbs and soak up beer foam. You'll feel the centuries of conviviality the minute you walk in the door of a really old, really *brown* brown café, and indeed some have been on their corners since Rembrandt's time. The best of them are on the Prinsengracht, below Westermarkt, at Dam Square, at Leidseplein, on Spui, or with a bit of looking, on tiny streets between the canals.

Besides my favorites listed below, here are some other brown cafés to seek out: **De Engelbewaarder,** Kloveniersburgal 59 (☎ **625-37-72**); **Café Eijlders,** Korte Leidsedwarsstraat

47 (☎ **624-27-04**); **Het Molenpad,** Prinsengracht 653 (☎ **625-96-80**); **Papeneiland,** Prinsengracht 2 (☎ **624-19-89**); and **Pieper,** Prinsengracht 424 (☎ **626-47-75**).

Café Bern, Nieuwmarkt 9. ☎ 622-00-34.

This popular brown café is famous for its cheese fondue and the arty crowd it attracts.

Café Chris, Bloemstraat 42. ☎ 624-59-42.

This brown café is said to be the place where the builders of Westerkerk were paid every week or two. Opened in 1624, Café Chris has been going strong ever since. There are a lot of curious old features to this bar that keep drawing people year after year, including the flushing system of the toilet in the bathroom—it flushes from outside the door.

Café de Druif, Rapenburg 83. ☎ 624-45-30.

This is one of those places that not too many people know about. De Druif ("The Grape") is located on the waterfront, and is mainly frequented by a friendly local crowd. The bar's mythology has it that the Dutch naval hero, Piet Heyn, was a frequent patron (he lived nearby); however, as happens so often when good beer is at hand, this seems to be a tall tale come of wishful thinking—the bar opened in 1631 and Heyn died in 1629.

Café Hoppe, Spuistraat 18–20. ☎ 623-78-49.

"Standing Room Only" is often the space situation here—the crowds sometimes even overflow out onto the street. It seems that, quite by accident, the Hoppe has become a tourist attraction. Locals love this spot, which dates from 1670, and often stop on their way home for a drink. It's worth stopping by just to see it.

Café Karpershoek, Martelaarsgracht 2. ☎ 624-78-86.

Opened in 1629, this bar was a favorite hangout of sailors and seamen. As it was in the 17th century, the floor is covered with sand.

Café 't Smalle, Egelantiersgracht 12. ☎ 623-96-17.

Opened by Pieter Hoppe in 1786 as a liquor distillery and tasting house, Café 't Smalle is a wonderfully cozy spot in which you're highly unlikely to get a seat, or even *see* one. If you really want the brown café experience, you should at least try to stop in.

In de Wildeman, Kolksteeg 3. ☎ 638-23-48.

In a medieval alley, this wood-paneled tavern lit by brass is loaded with atmosphere. The tile floor and rows of bottles and jars behind the counters are remnants from its earlier days, when it functioned as a pharmacy. Today its serves 150 kinds of beer.

Tasting Houses

The only differences between a brown café and a *proeflokaal,* or tasting house, are what one customarily drinks, how it's drunk, and who owns the place. The decor will still be basically brown and typically Old Dutch—and the age of the establishment may be even more impressive than that of its beer-swilling neighbors—but in a tasting house you will traditionally order jenever (Dutch gin, taken "neat," without ice) or another product of the distillery that owns the *proeflokaal.* Then, to drink your choice of libation, custom and ritual decree that you lean over the bar, with your hands behind your back, to take the first sip from your well-filled *borreltje* (small drinking glass).

De Drie Fieschjes, Gravenstraat 18. ☎ **624-84-43.**

Tidy and charming, this tasting house ("The Three Little Bottles") is located behind the Nieuwe Kerk. Since 1816 Heindrik Bootz liquors have been tasted here. The place is crowded with a diverse group of locals who will be more than happy to chat with you while you toss back a taste or two. Don't be afraid to ask for the local opinion on what's good. Open from noon to 8pm.

Café de Dokter, Rozemboomsteg 4. No phone.

Near Spui, the main square of the Student Quarter, is "The Little Doctor," an antique-filled tasting house. Ask to sample the homemade boeren jongen and boeren meisjes, the brandied fruits—raisins and apricots—that are traditional introductions to "spirits" for Dutch *jongen* and *meisjes,* boys and girls.

D'Admiral, Herengracht 319. ☎ **624-84-43.**

Along the canal and near Oude Spiegelstraat, this tasting house has a small and pleasant sort of outdoor café patio that's a joy in the summer months. There are also sofas and big comfortable armchairs. Open Monday through Friday from noon to midnight and on Saturday from 5pm to midnight.

A Wine & Sherry Bar

Continental Bodega, Lijnbaansgracht 246. ☎ **623-90-98.**

Another variation on the theme of drinking Dutch, and one step closer to a class act, is this wine and sherry bar where three-piece suits—his and hers—replace the dark-blue cotton work clothes of a brown café and conversation runs to witty asides more readily than to the latest bawdy joke. This cozy, cask-lined warehouse near the Leidseplein is regularly abuzz from 4pm to midnight.

Cocktails with a View

Ciel Blue Bar, in the Hotel Okura Amsterdam, Ferdinand Bolstraat 175. ☎ **678-71-11.**

Even a low-profile city like Amsterdam has a high-rise hotel with a rooftop cocktail lounge, located on the 23rd floor. The drink prices are a little higher than what you'll find when you've got your feet firmly on the ground, but the view is probably worth the cost: From a comfortable vantage point in Amsterdam South, the sweeping panorama takes in the city's residential neighborhoods, the river, and the harbor. Ciel Blue is a particularly enchanting place to be in the evening, when the sun is setting and the lights are beginning to twinkle on in the houses near the hotel. Open daily from 6pm to 1am.

Gay & Lesbian Bars

The gay scene in Amsterdam is quite large, a fact reflected in the number of gay bars and nightspots in town. Below you'll find listings of some of the most popular spots for gay men.

For lesbians, the scene is a little more difficult to discern. Rather than listing places that are hot now and might not be later, you'd be better off to call or visit **COC,** Rozenstraat 14 (☎ **626-30-87**), and ask.

For both gay men and lesbians, the *Use It* guide, which is available at the VVV Tourist Information Center, has listings for the day's most popular bars, clubs, and discos.

Amstel Taveerne, Amstelstraat 54. ☎ 623-42-54.

This is one of the oldest and most traditional gay bars in Amsterdam. It's one of those places where about an hour after happy hour everyone starts singing popular songs. Although the songs are in Dutch, the crowd welcomes visitors from other countries, so don't be intimidated. Open Sunday through Thursday from 4pm to 1am and Friday and Saturday from 3pm to 2am.

Admission: Free.

Café April, Reguliersdwarsstraat 37. ☎ 625-95-72.

It is said that almost every gay visitor to Amsterdam goes to the Café April at least once, so you're likely to make friends that hail from all over the world. A nice light menu is served. April's Exit, at Reguliersdwarsstraat 42 (☎ **625-87-88**), is close by, and many people from the Café April head over after happy hour. Open Sunday through Thursday from 2pm to 1am and Friday and Saturday from 2pm to 2am.

Admission: Free.

C-Ring, Warmoesstraat 96. ☎ 623-96-04.

Probably the most popular gay bar in town for men under 45. The music varies, and there's a video room. Open Sunday through Thursday from 10pm to 4am and Saturday from 10pm to 5am.

Admission: Free.

It, Amstelstraat 24. ☎ 625-01-11.

If you're interested in a place that attracts gay men, lesbians, and straight people, this is the place for you. The crowd is young, and the music is young—house music is popular here. There are sometimes drag shows, and there's a room that's quieter and more conducive to conversation. Open Thursday and Sunday from 11pm to 4am and Friday and Saturday from 10pm to 5am.

Admission: Free.

4 More Entertainment

EVENING CANAL-BOAT RIDES

Even if you took the daytime canal-boat ride through the canals of Amsterdam, come back for cocktails or dinner. There are special two-hour candlelight wine-and-cheese cruises that operate nightly year-round, except for December 31. Wine and cheese are served as you glide through the now-quiet canal district. It's a leisurely, convivial, and romantic way to spend an evening in Amsterdam. Or join the three-hour dinner cruise, nightly from April to November, Tuesday and Friday nights from November to April. Boats depart from the Holland International Pier at Prins Hendrikkade 33a, opposite Centraal Station. Operators are Holland International (% 622-77-88) and Key Tours (% 524-73-04). The two-hour cruise costs Dfl 46 ($24.20), the dinner cruise, Dfl 145 ($76.30) ($75). Reservations are necessary.

FILM

After a day of trudging to the sights, you may want to flop down in the nearest movie theater for a bit of stationary adventure. In most European cities it's either difficult or impossible to find a theater showing undubbed American and British films, whereas in Amsterdam you can probably find a dozen or more first-run features in English. Best of all, most of them will be shown at a theater on or near the Leidseplein, including the City Cinema, which has seven theaters in one building. Hotels post the *Uitlist,* which includes movie listings; for art films and film festivals, check the listings in *Time Out* or *Uitgaan.* Movie admission prices in Amsterdam are generally Dfl 10 to 20 ($5.25–$10.50), and tickets can be reserved in advance for a small charge. Don't worry if you're a few minutes late getting to your seat: A long string of commercials always precedes the feature.

The following are among the major movie houses of Amsterdam, which are conveniently located and frequently show first-run American films: **Alfa 1, 2, 3, and 4,** Kleine Gartmanplantsoen 4a, at Leidseplein (☎ **627-88-06**); **Alhambra 1 and 2,** Weteringschans 134, near Frederiksplein (☎ **623-31-92**); **Bellevue Cinerama,** Marnixstraat 400, near Leidseplein (☎ **623-48-76**); **Calypso 1 and 2,** Marnixstraat 402 (☎ **626-62-27**); **City 1-2-3-4-5-6-7,** Kleine Gartmanplantsoen 13–25, off Leidseplein (☎ **623-45-79**); and **Tuschinski 1-2-3-4-5-6,** Reguliersbreestraat 26–28, between Muntplein and Rembrandtsplein (☎ **626-26-33**).

Note: If all of a sudden there's a break in the film, don't fret over-much; it will last about 15 minutes, and it's called a *pauze.*

CASINOS

Gambling is a big attraction in Holland, and Amsterdam's casino is the **Lido,** Max Euweplein 64 (☎ **620-10-06**), near Leidseplein. There are casinos in other major cities as well, including the beach resort town of Zandvoort, near Haarlem, where the Dutch government opened Holland's first casino in 1976 (just 30 minutes by car or by train from Centraal Station). This is European gambling, with emphasis on the quiet games of roulette, baccarat, and blackjack, although the one-armed bandits, which the Dutch call "fruit machines," as well as blackjack, poker, and bingo machines (start

saving your guilder coins!) are in the casinos. You'll need correct attire to go into a casino in Holland (jacket and tie or turtleneck for
men). The minimum age to gamble is 18, and you'll need to bring
your passport to register at the door. Casinos are open from 2pm to
2am (to 3am in Amsterdam).

10

Easy Excursions from Amsterdam

Amsterdam is the bright star of a small galaxy of cities and towns that together form a conurbation the Dutch call the Randstad, or Rim City. The area offers a number of interesting possibilities for a day outside the city. It won't be a day in the country—not really—but you can see tulips, windmills, and cheese markets or take your choice of half a dozen museums of art and history. You can visit sites associated with the Pilgrims (who lived in Holland for years before sailing on the *Mayflower*) and tour the world's largest harbor. You can climb tall towers and view museums filled with music boxes and barrel organs, ride a steam train, eat fish at harbor side, and see giant locks and tiny canals. The area around Amsterdam is an introduction to the variety Holland offers its visitors.

You can't see everything in one day, but you can easily visit two, possibly three, cities if you get an early start. Several popular city combinations are The Hague and Rotterdam; Haarlem, Leiden, and The Hague; Rotterdam and Gouda; and Aalsmeer and Utrecht.

Excursions Orientation

BUS TOURS The major sightseeing companies of Amsterdam offer a wide variety of half- and full-day tours into the surrounding area, particularly between April and October; plus, there are special excursions offered at tulip time and at the height of the summer season (see the following pages for information on most destinations named here).

Two tours offered year-round are the "Grand Holland Tour," an 8- to 8^1/$_2$-hour drive that includes the Aalsmeer flower auction, The Hague and Scheveningen, Delft, and Rotterdam; and "Volendam and Marken," a 3^1/$_2$-hour trip to see the costumed villagers and their decorated houses, with a stop at a cheese farm along the way. An additional tour that generally is available during tulip time (early April to mid-May) is "Fabulous Flower Fields and Keukenhof," a 3^1/$_2$-hour drive through the bulb-growing district with a stop at the Keukenhof floral exhibition.

Tours generally available only between April and October (and varying dates in between) are "Delft and The Hague," a 4^1/$_2$-hour trip; "The Enclosing Dike and Zuiderzee," an 8-hour drive across the Enclosing Dike and around the IJsselmeer (IJssel Lake, formerly the Zuiderzee, an inland sea); "Windmills and Edam," a 3^1/$_4$-hour tour via Zaans Schans to Edam (a cheese town, no market); and "Alkmaar and Hoorn" (Friday only), a 4^1/$_2$-hour trip to visit the cheese market and 17th-century port of Hoorn.

The major Amsterdam-based sightseeing companies—all of which offer the same selection of tours at essentially the same prices—are **Holland International,** Damrak 7 (☎ **625-30-35**); **Key Tours,** Dam Square 19 (☎ **624-73-04**); and **Lindbergh,** Damrak 26 (☎ **622-27-66**). Prices for half-day tours are Dfl 28 to 40 ($14.75 to $21.05), and for full-day tours, Dfl 62 to 68 ($32.65–$35.80), children ages 13 and under are charged half fare, and children under 4 travel free.

CAR & CAMPER RENTAL To rent a car for an excursion outside Amsterdam you can expect to pay Dfl 45 to 85 ($23.70 to $44.75) per day plus Dfl 0.33 to 0.50 (15¢ to 25¢) per kilometer for a car with a stick shift and no frills such as a Renault 5, Ford Fiesta, or similar; or as much as Dfl 265 ($139.45) per day plus Dfl 1.08 (55¢) per kilometer for a fully equipped luxury car such as a Volvo 850. Plus gas, plus insurance, plus a whopping tax of 18.5%.

Unlimited-mileage/kilometerage rates represent a savings if you plan to do extensive wandering or want to keep the car long enough to make several successive excursions from Amsterdam, but some car-rental companies in Holland offer this option only with a minimum rental of seven days or more. During the winter season some Amsterdam firms offer special short-term unlimited-mileage plans.

By calling around you'll find that rates vary among companies, as do the makes or models of vehicles offered and the rental plans available, and the services you can expect in connection with your rental (such as free delivery to your hotel). Shop until you find the car—and the deal—that best suits your plans.

The major car-rental firms with offices in Amsterdam and, in some cases, with car pick up and return desks at Amsterdam's Schiphol Airport, are **ai/ANSA International,** Hobbemakade 6–7 (☎ **664-82-52**); **Avis,** Nassaukade 380 (☎ **683-60-61**); **Budget,** Overtoom 121 (☎ **612-60-66**); **Amcar,** Jacob Obrechtplein 13–15 (☎ **662-42-14**); **Europcar,** Overtoom 51–53 (☎ **618-45-95**); **Hertz,** Overtoom 333 (☎ **612-24-41**); **Autorent Kaspers & Lotte,** van Ostadestraat 232–234 (☎ **671-70-66**); and **Van Wijk,** Stromarkt 5 (☎ **526-23-95**). To rent a camper, if that idea appeals, call **Braitman & Woudenberg,** Droogbak 4 (☎ **622-11-68**), or **A-Point,** Kollenbergweg 11 (☎ **696-49-64**).

TRAIN SERVICES With a few exceptions, you can easily travel by train to the cities and towns described in this chapter and, once there, walk or take public transportation to the sights mentioned. Dutch cities are not large and railroad stations are located within a few blocks of the center of town, with buses or trams parked out front. Trains run frequently throughout the day and night from Amsterdam Centraal Station to many of the cities mentioned in the following pages; for example, there are trains at least every half hour to Alkmaar, to Rotterdam and points in between, and to Haarlem. You'll find that travel times are surprisingly short (Rotterdam, the farthest train destination in this chapter, is just one hour and six minutes away; Zaandam, the nearest, just eight minutes by train from Amsterdam Centraal Station).

Fares, too, are reasonable. For example a *dagretour* (one-day round-trip ticket at about 10% to 20% savings) to Haarlem is just Dfl 14.25 ($7.50) in first class or Dfl 9.50 ($5) in second class; to Leiden, Dfl 28 ($14.75) in first class, Dfl 28.50 ($10.80) in second class; or to Rotterdam, Dfl 49.50 ($26.05) in first class, Dfl 33 ($17.35) in second class.

The information office of Nederlandse Spoorwegen (☎ **06/9292**) is open Monday through Friday from 7am to 11pm and Saturday,

Sunday, and holidays from 8am to 11pm. **A special note:** Be sure to ask the time of the late trains back to Amsterdam; service is limited after 1am.

If you're trying to get information on Netherlands Railways before you leave the United States or Canada, you can call the Netherlands Board of Tourism offices in Chicago, New York, San Francisco, or Toronto (see Chapter 2).

TOURIST INFORMATION   Anywhere you travel in Holland you can expect to find a local **VVV Tourist Information Office** in one of two places—near the railway station or on the main square of town. If you're driving, you'll see blue-and-white VVV signs posted along major routes into town to direct you to the office. VVV tourism offices are open during regular business hours, including Saturday in some cities; in larger cities and towns, or during the busy seasons of spring and summer, extended hours and Sunday service are also possible.

1 The Hague & Scheveningen

Amsterdam may be the capital of the Netherlands, but The Hague (Den Haag, in Dutch) has always been the seat of government and the official residence of the Dutch monarchs, whether or not they chose to live there (Juliana, when she was queen, preferred to live near Utrecht, whereas Queen Beatrix has chosen Huis ten Bosch in the Hague Woods as a home for her rollicking brood of young princes).

The Hague is a beautiful and sophisticated city full of parks and elegant homes, with an 18th-century French look that suits its role as the diplomatic center of the Dutch nation and the site of the International Court of Justice (housed in the famous Peace Palace). Among its attractions are a number of fine antiques shops and a weekly antiques and curios market May through September, on Thursday and Sunday from 10am to 5pm; October to May, on Thursday from noon to 6pm.

So close it seems to be part of the same city is the beach resort and fishing port of Scheveningen, with its curious combination of costumed fishermen's wives near the harbor and tuxedoed croupiers from the casino at the beautifully restored 19th-century **Kurhaus Hotel.**

WHAT TO SEE & DO

Perhaps the most famous and popular attraction of The Hague is the impressive **Binnenhof,** or Inner Court, a complex of Parliament buildings located at Binnenhof 8a (open Monday through Saturday from 10am to 4pm). You can join a tour to visit the lofty, medieval Hall of Knights, in which the queen delivers the speech from the throne each year (if you're in Holland on the third Tuesday in September, be sure to be there to see her arrive and depart; she rides in a real golden coach—like Cinderella—drawn by high-stepping royal horses; it's quite a spectacle). Depending on the press of governmental business, you'll also tour one or the other of the two chambers of the States General, the Dutch Parliament. The last guided tour starts at

The Hague & Scheveningen

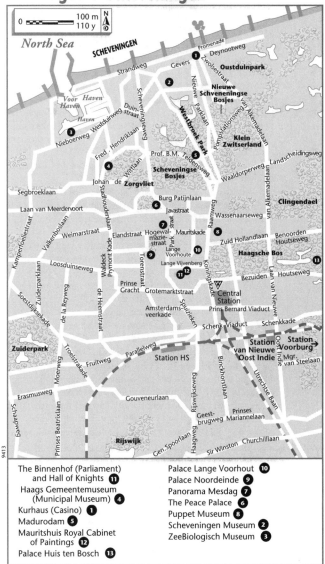

The Binnenhof (Parliament) and Hall of Knights 11
Haags Gemeentemuseum (Municipal Museum) 4
Kurhaus (Casino) 1
Madurodam 5
Mauritshuis Royal Cabinet of Paintings 12
Palace Huis ten Bosch 13

Palace Lange Voorhout 10
Palace Noordeinde 9
Panorama Mesdag 7
The Peace Palace 6
Puppet Museum 8
Scheveningen Museum 2
ZeeBiologisch Museum 3

3:55pm and the cost is Dfl 5 ($2.65) per person. It's requested that you book in advance by telephone(☎ **070/364-61-44**) if you intend to take the guided tour—call ahead in any case to make sure tours are being given on the day you intend to visit. Admission to the Parliament exhibition in the reception room of the Hall of Knights is free.

Adjacent to the Binnenhof Parliament complex is the elegant Italian Renaissance–style **Mauritshuis,** Korte Vijverberg 8, which was built in 1644 as the chic and architecturally innovative home of a young court dandy and cousin of the Orange-Nassaus. Today this small palace is officially known as the **Royal Picture Gallery,** and is the permanent home of an impressive art collection, given to the Dutch nation by King Willem I in 1816, which includes 13 Rembrandts, three Frans Hals, and three Vermeers (including the famous *View of Delft*), plus hundreds of other famous works by such painters as Breughel, Rubens, Steen, and Holbein (including his famous portrait of Jane Seymour, third wife of Henry VIII of England). The gallery is open Tuesday through Saturday from 10am to 5pm and Sunday from 11am to 5pm. Admission is Dfl 8 ($4.20) for adults, Dfl 6 ($3.15) for children under 18 and seniors over 65 (prices may be different during special exhibitions).

If you have an interest in royalty and palaces, take a ride on bus no. 4; its route passes four Dutch palaces built during the 16th and 17th centuries, including Palace Huis ten Bosch, the home of Queen Beatrix (no visits).

Venture beyond the the city center to visit the famous **Peace Palace,** Carnegieplein 2, donated by Andrew Carnegie as a home for the Permanent Court of Arbitration. Guided tours are given Monday through Friday at 10am, 11am, 2pm, and 3pm; from May to September, a tour is also given at 4pm. Tours will cost Dfl 6 ($3.15) for adults and Dfl 3.50 ($1.85) for children under 12. For information, call **070/346-96-80**. Also stop at the impressive center of popular sciences, **Museon,** Stadhouderslaan 41 (☎ **070/338-13-05**), located next to The Hague Municipal Art Museum. Museon is open Tuesday through Friday from 11am to 5pm and Saturday, Sunday, and holidays from noon to 5pm. Admission is Dfl 6 ($3.15) for adults, Dfl 3.50 ($1.85) for children 5 to 12 years old and seniors.

Not far away in the Scheveningen Woods is the enchanting **Madurodam,** Haringkade 175 (☎ **070/355-39-00**), a miniature village in 1-to-25 scale that represents the Dutch nation in actual proportions of farmland to urban areas and presents many of the country's most historic buildings in miniature, with lights that light, bells that ring, and trains that run efficiently—as all do in Holland. It's open daily: March through May from 9am to 10pm, June through August from 9am to 11pm, in September from 9am to 9pm, and October through January 3 from 9am to 6pm. Admission is Dfl 14 ($7.35) for adults, Dfl 9 ($4.75) for seniors 65 and older, and Dfl 7.50 ($3.95) for children 2 to 12.

In the **Rosarium** in Westbroekpark, more than 20,000 roses bloom each year between July and September. The grounds are open daily from 9am to one hour before sunset.

The attractions of **Scheveningen** are no longer limited to bicycling on the dunes, deep-sea fishing in the North Sea, and splashing in the waves at the beach or in a "wave pool" (an indoor/outdoor heated swimming pool that has mechanically produced surf). Added now to indoor amusements, including blackjack and roulette at the **casino** of the Kurhaus Hotel, are video games and pinball machines at the Pier, shopping, and "noshing" at the Palace Promenade shopping mall and, of course, fish dinners at the restaurants around the harbor (where you just might catch a glimpse of a fisherman's wife wearing the traditional costume of Scheveningen).

2 Rotterdam

For a change from the thick blanket of history settled around Amsterdam, consider a visit to a Dutch city that's almost completely modern, has a spacious and elegant shopping mall where most cities in Holland have a web of little streets and alleyways, and instead of miles and miles of canals, has the biggest and busiest ocean harbor in the world at its doorstep.

Rotterdam is a fascinating place to see and experience, particularly when you consider that this city also was a living monument to Holland's golden age until it was bombed to rubble during World War II. At the war's end, rather than try to re-create the old, Rotterdammers looked on their misfortune as an opportunity and approached their city as a clean slate. They relished the chance—unique in Holland—to create an efficient, elegant, and workable modern city. It's just the sort of challenge the Dutch take on with incomparable relish, and the results are a testimony to their ability to find impressive solutions to their problems. By the time they had finished with Rotterdam, the Dutch had dredged a long deep-water channel and filled in the shallow banks of the estuary that connected the city with the North Sea to create a 20-mile-long harbor called the **Europoort** that now handles more cargo and more ships every year than any other port in the world (250 million tons annually). Lest you think a harbor is boring business on a vacation, see Rotterdam and it'll make any other port you've ever seen look like a Fisher-Price toy!

WHAT TO SEE & DO

The first thing to do in Rotterdam is to take a **Spido Harbor Trip** (via Metro to Leuvehaven station; ☎ **010/413-54-00**). Departures are every 30 to 45 minutes from 9:30am to 5pm, April through September; two to four times per day, October through March. The season of the year will determine how much of the vast Europoort you'll be able to see, but it's an unforgettable experience to board a boat that seems large in comparison to the canal launches of Amsterdam—two tiers of indoor seating as well as open decks—and then feel dwarfed by the hulking oil tankers and container ships that glide like giant whales into their berths along the miles of docks. The basic harbor trip, offered year-round, is a 75-minute tour of the city's waterfront; between April and September, it's also possible to take an extended (2^1/4-hour) trip daily at 10am and 12:30pm; and on a limited schedule in July and August, you can make all-day excursions to the sluices of the Delta Works and along the full length of the Europoort. Prices vary according to the trip, but most run Dfl 12 to 42.50 ($6.30 to $22.35) for adults and Dfl 6 to 21.50 ($3.15 to $11.30) for children 3 to 12. There's also a music/dinner cruise offered from April to November that costs Dfl 95 ($50), which includes

Rotterdam

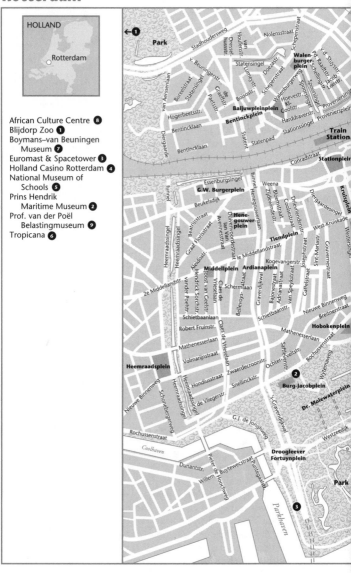

HOLLAND

Rotterdam

the cruise, a welcome cocktail, a four-course meal, two glasses of wine, and coffee. A reservation is absolutely necessary.

Back on dry land, the nearby **Boymans–van Beuningen Museum,** Museumpark 18–20 (☎ **010/441-94-00**), is another of Holland's treasure troves of fine art. In this case, however, Dutch painters share wall space with an international contingent that

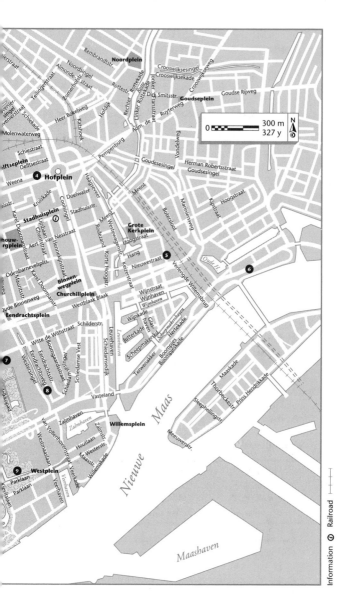

Information   ⊙ Railroad   ┼ ┼ ┼

includes Salvador Dalí and Man Ray, Titian and Tintoretto, Degas and Daumier. Plus, there are fine collections of porcelain, silver, glass, and Delftware. The museum also houses a gift shop and a restaurant where you can have a quick lunch. It's open Tuesday through Saturday from 10am to 5pm and Sunday and holidays from 11am to 5pm (closed New Year's Day and April 30). Admission is Dfl 6 ($3.15).

Not all of Rotterdam is spanking new and, thankfully, one of the neighborhoods spared by the German bombers is the tiny harbor area known as **Delftshaven** (Harbor of Delft), from which the Pilgrims sailed on the first leg of their trip to Massachusetts. It's a pleasant place to spend an afternoon, wandering into the church in which they prayed before departure, peeking into antiques shops and galleries, and checking on the progress of housing renovations in this historic area.

Two interesting places to visit there are the **Sack Carriers' Guild House,** Voorstraat 13–15 (☎ **010/477-26-64**), where artisans demonstrate the art of pewter casting, and **De Dubbelde Palmboom** (Double Palm Tree Historical Museum), Voorhaven 12 (☎ **010/476-15-33**), housed in two adjoining warehouses and displaying objects unearthed during the excavations of Rotterdam. Both are open Tuesday through Saturday from 10am to 5pm and Sunday and holidays from 1am to 5pm (closed New Year's Day and April 30).

3 Utrecht

When the Dutch Republic was established in the late 16th century, Utrecht was one of the more powerful political centers, having been an important bishopric since the earliest centuries of Christianity in Holland. (And here's a bit of trivia for you: Did you know that the only other non-Italian pope, beside John Paul II, was Pope Adrian VI of Utrecht?) As a result, this is a city of churches, with more restored medieval religious structures than any other city in Europe. Most are in the old heart of town, including the beautiful Domkerk and its adjacent Domtoren, or Dom Tower, the tallest in Holland (and worth a climb). Other sites, such as the St. Agnes and Catherine Convents, now house two of Utrecht's many fine museums; for centuries they filled a variety of roles (orphanages, hospitals, and so on) during the period of Protestant influence in the Netherlands.

Also unique to Utrecht is its bilevel wharf along the Oude Gracht canal through the Center, where restaurants, shops, and summer cafés have replaced the hustle and bustle of the commercial activity of former times, when Utrecht was a major port along the Rhine.

Commerce continues to be the city's major focus, as you quickly realize if you arrive by train. The Centraal Station is now in the midst of a multimillion-guilder renovation project called Hoog Catherijne (High Catherine)—a vast, multitiered, indoor shopping mall that spreads over a six-block area and traverses both a multilane highway and the web of railway tracks. Another part of this project is the new Jaarbeursplein, with its 40-room exhibition hall built especially to house the annual Utrecht Trade Fair, at which Dutch industry has presented its best products every year since 1916.

WHAT TO SEE & DO

Don't let Utrecht's modern face daunt your interest in visiting this well-preserved 2,000-year-old city. Take a **canal-boat ride,**

Oudegrachet at Lange Viestraat (☎ **31-93-77**); they're offered Monday through Sunday every hour on the hour from 11am to 5pm. At the end of the trip, visit **'t Hoogt,** Hoogt 4, at the corner of Slachstraat. It's a 17th-century burgher's house that fronts on two streets and is now an art cinema. It's open Monday through Sunday from noon to 1am, and admission is Dfl 10 ($5.25) per screening.

The major sight in Utrecht is the **Domplein,** where, if you have the stamina and the inclination, you can climb the 465 steps to the top of the **Domtoren** (Dom Tower). Guided tours are offered on weekends from October through the winter to April and daily during the summer. Also, visit the **Domkerk** (cathedral), the **Bisschopes Hof,** or Bishop's Garden (open daily from 11am to 5pm), and the **Dom Kloostergang,** a cloister arcade built in the 15th century, with magnificent stained-glass windows depicting scenes from the legend of St. Martin.

In another medieval church visit the merry **Rijksmuseum van Spielklok tot Pieremont** (National Museum from Music Box to Street Organ), Buurkerkhof 10 (☎ **030/31-27-89**), where you hear and see 600 different music makers, which makes it the largest museum of its kind in the world. There are hourly tours Tuesday through Saturday from 10am to 5pm and Sunday and holidays from 1 to 5pm. Admission is Dfl 7.50 ($3.95).

Also, be sure to see the exceptional collection of medieval religious art at **Het Catharijneconvent State Museum,** Nieuwegracht 63 (☎ **030/31-38-35**); it's open Tuesday through Friday from 10am to 5pm. The **Centraal Museum,** Agnietenstraat 1 (☎ **030/ 362-362**), has a ship from Utrecht that dates from A.D. 1200, a number of paintings of the Utrecht school of the 16th century, and a dollhouse that dates from 1680. An impressive collection of Dutch modern art and Dutch 20th-century applied art—the De Stijl group—is displayed in the former artillery mews on the grounds of the museum. An important item in the Centraal Museum collection is the Rietveld-Schroder House, Prins Hendriklaan 50, built in 1924 and designed by Gerrit Rietveld according to the ideas of the De Stijl group. The Rietveld-Schroder House is open Wednesday through Saturday from 11am to 5pm and Sunday noon to 5pm, or by appointment. The museum itself is open Tuesday through Saturday from 10am to 5pm and Sunday and holidays from noon to 5pm. Admission is Dfl 7.50 ($3.95) for adults, Dfl 4 ($2.10) for children 14 and under; prices vary for special exhibits.

4 The Historic Art Towns

DELFT

Yes, this is the city of the famous blue-and-white earthenware. And, yes, you can visit the factory of De Porceleyne Fles as long as you realize it's only a visit to a showroom and not the painting studios and other workrooms. But, please, don't let Delftware be your only reason to visit Delft. Not only is this one of the prettiest small cities in Holland, but also Delft is important as a cradle of the Dutch Republic and the traditional burial place of the royal family. Plus, it was the birthplace—and inspiration—of the 17th-century master of light and subtle emotion, the painter Jan Vermeer. Yet one of the nicest things about Delft is that in spite of its proximity to the big and ever-growing cities of The Hague (to which it is connected by tram, by the way) and Rotterdam, Delft remains a quiet and intimate little town, with flowers in its flower boxes and linden trees bending over its gracious canals.

WHAT TO SEE & DO The house where Vermeer was born, lived, and painted is long gone from Delft, as are his paintings. Instead, you can visit the **Oude Kerk,** at Roland Holstlaan 753, where he is buried. The Oude Kerk is also known for its 27 stained-glass windows of Joep Nicolas; it's open April to October, Monday through Saturday from 10am to 5pm. Also, you might want to visit the **Nieuwe Kerk,** on Markt near the VVV office. The Nieuwe Kerk, where Prince William of Orange and all other members of the House of Orange-Nassau are buried, is open Monday through Saturday: from 11am to 5pm; its tower is open from May to September only, Tuesday through Saturday from 10am to 4:30pm.

The **Prinsenhof Museum,** Agathaplein, on the nearby Oude Delft canal, is where William I of Orange (William the Silent) lived and had his headquarters in the years during which he helped found the Dutch Republic. It is also where he was assassinated in 1584 (you can still see the bullet holes in the stairwell). Today, however, the Prinsenhof is a museum of paintings, tapestries, silverware, and pottery; it's also the site of the annual Delft Art and Antiques Fair, held in late October or early November. Year-round, it's open Tuesday through Saturday from 10am to 5pm and Sunday from 1 to 5pm; from June to August, it's also open on Monday from 1 to 5pm.

In the same neighborhood you can also see a fine collection of old Delft tiles displayed in the wood-paneled setting of a 19th-century mansion museum called **Lambert van Meerten,** located at Oude Delft 199 and open Tuesday through Saturday from 10am to 5pm and Sunday from 1 to 5pm. Or to see brand-new Delftware, and one of the daily demonstrations of the art of handpainting Delftware, visit the showroom of **De Porceleyne Fles,** Rotterdamseweg 196 (☎ **015/56-92-14**). The showroom is open April to October, Monday through Saturday from 9am to 5pm and Sunday from 10am to 4pm; October to March, Monday through Friday from 9am to 5pm and Saturday from 10am to 4pm. Admission is free.

HAARLEM

Haarlem is a city of music and art just 12 miles west of Amsterdam. Near the beaches and the bulb fields, it's the gateway to the reclaimed Haarlemmermeer polder land, in the heart of an area dotted with elegant manor houses and picturesque villages. It's an easy drive from the massive locks of the North Sea Canal that have helped make Amsterdam a major European port. In short, if you have only one day to travel beyond Amsterdam, spend it in Haarlem, which is a charming town and the home of two of Holland's finest museums.

WHAT TO SEE & DO   Traditionally, Haarlem is the little sister city of Amsterdam. It was the destination of the first steam train in Holland, and it is the city where Frans Hals, Jacob van Ruysdael, and Pieter Saenredam were living and painting their famous portraits, landscapes, and church interiors during the same years that Rembrandt was living and working in Amsterdam. It also is a city to which both Handel and Mozart made special visits just to play the magnificent organ of the Church of St. Bavo, also known as **Grote Kerk,** Oude Groenmarkt 23. Look for the tombstone of painter Frans Hals, and for a cannonball that has been imbedded in the wall ever since it came flying through a window during the siege of Haarlem in 1572–73. And, of course, don't miss seeing the famous Christian Muller Organ, built in 1738. You can actually hear it at one of the free concerts given on Tuesday and Thursday from April to October. It has 5,068 pipes and is nearly 98 feet tall. The woodwork was done by Jan van Logteren. Mozart played the organ in 1766 when he was just 10 years old—when you see this organ you may be dumbstruck at the thought of the tiny Mozart reaching for one of the 68 stops. St. Bavo's is open Monday through Saturday from 10am to 4pm.

From St. Bavo's, it's an easy walk to the oldest and perhaps the most unusual museum in Holland, the **Teylers Museum,** Spaarne 16 (☎ **023/31-90-10**). It contains a curious collection of displays: drawings by Michelangelo, Raphael, and Rembrandt (which are shown on a rotating basis); fossils, minerals, and skeletons; instruments of physics and an odd assortment of inventions, including the largest electrostatic generator in the world (1784) and a 19th-century radarscope. The museum is open Tuesday through Saturday from 10am to 5pm and Sunday from 1 to 5pm. Admission is Dfl 6.50 ($3.40) for adults and Dfl 3 ($1.55) for children 15 and under, students, and seniors.

Saving the best for last, visit the **Frans Halsmuseum,** Groot Heiligeland 62 (☎ **023/16-42-00**), where the galleries are the halls and furnished chambers of a former pensioners' home and the famous paintings by the masters of the Haarlem school hang in settings that look like the 17th-century homes they were intended to adorn. It's a beautiful place to spend an hour or two at any time; it will be a high point of your trip to Holland. The museum is open Monday through Saturday from 11am to 5pm and on Sunday from 1 to 5pm. Admission is Dfl 6 ($3.15) for adults and Dfl 3 ($1.55) children 10 to 18, free for children under 10.

Also, near Haarlem, if you have time, are the graciously restored 18th-century manor house, **Beeckestljn,** in the town of Velsen-Zuid; the **Cruiquius Expo** steam-driven water mill and land-reclamation museum near Heemstede; and at IJmuiden, the three great locks of the **North Sea Canal.** And if you're an early bird, the **fish auctions** at IJmuiden, Halkade 4, are held Monday through Friday from 7 to 11am.

LEIDEN

Leiden is a town with an odd assortment of claims to fame and a smörgåsbord of interesting things to see. There's a windmill that sticks up like a sore thumb in the middle of town, and there's a 13th-century citadel still standing on a funny little bump of land between two branches of the river Rhine, the site of the oldest university in Holland—housed in a chapel, of course. And Leiden was the town in which the Pilgrims lived for 11 years before sailing for North America on the *Mayflower;* it's the birthplace of the Dutch tulip trade in 1593, and also of the famous painters Rembrandt van Rijn and Jan Steen. It was also the only Dutch city to withstand the Spanish siege of 1574.

WHAT TO SEE & DO   Probably the best way to see Leiden is to cruise its canals or follow one of four special city **walking tours**. One tour, called "The Pilgrim Fathers," makes a large circle around the old center of the city; the others, which are called "Town Full of Monuments," "In the Footsteps of Young Rembrandt," and "Along Leiden's Almhouses," make shorter circuits which can easily be combined to give you a comprehensive look at the sights near the university and also take you past that citadel.

One place worth stopping to see in Leiden is the **Botanical Gardens** of the university, at Rapenburg 73, which date from 1587—that's nearly 400 years of blooming flowers! The gardens are open Monday through Saturday from 9am to 5pm and Sunday from 10am to 5pm; the greenhouses are open Monday through Friday from 9am to 12:30pm and 1 to 4:30pm and Saturday and Sunday from 10:30am to 12:30pm and 1:30 to 3pm; everything is closed holidays year-round and on Saturday between October and April.

Also noteworthy is the **National Museum of Antiquities,** Rapenburg 28, which now houses the latest pride of Leiden—and Holland—the Temple of Taffeh, presented by the Egyptian government as a gift to the Dutch nation for helping to save the monuments prior to the construction of the Aswan High Dam (just as the Temple of Dendur, now in New York's Metropolitan Museum of Art, was a gift to the United States). It's open Tuesday through Saturday from 10am to 5pm and Sunday and most holidays from noon to 5pm (closed New Year's Day and October 3).

In the same neighborhood is the number-one destination for American visitors, the **Pilgrim's Documentation Centre,** Boisotkade 2a, where you hear a recorded commentary on the Pilgrims and see photocopies of documents relating to their 11 years of residence in Leiden. The center is open Monday through Friday from 9:30am to 4:30pm (closed weekends, holidays, and October 3).

On the other side of town, visit the **Stedelijk Museum de Lakenhal,** Oude Singel 32 (☎ **071/16-53-60**), to see works by the local boys—Rembrandt, Jan Steen, and Lucas van Leyden—plus period rooms from the 17th to 19th centuries, and the real pride of Leiden, the copper stew pot that it's said was retrieved by a small boy who crawled through a chink in the city wall within minutes of Leiden's liberation from the Spanish siege. He found this very pot full of boiling stew in the enemy's camp; it fed the starving inhabitants of Leiden. Ever since, stew has been a national dish of Holland, traditionally prepared for the Leiden city holiday, October 3, which is the anniversary of their lucky day. Modern art is now being regularly shown in temporary exhibitions. Open Tuesday through Saturday from 10am to 5pm and Sunday and holidays (except Christmas and New Year's Day) from 1 to 5pm. Admission is Dfl 5 ($2.65) for adults and Dfl 2.50 ($1.30) for children 6 to 16.

LAREN

The Dutch legacy of impressive art was not a one-shot, golden age phenomenon, nor were the later 19th-century contributions solely the work of Mijnheer Vincent van Gogh. Visit the pretty little suburban town of Laren, 15 miles east of Amsterdam in the district Het Gooi, and you'll discover a less well known Dutch art center, where a number of important painters chose to live and work at the turn of the century. Among the town's star residents were Anton Mauve, the Dutch impressionist who attracted other members of the Hague school, and the American painter William Henry Singer, Jr., who chose to live and paint in the clear light of Holland rather than follow his family's traditional path to fame and fortune by the light of their fiery steel mills in Pittsburgh. Today it is Singer's former home, once called the Wild Swans, that is the principal attraction of Laren. Now called simply the **Singer Museum,** Oude Drift 1 (☎ **021/531-56-56**), it houses both the works of the former occupant and also his collection of some 500 works by American, Dutch, French, and Norwegian painters. It's open Tuesday through Saturday from 11am to 5pm and Sunday and holidays from noon to 5pm (closed January 1, April 30, and December 25).

5   The Flower Centers

KEUKENHOF GARDENS AT LISSE

Flowers at their peak and Keukenhof Gardens (☎ **025/211-90-34** or **211-91-44**) both have short but glorious seasons, and you'll never forget a visit to this park. It's a meandering 70-acre wooded park in the heart of the bulb-producing region, planted each fall by the major Dutch growers (each plants his own plot or establishes his own greenhouse display). Then, come spring, the bulbs burst forth and produce not hundreds of flowers, or even thousands, but millions and millions (6,000,000 at last count) of tulips and narcissi, daffodils and hyacinths, bluebells, crocuses, lilies, amaryllis, and many others. The blaze of color is everywhere in the park and in the greenhouses, beside the brooks and shady ponds, along the paths and in the neighboring fields, in neat little plots and helter-skelter on the lawns. By its own report it's the greatest flower show on earth—and it's Holland's annual Easter/Passover/spring gift to the world. There are plans to build a one-mile track for a soundless, slow-moving shuttle train for those who would be more comfortable riding than walking. Currently there are four self-serve cafeterias where you can grab a quick lunch so you don't have to go running around looking for a place to eat when you'd rather be enjoying the flowers.

The park is open late March to mid-May only, daily from 8am to 6:30pm. There are special train-bus connections via Haarlem and the small community of Leiden. Admission is Dfl 17 ($8.95) for adults, Dfl 13 ($6.85) for seniors, and Dfl 7.50 ($3.95) for children 4 to 12.

AALSMEER FLOWER AUCTION

In Holland, flowers are a year-round business that nets more than a billion guilders a year at the Aalsmeer Flower Auction (☎ 02977/ 34567 or 32185), held in the lakeside community of Aalsmeer, near Schiphol Airport. Every year, 4 billion flowers and 400 million plants are sold, coming from 8,000 nurseries. Get there early to see the biggest array of flowers in the distribution rooms, and to have as much time as possible to watch the computerized auctioning process—it works basically like the old "Beat the Clock" game on television: The first one to press the button gets the posies. In keeping with a Dutch auctioneering philosophy that demands quick handling for perishable goods, the bidding on flowers goes from high to low instead of proceeding in the usual manner of bidding up. There are mammoth bidding clocks that are numbered from 100 to 1. The buyers, many of whom are buying for the French and German markets, sit in rows in the four auditorium-style auction halls; they have microphones to ask questions and buttons to push to register their bids in the central computer (which also takes care of all the paperwork). As the bunches of tulips or daffodils go by the stand on carts, they are auctioned in a matter of seconds, with the first bid—which is the first bid to stop the clock as it works down from 100 to 1—as the only bid. Whether or not it's really for the sake of the freshness of the flowers, the Aalsmeer Flower Auction is smart Dutch business.

The auction is held Monday through Friday from 7:30 to 11am; bus 172 will take you there from Centraal Station. The entrance fee to the auction is Dfl 6 ($3.15) per person—children under 12 are admitted free.

6 The Cheese Towns

ALKMAAR

Every Friday morning during the long Dutch summer season there's a steady parade of tourists leaving Amsterdam to visit the **Alkmaar Cheese Market** in the small city of Alkmaar, northwest of Amsterdam, and it's quite a show they're on their way to see. Cheeses are piled high on the cobblestone square and the carillon in the Weigh House tower is drowning the countryside in Dutch folk music. Around the square dart the white-clad cheese carriers whose lacquered straw hats tell you which of four sections of their medieval guild they belong to: red, blue, yellow, or green. The bidding process is carried on in the traditional Dutch manner of hand clapping to bid the price up or down, and a good solid hand clap to seal the deal. Then, once a buyer has accumulated his lot of cheeses, teams of guild members move in with their shiny, shallow barrows, or carriers, and using slings that hang from their shoulders, carry the golden wheels and balls of cheese to the Weigh House for the final tally of the bill. The market goes on from mid-April to mid-September, on Friday from 10am to noon.

While you're in Alkmaar, there are a few other attractions you may want to see, including the **Old Craft Market** (also held on Friday from 10am to noon); the **House with the Cannonball,** presumably a souvenir of the Spanish siege; and the **Remonstraat Church,** a clandestine church in a former granary.

GOUDA

If the showmanship of the Alkmaar Cheese Market seems a bit much to you—or if you can't wait until Friday—go to the **Gouda Cheese Market,** held in the small city of Gouda, near Rotterdam, mid-June through the end of August on Thursday from 9:30am to noon. It's a real market, in the words of the locals, with the dairy farmers in their everyday overalls and the only musical accompaniment the sound of the hand clapping that seals a deal in any Dutch market and the half-hourly tinkling of the carillon with moving figures that graces the 15th-century Gothic town hall (take a close look at it— it's the oldest town hall in Holland).

Also worthy of attention while you're in Gouda (which is pro-nounced "*How*-dah," by the way) are the **Catherine Guesthouse Municipal Museum,** Oosthaven 9 (☎ **01820/88440**), with period rooms and a torture chamber, modern art, silverware, religious art, altarpieces, toys, and other paintings; the 14th-century **Janskerk,** with the longest nave in the country and 70 big, bright, 16th-century stained-glass windows; plus the **Moriaan Pipe and Pottery Museum,** Westhaven 29 (☎ **01820/88444**), located in a 17th-century house. Both museums are open Monday through Saturday from 10am to 5pm and Sunday and holidays from noon to 5pm. Admission (a combination ticket for both) is Dfl 3.50 ($1.85) for adults and Dfl 2 ($1.05) for children under 16.

PURMEREND

Also held on Thursday in the midsummer months is the mini-Alkmaar market, **Purmerend Cheese Market,** which takes place in the small city of Purmerend, north of Amsterdam, from July through August on Thursday from 11am to 1pm. Or you can come here on Thursday mornings from July through August for a cattle-and-produce market.

---

7   Windmills & Wooden Shoes

THE WINDMILLS OF KINDERDIJK

There are three things that stir the soul of a true Hollander: his or her flag, his or her anthem, and the sight of the windmill sails spin-ning in the breeze at Kinderdijk. There are 19 water-pumping wind-mills on the horizon at Kinderdijk, a tiny community approximately 66 miles south of Amsterdam, between Rotterdam and Dordrecht;

that means 76 mill sails, each with a 14-yard span, all revolving on the horizon on a summer day. It's a spectacular sight and one of the must sees of Holland in the summer. The mills are in operation on Saturday afternoons in July and August from 2:30 to 5:30pm; the visitor's mill is open April through September, Monday through Saturday from 9:30am to 5:30pm.

VOLENDAM & MARKEN

There are differences between these two towns—one is Catholic, the other Protestant; one is on the mainland, the other on a former island; in one women wear white caps with wings, and in the other, caps with ribbons—but Volendam and Marken have been combined on bus-tour itineraries for so long that soon they may contribute a new compound word to the Dutch language. Unfortunately, *volendammarken* will probably take on the meaning of "tourist trap," or being slightly kinder, it will stand for "Packaged Holland and Costumes-to-Go," but it is possible to have a delightful day in the bracing air of these waterside communities.

If you simply must have a snapshot of the missus surrounded by fishermen in little caps and balloon-legged pants, or if you want to flip the ringlets of a *Markenervrouw* (Mrs. Marken), these are the villages to visit. You'll enjoy the day as long as you realize what the villagers understand quite well: Dutch costumes are a tradition worth preserving, as is the economy of two small towns that lost their fishing industry when the enclosure of the Zuiderzee cut them off from the North Sea. Tourism isn't a bad alternative, they figure—it brought the Wimpyburger to town to join such attractions as the fish auction, the diamond cutter, the clog maker, and the house with a room entirely papered in cigar bands.

ZAANSE SCHANS

Just 10 miles northwest of Amsterdam is a district known as the Zaan area. Much of it is now taken up with the ugliness of shipping and industry, but nestled in its midst is also the charm of **De Zaanse Schans** near KoogZaandijk. De Zaanse Schans is a planned replica-village, made up of houses moved to the site when industrialization leveled their original locations. Although most of these houses are still lived in by the sort of Amsterdam expatriates who can afford and appreciate their historic timbers (and have the patience for the pedestrian traffic from the tour buses), a few can be visited under the guise of being museums. To the pleasure of just walking in this tiny little "town," add a visit to four different kinds of windmill—one for lumber, one for paint, one for oil (vegetable oil), and one for mustard—a stop at an 18th-century grocery or old-style bakery, and a cruise on the river Zaan. And in nearby Zaandam, you also can see the Tsar Peter Cottage, where the Russian monarch lived in 1697 when he studied shipbuilding with the craftsmen whom he—an avid nautical student—considered to be the world's best.

8 | Castles & Moats

MUIDEN

The perfect starting point for a lovely day in the Middle Ages is the **Rijksmuseum Muiderslot,** near the small town of Muiden at Herengracht 1 (☎ **02942/1325**). This is a turreted, fairy-tale princess sort of castle—complete with moat—that perches on the far bank of the river Vecht, just eight miles east of Amsterdam. You may have seen Muiderslot from the air when your plane landed at Amsterdam's Schiphol Airport (it regularly draws gasps from passengers in window seats), or you may remember Muiden (as it is usually called) from an otherwise unremarkable Hollywood thriller of several years ago called *Puppet on a Chain.* But never mind—just go to see where Count Floris V was living when he granted toll privileges and thereby officially recognized the small, new community of "Amstelledamme" in 1275, and where he was murdered just 20 years later.

Muiderslot is also where Dutch poet P. C. Hooft found both a home and employment—and, we suppose, inspiration for romantic images and lofty phraseology—when he served as castle steward and local bailiff for 40 years in the early 17th century. The castle is furnished essentially as Hooft and his artistic circle of friends (known in Dutch literary history as the Muiden Circle) knew it, with plenty of examples of the distinctly Dutch carved cupboard beds, heavy chests, fireside benches, and mantelpieces.

The castle is open April through September, Monday through Friday from 10am to 5pm and Sunday from 1 to 5pm; from October through March it closes one hour earlier. Admission is Dfl 6 ($3.15) for adults; children under 18 and seniors over 65 are charged Dfl 4.50 ($2.35).

NAARDEN

Just beyond Muiderslot is the still-fortified small town of Naarden, where, much in the manner of locking the barn door after the horse was gone, the local inhabitants erected their beautiful star-shaped double fortifications *after* the town was brutally sacked by Don Frederick of Toledo and his boys in the late 16th century. Beneath the Turfpoort Bastion, you can visit the casemates (the artillery vaults) at the **Dutch Fortifications Museum** (Nederlands Vestingmuseum), Westwalstraat 6 (☎ **02159/45459**), open from the Monday before Easter to October 31, Monday through Friday from 10am to 4:30pm and Saturday, Sunday, and holidays from noon to 5pm.

Also see the 15th-century **Grote Kerk,** on Markstraat (☎ **02159/43027**), well known for its fine acoustics and annual performances of Bach's *St. Matthew Passion.* The Grote Kerk is open from April 30 to September 30, Saturday through Thursday from 2 to 4pm.

DE HAAR

One of the more richly furnished castles you can visit in Holland—and one that's still owner-occupied part of the year—is **Castle de Haar,** Kasteellaan 1 (☎ **03407/3804**), at Haarzuilens near Utrecht. Like most castles, De Haar has had its ups and downs, fires and ransackings and the like, over the centuries, but thanks to an infusion of Rothschild money in the early 1900s, it now sits in all its 15th-century moated splendor in the middle of a gracious Versailles-like formal garden. Its walls are hung with fine paintings and precious Gobelin tapestries of the 14th and 15th centuries; its floors are softened with Persian rugs; and its chambers are furnished in the styles of Louis XIV, XV, and XVI of France. The castle is open between March 1 and August 15 and from October 7 to November 15, Monday through Friday from 11am to 4pm and Sunday and public holidays from 1 to 4pm.

Appendix

A Basic Vocabulary & Numbers

English	Dutch	Pronunciation
Hello	Hallo	ha-loh
How are you?	Hoe gaat hot met U?	hoo haht ut met oo?
Very well	Uitstekend	out-stayk-end
Thank you	Dank U	Dahnk ew
Good-bye	Dag	dahk
Please	Alstublieft	ah-stoo-bleeft
Yes	Ja	yah
No	Nee	Nay
Excuse me	Pardon	par-dawn
Give me . . .	Geeft U my . . .	hayft oo may . . .
Where is . . . ?	Waar is . . . ?	vahr iz . . . ?
the station	het station	het stah-ssyonh
a hotel	een hotel	uhn ho-tel
a restaurant	en restaurant	uhn res-to-rahng
the toilet	het toilet	het twah-let
To the right	Rechts	rekhts
To the left	Links	links
Straight ahead	Rechtdoor	rekht-dour
I would like . . .	Ik zou graag . . .	ik zow hrah . . .
to eat	eten	ay-ten
a room	een kramer	uhn kah-mer
for one night	voor een nacht	voor ayn nakht
How much is it?	Hoe veel kost het?	hoo fayl kawst het?

English	Dutch	Pronunciation
The check	De rekening	duh ray-ken-ing
When?	Wanneer?	vah-neer
Yesterday	Gisteren	his-ter-en
Today	Vandaag	van-dahkh
Tomorrow	Morgen	mor-hen
Breakfast	Ontbijt	ohnt-bayt
Lunch	Lunch	lunch
Dinner	Diner	dee-nay

Numbers

1 een (ayn)
2 twee (tway)
3 drie (dree)
4 vier (veer)
5 vijf (vayf)
6 zes (zes)
7 zeven (zay-vun)
8 acht (akht)
9 negen (nay-hen)
10 tien (teen)
11 elf (elf)
12 twaalf (tvahlf)
13 dertien (dayr-teen)
14 veertien (vayr-teen)

15 vijftien (vayf-teen)
16 zestien (zes-teen)
17 zeventien (zay-vun-teen)
18 achtien (akh-teen)
19 negentien (nay-hen-teen)
20 twinting (twin-tukh)
30 dortig (dayr-tukh)
40 veertig (vayr-tukh)
50 vijftig (vahf-tukh)
60 zestig (zes-tukh)
70 zeventig (zay-vun-tukh)
80 tachtig (takh-tukh)
90 negentig (nay-hen-tukh)
100 honderd (hon-dayrt)

B   Menu Savvy

Basics

ontbijt breakfast
lunch lunch
diner dinner
boter butter
brood bread
honing honey

jam jam
kaas cheese
mosterd mustard
peper pepper
suiker sugar
zout salt

Soup (Soepen)

aardappelsoep potato soup
bonensoep bean soup
erwtensoep pea soup
groentesoep vegetable soup

kipponsoep chicken soup
soep soup
tomatensoep tomato soup
uiensoep onion soup

Eggs (Eier)

eieren eggs
hardgekookte eieren hard-
boiled eggs
roereieron scrambled eggs

spiegeleieren fried eggs
zachtgekookte eieren boiled
eggs

Fish (Vis)

forel trout
gerookte zalm smoked salmon
haring herring
kabeljauw haddock
kreeft lobster

makreel mackerel
mosselon mussels
oesters oysters
sardientjes sardines
zalm salmon

Meat (Vleeswarer)

biefstuk steak
chateaubriand filet steak
eend duck
gans goose
kalkoen turkey
kip chicken
konin rabbit

koude schotel cold cuts
lamscotelet lamb chops
lever liver
ragout beef stew
runder bief beef
spek bacon
worst sausage

Vegetables/Salads (Groente/Sla)

aardappelen potatoes
asperges asparagus
augurkjes pickles
bonen beans
bieten beets
erwtjes peas
groente vegetables
komkommersla cucumber
salad
kool cabbage
patates frites french-fried potatoes

prinsesseboontjes green beans
purée mashed potatoes
radijsjes radishes
rapen turnips
rijst rice
sla lettuce, salad
spinazie spinach
tomaten tomatoes
worteltjes carrots
zuurkool sauerkraut

Fruits (Vruchten)

appelen apples
bananen bananas
citroenen lemons
druiven grapes
frambozen raspberries

fruit fruit
kersen cherries
pruimen plums
sinaasappelen oranges
zwateo bessen blackberries

Dessert (Desserts)

ananas pineapple
cake cake
compôte stewed fruits

ijs ice cream
nagerecht dessert
omelette omelet

Beverages (Dranken)

bier beer
cognac brandy
koffie coffee
melk milk

rode wijn red wine
thee tea
water water
witte wijn white wine

Cooking Terms

gebakken fried
gekookt boiled
geroosterd boiled

goed doorgebakken well done
niet doorgebakken rare

C Metric Measures

Length

1 millimeter (mm)	=	.04 inches (*or* less than $^1/_{16}$ in.)
1 centimeter (cm)	=	.39 inches (*or* just under $^1/_2$ in.)
1 meter (m)	=	39 inches (*or* about 1.1 yards)
1 kilometer (km)	=	.62 miles (*or* about $^2/_3$ of a mile)

To convert kilometers to miles, multiply the number of kilometers by .62. Also use to convert kilometers per hour (kmph) to miles per hour (m.p.h.).

To convert miles to kilometers, multiply the number of miles by 1.61. Also use to convert from m.p.h. to kmph.

Capacity

1 liter (l)	=	33.92 fluid ounces	=	2.1 pints	=	1.06 quarts
	=	.26 U.S. gallons				
1 imperial gallon	=	1.2 U.S. gallons				

To convert liters to U.S. gallons, multiply the number of liters by .26.

To convert U.S. gallons to liters, multiply the number of gallons by 3.79.

To convert imperial gallons to U.S. gallons, multiply the number of imperial gallons by 1.2.

To convert U.S. gallons to imperial gallons, multiply the number of U.S. gallons by .83.

Weight

1 gram (g)	=	.035 ounces (*or* about a paper clip's weight)
1 kilogram (kg)	=	35.2 ounces
	=	2.2 pounds
1 metric ton	=	2,205 pounds (1.1 short ton)

To convert kilograms to pounds, multiply the number of kilograms by 2.2.

To convert pounds to kilograms, multiply the number of pounds by .45.

Area

1 hectare (ha)	=	2.47 acres		
1 square kilometer (km²)	=	247 acres	=	.39 square miles

To convert square miles to square kilometers, multiply the number of square miles by 2.6.

To convert hectares to acres, multiply the number of hectares by 2.47.

To convert square kilometers to square miles, multiply the number of square kilometers by .39.

Temperature

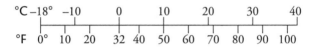

To convert degrees Fahrenheit to degrees Celsius, subtract 32 from ºF, multiply by 5, then divide by 9.

To convert degrees Celsius to degrees Fahrenheit, multiply ºC by 9, divide by 5, and add 32.

Index

Accommodations

Restaurants

Notes

Now Save Money On All Your Travels By Joining
FROMMER'S™ TRAVEL BOOK CLUB
The World's Best Travel Guides
At Membership Prices!

Frommer's Travel Book Club is your ticket to successful travel! Open up a world of travel information and simplify your travel planning when you join ranks with thousands of value-conscious travelers who are members of the Frommer's *Travel Book Club.* Join today and you'll be entitled to all the privileges that come from belonging to the club that offers you travel guides for less to more than 100 destinations worldwide. **Annual membership is only $25.00 (U.S.) or $35.00 (Canada/Foreign).**

The Advantages of Membership:

1. Your choice of **three free** books (any **two** Frommer's Comprehensive Guides, Frommer's $-A-Day Guides, Frommer's Walking Tours or Frommer's Family Guides—plus **one** Frommer's City Guide, Frommer's City $-A-Day Guide or Frommer's Touring Guide).

2. Your own subscription to the **TRIPS & TRAVEL** quarterly newsletter.

3. You're entitled to a **30% discount** on your order of any additional books offered by the club.

4. You're offered (at a small additional fee) our **Domestic Trip-Routing Kits.**

Our **Trips & Travel** quarterly newsletter offers practical information on the best buys in travel, the "hottest" vacation spots, the latest travel trends, world-class events and much, much more.

Our **Domestic Trip-Routing Kits** are available for any North American destination. We'll send you a detailed map highlighting the best route to take to your destination—you can request direct or scenic routes.

Here's all you have to do to join:

Send in your membership fee of $25.00 ($35.00 Canada/Foreign) with your name and address on the form below along with your selections as part of your membership package to the address listed below. Remember to check off your three free books.

If you would like to order additional books, please select the books you would like and send a check for the total amount (please add sales tax in the states noted below), plus $2.00 per book for shipping and handling ($3.00 Canada/Foreign) to the address listed below.

FROMMER'S TRAVEL BOOK CLUB
P.O. Box 473
Mt. Morris, IL 61054-0473
(815) 734-1104

[ ] **YES!** I want to take advantage of this opportunity to join Frommer's Travel Book Club.

[ ] My check is enclosed. Dollar amount enclosed_____*
(all payments in U.S. funds only)

Name _____

Address _____

City _____ State _____ Zip _____

Phone (   ) _____(In case we have a question regarding your order).

All orders must be prepaid.

To ensure that all orders are processed efficiently, please apply sales tax in the following areas: CA, CT, FL, IL, IN, NJ, NY, PA, TN, WA and CANADA.

*With membership, shipping & handling will be paid by Frommer's Travel Book Club for the three FREE books you select as part of your membership. Please add $2.00 per book for shipping & handling for any additional books purchased ($3.00 Canada/Foreign).

Allow 4-6 weeks for delivery for all items. Prices of books, membership fee, and publication dates are subject to change without notice. All orders are subject to acceptance and availability.

Please send me the books checked below:

FROMMER'S COMPREHENSIVE GUIDES

*(Guides listing facilities from budget to deluxe,
with emphasis on the medium-priced)*

	Retail Price	Code		Retail Price	Code
☐ Acapulco/Ixtapa/Taxco, 2nd Edition	$13.95	C157	☐ Jamaica/Barbados, 2nd Edition	$15.00	C149
☐ Alaska '94-'95	$17.00	C131	☐ Japan '94-'95	$19.00	C144
☐ Arizona '95 (Avail. 3/95)	$14.95	C166	☐ Maui, 1st Edition	$14.00	C153
☐ Australia '94'-'95	$18.00	C147	☐ Nepal, 2nd Edition	$18.00	C126
☐ Austria, 6th Edition	$16.95	C162	☐ New England '95	$16.95	C165
☐ Bahamas '94-'95	$17.00	C121	☐ New Mexico, 3rd Edition (Avail. 3/95)	$14.95	C167
☐ Belgium/Holland/ Luxembourg '93-'94	$18.00	C106	☐ New York State '94-'95	$19.00	C133
☐ Bermuda '94-'95	$15.00	C122	☐ Northwest, 5th Edition	$17.00	C140
☐ Brazil, 3rd Edition	$20.00	C111	☐ Portugal '94-'95	$17.00	C141
☐ California '95	$16.95	C164	☐ Puerto Rico '95-'96	$14.00	C151
☐ Canada '94-'95	$19.00	C145	☐ Puerto Vallarta/ Manzanillo/Guadalajara '94-'95	$14.00	C135
☐ Caribbean '95	$18.00	C148			
☐ Carolinas/Georgia, 2nd Edition	$17.00	C128	☐ Scandinavia, 16th Edition (Avail. 3/95)	$19.95	C169
☐ Colorado, 2nd Edition	$16.00	C143	☐ Scotland '94-'95	$17.00	C146
☐ Costa Rica '95	$13.95	C161	☐ South Pacific '94-'95	$20.00	C138
☐ Cruises '95-'96	$19.00	C150	☐ Spain, 16th Edition	$16.95	C163
☐ Delaware/Maryland '94-'95	$15.00	C136	☐ Switzerland/ Liechtenstein '94-'95	$19.00	C139
☐ England '95	$17.95	C159	☐ Thailand, 2nd Edition	$17.95	C154
☐ Florida '95	$18.00	C152	☐ U.S.A., 4th Edition	$18.95	C156
☐ France '94-'95	$20.00	C132	☐ Virgin Islands '94-'95	$13.00	C127
☐ Germany '95	$18.95	C158	☐ Virginia '94-'95	$14.00	C142
☐ Ireland, 1st Edition (Avail. 3/95)	$16.95	C168	☐ Yucatan, 2nd Edition	$13.95	C155
☐ Italy '95	$18.95	C160			

FROMMER'S $-A-DAY GUIDES

(Guides to low-cost tourist accommodations and facilities)

	Retail Price	Code		Retail Price	Code
☐ Australia on $45 '95-'96	$18.00	D122	☐ Israel on $45, 15th Edition	$16.95	D130
☐ Costa Rica/Guatemala/ Belize on $35, 3rd Edition	$15.95	D126	☐ Mexico on $45 '95	$16.95	D125
☐ Eastern Europe on $30, 5th Edition	$16.95	D129	☐ New York on $70 '94-'95	$16.00	D121
☐ England on $60 '95	$17.95	D128	☐ New Zealand on $45 '93-'94	$18.00	D103
☐ Europe on $50 '95	$17.95	D127	☐ South America on $40, 16th Edition	$18.95	D123
☐ Greece on $45 '93-'94	$19.00	D100			
☐ Hawaii on $75 '95	$16.95	D124	☐ Washington, D.C. on $50 '94-'95	$17.00	D120
☐ Ireland on $45 '94-'95	$17.00	D118			

FROMMER'S CITY $-A-DAY GUIDES

	Retail Price	Code		Retail Price	Code
☐ Berlin on $40 '94-'95	$12.00	D111	☐ Madrid on $50 '94-'95	$13.00	D119
☐ London on $45 '94-'95	$12.00	D114	☐ Paris on $50 '94-'95	$12.00	D117

FROMMER'S FAMILY GUIDES

*(Guides listing information on kid-friendly
hotels, restaurants, activities and attractions)*

	Retail Price	Code		Retail Price	Code
☐ California with Kids	$18.00	F100	☐ San Francisco with Kids	$17.00	F104
☐ Los Angeles with Kids	$17.00	F103	☐ Washington, D.C.		
☐ New York City			with Kids	$17.00	F102
with Kids	$18.00	F101			

FROMMER'S CITY GUIDES

*(Pocket-size guides to sightseeing and tourist
accommodations and facilities in all price ranges)*

	Retail Price	Code		Retail Price	Code
☐ Amsterdam '93-'94	$13.00	S110	☐ Montreal/Quebec City '95	$11.95	S166
☐ Athens, 10th Edition			☐ Nashville/Memphis,		
(Avail. 3/95)	$12.95	S174	1st Edition	$13.00	S141
☐ Atlanta '95	$12.95	S161	☐ New Orleans '95	$12.95	S148
☐ Atlantic City/Cape May,			☐ New York '95	$12.95	S152
5th Edition	$13.00	S130	☐ Orlando '95	$13.00	S145
☐ Bangkok, 2nd Edition	$12.95	S147	☐ Paris '95	$12.95	S150
☐ Barcelona '93-'94	$13.00	S115	☐ Philadelphia, 8th Edition	$12.95	S167
☐ Berlin, 3rd Edition	$12.95	S162	☐ Prague '94-'95	$13.00	S143
☐ Boston '95	$12.95	S160	☐ Rome, 10th Edition	$12.95	S168
☐ Budapest, 1st Edition	$13.00	S139	☐ St. Louis/Kansas City,		
☐ Chicago '95	$12.95	S169	2nd Edition	$13.00	S127
☐ Denver/Boulder/Colorado			☐ San Diego '95	$12.95	S158
Springs, 3rd Edition	$12.95	S154	☐ San Francisco '95	$12.95	S155
☐ Dublin, 2nd Edition	$12.95	S157	☐ Santa Fe/Taos/		
☐ Hong Kong '94-'95	$13.00	S140	Albuquerque '95		
☐ Honolulu/Oahu '95	$12.95	S151	(Avail. 2/95)	$12.95	S172
☐ Las Vegas '95	$12.95	S163	☐ Seattle/Portland '94-'95	$13.00	S137
☐ London '95	$12.95	S156	☐ Sydney, 4th Edition	$12.95	S171
☐ Los Angeles '95	$12.95	S164	☐ Tampa/St. Petersburg,		
☐ Madrid/Costa del Sol,			3rd Edition	$13.00	S146
2nd Edition	$12.95	S165	☐ Tokyo '94-'95	$13.00	S144
☐ Mexico City, 1st Edition	$12.95	S170	☐ Toronto '95 (Avail. 3/95)	$12.95	S173
☐ Miami '95-'96	$12.95	S149	☐ Vancouver/Victoria '94-'95	$13.00	S142
☐ Minneapolis/St. Paul,			☐ Washington, D.C. '95	$12.95	S153
4th Edition	$12.95	S159			

FROMMER'S WALKING TOURS

*(Companion guides that point out the places
and pleasures that make a city unique)*

	Retail Price	Code		Retail Price	Code
☐ Berlin	$12.00	W100	☐ New York	$12.00	W102
☐ Chicago	$12.00	W107	☐ Paris	$12.00	W103
☐ England's Favorite Cities	$12.00	W108	☐ San Francisco	$12.00	W104
☐ London	$12.00	W101	☐ Washington, D.C.	$12.00	W105
☐ Montreal/Quebec City	$12.00	W106			

SPECIAL EDITIONS

	Retail Price	Code		Retail Price	Code
☐ Bed & Breakfast Southwest	$16.00	P100	☐ National Park Guide, 29th Edition	$17.00	P106
☐ Bed & Breakfast Great American Cities	$16.00	P104	☐ Where to Stay U.S.A., 11th Edition	$15.00	P102
☐ Caribbean Hideaways	$16.00	P103			

FROMMER'S TOURING GUIDES

*(Color-illustrated guides that include walking tours,
cultural and historic sites, and practical information)*

	Retail Price	Code		Retail Price	Code
☐ Amsterdam	$11.00	T001	☐ New York	$11.00	T008
☐ Barcelona	$14.00	T015	☐ Rome	$11.00	T010
☐ Brazil	$11.00	T003	☐ Tokyo	$15.00	T016
☐ Hong Kong/Singapore/ Macau	$11.00	T006	☐ Turkey	$11.00	T013
☐ London	$13.00	T007	☐ Venice	$9.00	T014

*Please note: If the availability of a book is several months away, we may
have back issues of guides to that particular destination.
Call customer service at (815) 734-1104.*

Frank Lloyd-Wright. Triptych window from Avery Coonley Playhouse, Riverside, Illinois, 1912; 11cb Saint-Louis Factory, France. 'Lampwork Paperweight: Clematis, c. 1848–55'
BROOK COLLINS/ CHICAGO PARK DISTRICT: 98tl
BUENA VISTA: 60bl
CHICAGO OFFICE OF TOURISM: 50tl (Peter J. Schulz); 85bl; 92tr (Peter J. Schulz); 106tc (Mark Montgomery); 112c (Willie Schmidt)
COLUMBIA PICTURES: 60 tr
CORBIS: 1c (Jon Hicks); 12–13c (Alan Schein Photography); 30cla (Sandy Felsenthal) 30clb (Thomas A. Heinz); 35tl (Bettmann)
COURT THEATRE: 48cla, Mary Stuart by Friedrich Schiller. Translated by Robert David MacDonald. Directed by Joanne Akalaitis. Left to Right: Jenny Bacon and Barbara E. Robertson.
DUSABLE MUSEUM: 99tr
THE FIELD MUSEUM: 6c; 14cla, 14c, 14br; 15tl, 15clb, 93c
FUNKY BUDDHA LOUNGE: 44tl
GENE SISKEL FILM CENTER: 48tr
GOLD COAST GUEST HOUSE: 114tl; 117tl; Courtesy of
HERSHEY'S CHICAGO: 81br;
INTERNATIONAL MUSEUM OF SURGICAL SCIENCES: 39tl
JOHN HANDLEY: 50bl; 64tl; 106tr; 108tr; JAMES LEMASS: 31clb; 106–107; JOHN G. SHEDD AQUARIUM 22cb, 22bl, 22–23c, 23tr, 23cr, 23bl; 56c; 92c (Edward G. Lines, Jnr); LEONARDO MEDIA LIMITED: 115tl; 116tl; 116tr

LINCOLN PARK ZOO: 7tl; 24cla; bc; 24-25c, 25cr, 25clb, 56tl (Todd Rosenberg);
MARY EVANS PICTURE LIBRARY: 34t; 35d; MAYOR'S OFFICE OF SPECIAL EVENTS: 3tr; 50tc, 50tr; 51tl; MEXICAN MUSEUM OF FINE ART: 38bl, Work by Jesus Helguera (Courtesy of Garrison and Rosslyn Valentine); MUSEUM OF CONTEMPORARY ART: 79c (Memorial to the Idea of Man If He Was an Idea by H.C. Westermann); MUSEUM OF SCIENCE & INDUSTRY: 16bl, 16bcl, 17tr; 18 tc, 18tr, 18c; 19c; 56tl; 98cr (Dirk Fletcher);
NATIONAL VIETNAM VETERANS MUSEUM: 38tl (Goodbye Vietnam by David A. Sessions); 95tl
NAVY PIER: 3bl; 6bl; 20cla, 20cb; 20–21c; 21tr, 21bl; 57tr
OLD TOWN SCHOOL OF FOLK MUSIC: 49tr
PARAMOUNT PICTURES: 60 tl
PEGGY NOTEBAERT NATURE MUSEUM: 84tr
RUSSIAN TEA-TIME: 75tl
SOUTH SHORE CULTURAL CENTER: 98tl (Brook Collins/ Chicago Park District)
STEPPENWOLF THEATRE: 48tl
TERRA FOUNDATION OF THE ARTS: 81tl; UNIVERSITY OF CHICAGO: 7b; 29 tl, 29cla, 29clb; 98tr; WATER TOWER PLACE: 107tr; WHEELER MANSION: 117tr

All other images are © Dorling Kindersley. For further information see www.dkimages.com

---

Street Index

Selected Street Index

Chicago's Grid System

Nearly all streets in Chicago run east-west or north–south. The zero point is at the intersection of Madison Street (running east-west) and State Street (running north-south). All streets are labelled in relation to this point: for example, the section of State Street north of Madison is known as North State Street. Numbering also begins at the zero point and odd numbers are on the east sides of north-south streets and the south sides of east-west streets.